No More Vietnams?

THE WAR AND THE FUTURE
OF AMERICAN FOREIGN POLICY

EDITED BY Richard M. Pfeffer

PUBLISHED FOR THE

Adlai Stevenson Institute of International Affairs
BY HARPER & ROW, PUBLISHERS
NEW YORK, EVANSTON, AND LONDON

Grateful acknowledgment is made to the *Atlantic Monthly* for allowing use
of portions of the article by James C. Thomson, Jr., "How Could Vietnam
Happen?" *Atlantic Monthly* (April, 1968).

NO MORE VIETNAMS?

Contributors:

EQBAL AHMAD

RICHARD J. BARNET

CHESTER COOPER

THEODORE DRAPER

LUIGI EINAUDI

DANIEL ELLSBERG

JOHN KING FAIRBANK

FRANCES FITZGERALD

COL. FRED HAYNES

STANLEY HOFFMANN

SAMUEL P. HUNTINGTON

GEORGE MCTURNAN KAHIN

HENRY KISSINGER

JOHN MCDERMOTT

HANS MORGENTHAU

RICHARD M. PFEFFER

WILLIAM R. POLK

ITHIEL DE SOLA POOL

EDWIN REISCHAUER

JOHN E. RIELLY

ARTHUR SCHLESINGER, JR.

SIR ROBERT THOMPSON

JAMES C. THOMSON, JR.

LEROY WEHRLE

ALBERT WOHLSTETTER

ADAM YARMOLINSKY

Contents

THE ADLAI STEVENSON INSTITUTE OF INTERNATIONAL AFFAIRS was founded on February 5, 1967, as a private, nonprofit, nonpartisan, educational foundation.

The Institute assembles each year a group of Fellows, men and women with ten or more years of experience in public policy problems who need a year of research and consultation in order to make major strides in areas of their commitment. Fellows are brought to the Institute, encouraged to undertake research projects within their specialties, broaden their understanding of related subjects through discussions with colleagues and reading or study, and contribute to the enrichment of their own and others' understanding of these problems by meetings with faculty and students in leading American colleges and universities.

Preface

In a year-long seminar on the problems of political violence, distinguished social scientists and government officials at the Adlai Stevenson Institute of International Affairs repeatedly commented that the United States had come to the end of an era of foreign policy. Yet in all of the agonized public discussion of the Vietnamese problem very little constructive comment on the implications of this fact for future foreign policy had taken place. As a contribution to public understanding, the Institute decided to hold a meeting of current and former government officials, scholars with relevant expertise, and journalists in June 1968 to discuss this broad issue.

Participants in the conference were carefully selected to ensure a full range of viewpoints. The foreign affairs advisors of the major presidential candidates were included. And as will be noted from their biographies, most of the participants combine a rare degree of distinction in government service and academic pursuits. The basis of their discussion was provided by six papers, each of which was criticized in advance in writing by someone with a different point of view, on such topics as the national security organizations, the strategy of intervention, "flexible response" and progressive involvement, the concept of American national interest, and lastly the aftermath of Vietnam. The participants had the advantage of having read the papers and the critiques of them before meeting. Thus they were able to base their discussion on a common foundation as well as to enrich the meetings by their individual experiences.

At the end of two and a half days of intense discussion we agreed that it would be a mistake to attempt to homogenize the differing viewpoints into a report. We judged that, at this stage of our awakening understanding of the implications of Vietnam, conflicts in interpretation and opinion need to be emphasized rather than synthesized. With this purpose in mind this book has been organized in dialectical form. To emphasize the topics and the variety of points of view, substantial editing of the written materials has been required. In short, we have blended the oral and written *presentation* in order not to have to blend the *substance* of the discussion. While each author naturally has a pride in his draftsmanship, each has graciously allowed the editor more than normal liberty in highlighting the issues by selective editing of the papers.

Many people have contributed to the success of this project. The conference was organized by Mr. Pfeffer, a Fellow of the Stevenson Institute, who is the editor of this book. Sidney Hyman, a Fellow of the Institute in 1968–69 suggested the format of the book and has helped considerably in putting it together. John King Fairbank, by his judicious and impartial chairmanship of the conference, won increased respect and gratitude from us all. James C. Thomson, Jr., contributed substantially at all stages of the project, and Rosalie Smith helped to coordinate the conference.

In order to guide the reader, we have inserted the symbol "§§" in the text to indicate which sections are extracted from the papers and written critiques.

One basic purpose of the Adlai Stevenson Institute of International Affairs is to help raise the level of dialogue on major public issues. No issue before the American people is of more importance today than the Vietnamese problem. It is our hope that this book will initiate a reasoned public discussion on the meaning of the Vietnamese experience and the future course of American foreign policy.

—WILLIAM R. POLK
Director

NO MORE VIETNAMS?

Prologue:

I History as a Teacher

§§ ADAM YARMOLINSKY: President Kennedy once remarked, "If this planet is ever ravaged by nuclear war—if the survivors of that devastation can then endure the fire, poison, chaos and catastrophe—I do not want one of those survivors to ask another, 'How did it all happen?' and to receive the incredible reply, 'Ah, if only one knew.' " The process of U.S. involvement in Vietnam seems, in retrospect, just this kind of process. And yet there were all kinds of warnings, from within the government as well as from outside, warnings that were heard and even listened to at the highest levels of government. At no point could anyone properly say, "We didn't know it was loaded."

§§ SAMUEL P. HUNTINGTON: All of us have long been familiar with Santayana's warning that if we do not remember the past, we shall be condemned to repeat it. In the debates over Vietnam a counterwarning has frequently been voiced, most insistently by Arthur Schlesinger, Jr., that if we remember the past, we are condemned to misread it. At one time or another the historical analogies of Munich, Berlin, Cuba, Korea, Algeria, and, not least, the first Indochinese war have all been suggested, and all have been denounced as irrelevant and misleading. Whatever one may think of individual analogies, it would seem almost inevitable that past history has provided more mislessons than lessons for Vietnam. What will Vietnam provide for future history and historians?

I begin with the subversive idea that this conference may well mark the formal beginning of the misreading of the Vietnam experience. If

1

the legacy of misplaced analogies which the past has bequeathed to the Vietnam debates is even half equaled by the misplaced analogies which Vietnam bequeaths to the future, error will compound error in positively horrifying manner. It is conceivable that our policy-makers may best meet future crises and dilemmas if they simply blot out of their minds any recollection of this one. The right lesson, in short, may be an unlesson.

The usefulness of drawing no lessons from Vietnam is enhanced by two other considerations. First, the situational characteristics of our Vietnamese entanglement are in many respects unique. The Vietnam problem is a legacy of Western colonial rule, which has just about disappeared from world politics. Vietnam was, in addition, the one European colony in which, for a variety of unique and complex historical factors, communist groups established an early ascendancy in the nationalist movement. In no other European colony—much less any American one—have communism and nationalism been more closely linked. The resulting problems were compounded by a combined heritage of Chinese and French cultural primacy, in which each group reinforced the other in maintaining rule by an intellectual-administrative elite culturally and socially divorced from the mass of the population. The struggle for independence led to a divided country, again a sequence of events which seems unlikely to be duplicated in the future. Finally, the American involvement in Vietnam came at the end of a cycle of active American concern with foreign affairs, which seems unlikely to be repeated for some time in the future. Every historical event or confluence of events is obviously unique; Vietnam may also be irrelevant.

The second qualification about Vietnam concerns the dangers, not of drawing any lesson from Vietnam, but rather of drawing the wrong lessons. At the present moment it is obvious that our involvement has imposed on us severe costs—in men, money, and psychological composure—which make it all look like a horrible mistake. It is desirable, however, to raise a word of caution here, and I would like to apply in reverse the very salutary qualifications which Abraham Lowenthal has suggested with respect to the lessons to be drawn from the Dominican imbroglio.[1] At the moment the dominant tendency is to view that intervention as a success. Whether or not there was a

---

[1] Abraham Lowenthal, "Lessons of the Dominican Crisis" (unpubl. paper, Harvard University, Center for International Affairs, Feb. 1968), p. 5.

threat of communist takeover on the island, we were able to go in, restore order, negotiate a truce among conflicting parties, hold reasonably honest elections which the right man won, withdraw our troops, and promote a very considerable amount of social and economic reform. For those of us who thought in 1965 that there were good political and moral grounds for escalation in Vietnam but none whatsoever for intervening in the Dominican Republic, the apparent results of the two operations are a useful reminder that results are all that count. On the other hand, the Dominican intervention may not be the complete success which so many people now claim it to be. We are in danger of being prisoners of the moment in our interpretations of both the Dominican and Vietnamese affairs. If we are to produce anything other than profound mislessons for the future, we cannot assume one to be an over-all success and the other a total failure.

Undoubtedly there is something to be learned from the Vietnamese experience which may be relevant in the future, but there are a lot more mislessons to be learned that quite clearly will be learned. We have had the experience of a Secretary of State who has been attending to Vietnam in terms of his experience with Korea fifteen years ago, and I can just see future policy makers developing a Vietnam hang-up and approaching the future in terms of their experience with Vietnam.

HANS MORGENTHAU: While listening here, I imagined that in the spring of 1919 an institute, perhaps like this one, might have convened a conference to draw lessons from World War I. To this meeting they would have invited the military and political advisors responsible for the disastrous strategy of the war. All of them would have maintained that World War I was a unique phenomenon, that absolutely nothing could be learned from it for future wars.

Now, it is not a new discovery that historic phenomena are unique in one sense, but it is also an obvious fact that they are typical in another sense. If they were only unique, historical phenomena would simply be oddities, of whose existence we could keep a record but from which obviously we could not learn anything.

DANIEL ELLSBERG: I take it that Professor Huntington's comment that this conference may well begin the formal misreading of the Vietnam experience—unless he was warning us about his own remarks—must be an invidious comment on what he is likely to hear from the rest of us.

§§ ALBERT WOHLSTETTER: Not from me. I am painfully aware that, of all the disasters of Vietnam, the worst may be the "lessons" that we'll draw from it. The disasters so far are real enough; as is our responsibility in them. I have disagreed with our policy there. But one precedent that should make us thoughtful is the wrong lessons that were drawn in Vietnam from Korea. And I do not mean the polemical analogies with Korea—mentioned by Sam Huntington—that were used by one side or another in debate. I am thinking of matters that had greater consequence: the inferences drawn from Korea by our decision-makers in making decisions in Vietnam. For example, U.S. advisors expected another conventional invasion across a parallel separating a communist north from a noncommunist south.[2] To repel it they centered almost all our effort on organizing some 140,000 South Vietnamese into large conventional Army divisions. In the process they created commanders of vast independent political power and thus increased the danger of military coups. This reinforced Diem's natural suspiciousness, nepotism, and tendency to avoid any delegation of power, and it further reduced the chance that the Vietnamese, in spite of internal attack, would be able to advance in economic and political self-development and to operate under the rule of law. That, in turn, encouraged subversion, terror, and counter-terror, and helped make a discriminate response unlikely. Our advisors were responding to a "lesson" of Korea.

Lessons from such complex events require much reflection to be of more than negative worth. But reactions to Vietnam, even more than to Korea, tend to be visceral rather than reflective. We hear now that the United States has no valid concern with the physical security or political and economic development of distant peoples, or of people ethnically distinct from us (that is, those of "us" descended from West

[2] "Q. With command in your own hands from that point on, what were you trying to achieve?
"A. First of all, to organize the armed forces to repel an invasion coming down from the Communist North." Interview with Lieutenant General Samuel T. Williams (Ret.), chief U.S. military advisor in South Vietnam from 1955 to 1960, in *U.S. News and World Report*, Nov. 9, 1964.

Europeans); that U.S. power is the greatest danger to the world; that our problem is not the use of our power discriminately and for worthy ends, but the fact of power itself, that we are better off reducing the choices available to us; that even the policy of massive retaliation, which tended to make every confrontation a choice between nuclear war or doing nothing, was not so bad after all (it was and would be fine because we would always do nothing rather than something in between—according to the hopeful left; according to the hopeful right, it is fine because our *adversaries* would always do nothing in order to avoid our massive retaliation, and if not, they would be overwhelmed by it); that our concerns for security should be limited to direct physical attacks on the continental United States and that we should depend for this purpose on the Navy and an intercontinental nuclear missile force (there is an odd coalition one might discern forming between the old defenders of Fortress America and the New Left—a kind of SAC-SDS position).

I think that such cures would be far worse than the disease. In fact, they would make likely a sharp deterioration of the international system, including an increased expectation of the spread of nuclear weapons and a greater likelihood of nuclear war. The new isolationism has been justified variously on moral, strategic, economic, and ethnic grounds. In my view, none of those grounds can sustain examination.[3]

§§ STANLEY HOFFMANN: The question which the Vietnam fiasco raises is both crucial and difficult to answer. Has Vietnam been an accident, an aberration, an exception, or as Walt Rostow's preaching would have us believe and as so many "revisionists" assert, has it been a logical and necessary development in American foreign policy? If they are right, then our failure there should oblige us to revise drastically our whole policy, to follow a totally new course in the future, and also to re-examine more critically our past successes so as to find in them the germs of our later failure. If they are wrong, then the only lesson of Vietnam is that we applied valid concepts clumsily and that in future interventions we ought to be more careful about the means and strategy we use to reach our goals.

My own contention is somewhere in between. On the one hand,

[3] I examine several of these grounds in "Illusions of Distance," *Foreign Affairs,* Jan. 1968.

Vietnam is an extreme case: the most inappropriate terrain for the application of concepts that have proved fertile and adequate elsewhere. On the other hand, the very attempt, indeed the massive and often frenzied effort, at pursuing goals, applying notions, and devising strategies that turned out to be irrelevant, self-defeating, and dangerous in so unrewarding an area with such persistence in wishful thinking and self-delusion, tells us a great deal about what ought to be discarded in the future. It reveals flaws that come from the depths of our political style and machinery, but had never been so clearly brought to light in any previous operation.

An extreme case that is an aberration teaches little. An extreme case which is at the margin, in the sense of disclosing either a logic or a set of contradictions that are not apparent in run-of-the-mill cases and of forcing one to make explicit choices that are normally made without much thought or pain, can perform the same functions as an ideal type: it is an intensification, an enlargement, of normally blurred features. Vietnam is like a blowup of many of our flaws.

Throughout the conflict we have made the mistake of not facing clearly enough the circumstances peculiar to Vietnam which vitiated our analysis and defeated our expectations. We should not now make the opposite mistake of putting all the blame on "circumstances beyond our control": for unless we recognize our errors, our contribution to the tragedy, we may well, by our own action, reproduce elsewhere the circumstances that we found in Vietnam—say, in Thailand. Of all the disasters of Vietnam the worst could be our unwillingness to learn enough from them.

The Roots
II of Misconceptions

American National Character

ARTHUR SCHLESINGER, JR.: Like everyone else, I have had enormous trouble in working out how we got into the ghastly business of Vietnam. There is, however, a historical framework which may help throw some light on our readiness to undertake an act of intervention which, in the end, bore no relationship to any rational assessment of our interest. The historical framework is comprised of two traditional and entirely honorable strands in American thinking about our role in the world. In time past these two strands were responsible for some of the most splendid moments of our international behavior, but they reached a final and tragic misapplication in Vietnam.

For the lack of a better word one of the strains can be called Stimsonianism. This is the view that an orderly world requires a single durable structure of world security, which must everywhere be protected against aggression: if aggression were permitted to go unpunished in one place, this by infection would lead to a general destruction of the system of world order. I call this Stimsonianism because it was the basis of Secretary of State Henry Stimson's reaction to the Japanese incursion into Manchuria. The underlying idea, nourished by the thinking associated with the League of Nations, gave rise to the phrase "collective security," which gained currency in the 1930's. The idea was nourished by the events of World War II.

The genealogy of Stimsonianism is clear. It extends from Stimson

7

as Secretary of State to his Assistant Secretary, Harvey Bundy, to Bundy's sons, one as Special Assistant for National Security Affairs in the administrations of Presidents John F. Kennedy and Lyndon Johnson and another as Assistant Secretary of State for Far Eastern Affairs. On a parallel line of descent it extends from Stimson, when he was Secretary of War during World War II, through General George C. Marshall, then Chief of Staff of the U.S. Army and later Secretary of State and Secretary of Defense, and from there to Marshall's aide and protégé, now Secretary of State, Dean Rusk. McGeorge and William Bundy and Dean Rusk are, in a sense, the personal executors of the Stimsonian tradition. They argued conscientiously and powerfully for its overextension to Vietnam.

The second honorable tradition is the concept that the United States has a saving mission to the world. It is an old idea, rekindled by Woodrow Wilson in 1917–20 and enlarged by World War II into a kind of global New Dealism. Global New Dealism meant that we have an obligation to deal with poverty, repression, and injustice "everywhere in the world." The concept led to many excellent post–World War II undertakings such as UNRRA, the Marshall Plan, and economic development and technical assistance programs. The human carriers for this idea have a direct line of descent, extending from Woodrow Wilson through Franklin D. Roosevelt to Lyndon Johnson and Hubert Humphrey—two fervent young New Dealers of the 1930's and 1940's. The sense that our duty was to create New Deals on a global basis helped make us vulnerable to an entrapment in Vietnam.

This second strand of thinking—the liberal evangelism which came out of the New Deal and World War II—was reinforced by a third factor: the impact of Stalinism. Because of the tremendous power vacuums created by the war, America and Russia appeared for a moment in history after 1945 to be the world's two superpowers. At the same time, the phenomenon of Stalinism gave rise to an American anticommunism which rightly saw communism as a relatively unified world movement directed from a single center. For many people in the 1940's this necessary and correct anticommunism hardened into a series of conditioned reflexes which continued to guide their thoughts after communism itself was beginning to be transformed under the stress of nationalism. Thus, for example, when Vice-President Hubert Humphrey in October 1967 declared that the threat to peace was militant, aggressive Asian communism with headquarters in Peking, of which the action in Vietnam was the current and immediate expression, he was talking from the conditioned reflexes of the liberal evangelism of the forties.

I was among those who subscribed to the anticommunism of the 1940's in response to Stalinist communism, and I have absolutely no regret about this. Until 1965 I also sympathized with the strands of Stimsonianism and global New Dealism which established the framework for American thinking about foreign affairs. Yet one must now recognize the measure of the tragedy we got into in Vietnam, a tragedy that is all the more poignant because of its conceptual roots—the noble traditions of Stimsonianism and of liberal evangelism—both of which, in times past, expressed some of the best moments in American foreign policy.

EQBAL AHMAD: It seems to me that other aspects inherent in American political culture should be singled out as being driving factors in pushing the United States toward relationships that are likely to lead to intervention.

The first is an extraordinary tradition, clearly characteristic of American political culture: the management of dissent par excellence, a management growing out of the immigrant character of American society.

It now appears, however, that the same immigrant nature of American society which gave this political culture its extraordinarily flexible character also makes for a certain kind of intolerance. It makes for a greater need to insist on the general consensus—on a rather authoritarian superstructure—within whose boundaries bargaining can take place.

Now it seems to me that Americans very often carry this particular attitude to countries abroad. They expect that a certain amount of bargaining will take place, and may often quite unconsciously define its boundaries. But when they find dissent unfolding outside the defined boundaries in totally unmanageable ways, they become intolerant, just as they do at home when they face movements which seem to threaten fundamentals. It also seems to me that when the United States finds itself in a situation where it feels dissent to be quite unmanageable, its immediate, intolerant response reinforces its belief in the efficacy of violence.

ARTHUR SCHLESINGER, JR.: I disagree. I do not think American society responds in any unified way in terms of tolerance or intolerance on questions of dissent. The diverse responses to the war in Vietnam make this clear. By the terms of your thesis, there should have been a united American support for the policy of escalation, whereas in fact the division within American society is tremendous.

Your remark about violence raises another question. Most of the theories of imperialism were inspired by European experience. I think it is interesting as an exercise to try to apply these theories to Vietnam. Lenin's theory that imperialism is the result of a search for investment outlets obviously does not apply to Vietnam. No one seriously supposes that the United States is in Vietnam for economic reasons. But it does seem to me that in a special sense one view of imperialism does explain a good deal of the Vietnam business.

You will remember that Schumpeter argues that the essence of nineteenth-century imperialism in Europe was a reversion to the habit and outlook of a warrior caste which felt itself squeezed out of the picture by the rise of a commercial society. Now, not all of this view applies to the case of Vietnam. Yet it seems to me that a great deal of the pressure leading to an enlargement of the war in Vietnam resulted from the creation in the United States—during World War II and for the first time in American history—of what might be described as a warrior caste in American society. The policies on which our Vietnam course were based as well as the internal momentum to enlarge these policies were largely generated by the military machine. This included the determination to visualize the problem as a military problem, the desire on the part of the military to have testing grounds for tactics and weapons, and the pressures that a concentrated military lobby had in the government and in the Congress.

All this coincided with the ideological susceptibility in the foreign policy establishment resulting from Stimsonianism and liberal evangelism. But the hard thrust which pushed through the policy of enlarging the Vietnamese war was the existence of a "warrior caste," a sort of self-generating, escalating type of machine. This, as you will agree, is a very important factor which ought to be considered when we are trying to avoid getting into future difficulty.

ADAM YARMOLINSKY: I must take issue both with Mr. Ahmad and with Mr. Schlesinger. The point that Mr. Ahmad advanced is inconsistent with the events of the last few months, particularly with the impact of growing dissent within the United States. In fact, it is fair to say that the decision of President Johnson to step down was largely effected by the dissent from his policies.

I would suggest that what Mr. Ahmad is talking about really concerns the way the bureaucracy works. A bureaucracy will tolerate a good deal of dissent within the organization because dissent is necessary to make the organization work. On the other hand, because bureaucracy is so preoccupied with making the organization work, it tends to see everything outside as dimmer and smaller than it in fact is, and therefore is relatively intolerant of external dissent. Further, when the bureaucracy functions outside its natural boundaries and even outside the hemisphere in which we live, it shows an even greater degree of misunderstanding—or nonunderstanding—and is even more disposed to ride roughshod over things standing in its way.

As for Arthur Schlesinger's point about the "warrier caste," the influence it wields is really more of a long-run than a short-run factor. It is more likely to affect the general atmosphere in which decisions are made than to determine any particular decision by bringing direct pressure to bear on it. I don't think the military tell the civilians what to do. But the military alternative attracts more people, more talk, more preparation, more money. The general climate is thus affected, rather than there being a direct conflict about a particular situation in which the warrior caste takes one position.

HENRY KISSINGER: It seems to me that many of our difficulties in Vietnam have turned out to be conceptual failures; and almost all of our concepts, the military ones as well as some of the traditional liberal ones, have really failed, and failed for two reasons.

One of these reasons is that many of them were irrelevant to the situation. Secondly, they failed for a reason that requires careful study: the degree to which our heavy, bureaucratic, and modern government creates a sort of blindness in which bureaucracies run a competition with their own programs and measure success by the degree to which they fulfill their own norms, without being in a position to judge whether the norms made any sense to begin with.

It is a source of infinite wonder to me how General Westmoreland, for example, could continue to come back every time repeating exactly the same phrases, impervious to the lessons that were learned. The official military line for as long as I can remember is that the Viet Cong meant to cut the country into two pieces. Now, why should they want to do that when they already have it cut into fifty pieces? Why should they want to hold territories when their whole strategy depends on the fact that they never have an identifiable territory that is their own. Our blindness here really reflects the predominance of our traditional concepts, under which you measure success and failure by the control of territories.

The liberal concept that you can remove the causes of war by removing economic distress has led to another sort of massive difficulty in Vietnam. Applying lessons learned in the New Deal, we try to alleviate distress—which may not even have been felt as distress by the rural population—at the price of destroying whatever small vestiges of local responsibility there may be. I don't know enough about Vietnamese culture to judge, but I have been very impressed by some things I have plagiarized from John Fairbank. On that basis I doubt whether in a Chinese type of culture legitimacy is established, as is the case in the United States, by a pluralistic sort of election. It seems that our insistence on the elective process in Vietnam may also be an example in which we are simply running a competition with our own criteria.

There is a tendency in the United States to believe that altruism is a guarantee for the correctness of a policy. I would not accept the proposition that we have to support every moral government in the world which gets into difficulty, and I would think that in the kind of world toward which we are heading we will have trouble enough establishing a conception of the American interest without getting into a global conception by which we judge everything in terms of perfectibility.

The problem of defining a national interest under present circumstances is most elusively complicated. We all talk, for example, in terms of balance of power, equilibrium, and the traditional concepts of international relations. But even if our original assumption had been correct—even if Peking were the seat of aggressive Asian communism—we come up against a curious paradox: the acquisition of Vietnam by Peking would be infinitely less significant in terms of the balance of power than the acquisition of nuclear weapons by Peking.

We have no real concepts suitable for guiding our response to nonterritorial change. We have no real concepts suitable for guiding our response to the most significant source of change that may be occurring at the moment, the sort of moral wave going through the world whereby one sort of rebellion leads to another. This process, in turn, cannot be encompassed at all by traditional theories of balances of power. Vietnam is more than a failure of policy. It is really a very critical failure of the American philosophy of international relations.

Moreover, as Stanley Hoffmann has argued in his book, there is a kind of national psychology which leads Americans to conduct their foreign policies with a lack of historical knowledge. For example, it is amazing that no one seems to have systematically studied, before we went there, what the French experience was in Vietnam. I never understood, even before I knew anything about Vietnam, why we thought we could achieve with sixteen thousand men what the French could not do with two hundred thousand men.

When one is asked for advice, the constant American tendency has been to respond by looking for a gimmick. Every year we have had a new program in Vietnam, and we have carried out each program with the obsessive certainty that it was the ultimate solution to the problem.

I don't know whether there will be "another Vietnam." But I feel that we have to make a really prayerful assessment of what we went in there for, not to pin blame on any people or particular set of conditions but to assess the whole procedure and concepts that got us involved there. We have to do this if we are not going to have another disaster that may have a quite different look but will have the same essential flaws.

§§ EQBAL AHMAD: Let me spell out what I meant in my previous remarks. The United States, the protestations of its leaders and scholars notwithstanding, has been, in effect, opposed to third-world nationalism, historically in South America and recently in its client states. This opposition, however, has been manifest, not in the initial stages of the demand for self-determination with respect to Spanish, French, Dutch or British colonialism, but in the stage when a particular nationalism has begun to acquire a diplomatic, economic, and social expression. The antinationalist thrust of the United States, as well as its interventionist tendencies, is not rooted in American ideology. It is related, perhaps, to certain aspects of American political culture:

(1) *The paranoid strain in American politics,* which has been analyzed at some length by Richard Hofstadter. It forms the basis, at least in part, of America's crusading zeal, which the realists like Morgenthau and Kennan have bewailed. It also constitutes the most important component of a conspiratorial view of history, a sort of Manichaean outlook which panics over the imagined subversion of the forces of good by the forces of evil. Hofstadter states: "The distinguishing thing about the paranoid style is not that its exponents see conspiracies here and there in history but that they regard a vast and gigantic conspiracy as the motive force in historical events. History is a conspiracy, set in motion by demonic forces of almost transcendent power, and what is felt to be needed to defeat it is not the usual methods of political give and take but an all-out crusade."

The deep hold of an almost theological anticommunism on the American people becomes more understandable when viewed in this light. The habit of viewing historical events and social processes in *ad hoc,* technical terms derives partly, too, from this view of history. Even the social scientists are conditioned by it. The official literature on counterinsurgency is a case in point. Revolutionary warfare is viewed essentially as a technical problem, i.e., a problem of plotting and subversion on the one hand and of intelligence and suppression on the other. As the chief conspiratorial groups the communists are believed to be the most likely initiators and beneficiaries of revolution. This belief produces a pessimistic posture toward a world in transformation and underlies the nearly unqualified commitment of the United States to stability and order in the countries under its influence. It was this attitude which led to the quashing of what was construed as the "Dominican communist conspiracy."

A logical extension of this attitude is the belief that any revolutionary movement is inspired, directed, and controlled from abroad.

In times of stress it may lead to a ridiculously simplified "puppeteer view" of history, which disregards the force of nationalism. Dean Rusk's famous description of China as being a "Soviet Manchukuo" is now legend. The Johnson Administration's belief, perhaps once sincere, that the National Front for Liberation (South Vietnam) was a puppet of the northern regime and that the Democratic Republic of Vietnam (North) was in turn a puppet of one or the other of the larger communist powers, may fly in the face of facts, but it has been held with tenacity in this country and is still plausible to most people.

(2) *The tradition of management of dissent.* Owing perhaps to its immigrant character, which necessitated the successful integration of diverse groups within the system, the American political culture is management-oriented. Historically group demands have been managed through the process of political bargaining and selective rewards. Ideological and social dissent have been managed by the co-optation both of individuals and ideas. Insofar as the society was endowed with expanding resources as well as an extremely mobile social structure, the politics of management within a pluralistic framework was possible. It was further facilitated by the existence of a basic consensus to which all aspiring groups tended to subscribe.

Yet the same forces which produced a flexible tradition of bargaining and co-optation also produced an overemphasis on the maintenance of a basic consensus which would admit of differences but not cleavages on how society was to be organized. Unmanageable dissent has, therefore, often encountered swift and ruthless repression in America. The I.W.W. immediately comes to mind. Those groups that were defined as being outside of the political boundary faced extermination, as did the Indians, or were forcibly kept on the outer limits, as were the blacks. The result is an authoritarian superstructure, allowing for a well-defined but extremely permissive infrastructure. This cultural complex has important ramifications for the American response to the stresses of social change in underdeveloped countries.

First, there is an expectation that the Asian and Latin versions of robber barons and party bosses will, out of self-interest, get around seriously to introducing reforms and will achieve an orderly resolution of conflicts arising from the pressures of participation and distribution. Hence the tendency to cling obstinately to the hope that institutions will be promoted and social progress will be achieved under a Diem, the Thai generals, or the Filipino politicians. This view misconstrues the value system and class characteristics of the rulers in a traditional and feudal society, their concept of self-interest, and their relationship to the society, upon all of which their defense of the status quo is predicated. It is the reason for America's alliance with conservative nationalism whose legitimacy erodes as social pressures mount and foreign involvements augment. The United States, in turn, becomes progressively committed to defending conservative factions.

Second, since rewards and bargains are essential aspects of the American political style, the United States increases its economic and military commitments to client states often in the hope of using these commitments as a leverage to press for reforms.

Third, the consensus upon which the American system of bargaining and boundary management is predicated does not exist in underdeveloped countries. It is likely to be particularly lacking in the client states where foreign alignments tend to exacerbate internal divisions. There is a growing trend in the third world toward the radicalization of conflict. The superimposition and infiltration of modern technology and values are drastically altering the social and economic configurations which in the traditional societies had circumscribed discontent within the boundaries of religiosity and rebellions. These countries are witnessing a fundamental shift in the equation of human condition, and this change marks their transition from rebellion to a revolution whose basic drive is not merely the fulfillment of limited goals, like raising the per-capita income and level of food consumption, but the transformation of all relationships—political, economic, and social —between groups and individuals. As new groups of people, previously outside the political realm, force their way into politics, the common man becomes politically relevant. For many newcomers in politics this mass constitutes the only capital. Politics thus ceases to be a mere struggle within a privileged minority for spoils of power. It becomes progressively a contest between the contenders of different social systems and political ideals. The opposition in such societies is frequently unmanageable because it does not share the values of an often ill-defined and sometimes illegitimate authority.

In such conflictive cultures the United States is aligned, by inclination no less than by reason of diplomatic priority, with the ruling, generally conservative regimes. When faced with unmanageable dissent in countries where American influence is paramount, the United States is inclined to intervene, responding in a traditional American way. The opposition is defined as being outside the legitimate political boundary (often it does not matter if both legitimacy and a defined boundary are absent).

Paranoia seeks plausible enemies; the conspiratorial theory is invoked; radical nationalists, socialists, all become "communists"; repression against "outside agitators" is carried out. After listening to a State Department official's defense on Vietnam at Tougaloo College, Mississippi, a black woman remarked that he spoke exactly like the white leaders in the South: there was the assertion that Negroes in the South were generally satisfied; trouble began only when agitators from the North infiltrated; there was communist subversion. For the same reason Ambassador Nolting came to remind David Halberstam "of some white community leaders in Mississippi and Tennessee."

(3) Perhaps the most important single factor in influencing *American* style in the underdeveloped countries has been its *experience in Latin America*. Before becoming a world power, America had exercised its power outside its own boundaries mainly in the Latin American countries; and this seems to have shaped its attitudes and methods of dealing with weaker nations. Here radical nationalism has been the greatest threat to American interests; here the pattern of alliance with oligarchies was established, and it paid economic and political dividends. The dialectic of intervention that developed in South America confirmed America's belief in the efficacy of violence as an instrument of foreign policy.

(4) *Belief in the efficacy of violence.* There has been some discussion in recent years of the role of violence in American culture. However, I have seen insufficient analysis of the extent to which a belief in the efficacy of violence appears to be an important aspect of the historical outlook and socialization in the United States. As a newcomer I was struck by the thematic consistency of films on American colonization ("Westerns") and by the reactions of American audiences to them. The whites are a human grouping in all their

diversities, emotions, and failings. Tension builds up around the pioneer group united by a common enterprise and threatened by an invisible, elemental enemy. The Indian is an outsider, and dehumanized. One does not learn of his family life, hopes, fears, and grievances. Indians come in hordes, screaming primitives. White guns, strategically placed and skillfully fired, wipe them out. They fall in stylized movements which bring smiles or laughter to the audience. Efficiency and superior technology in the service of a mission overcome the Indian; violence is seen as an instrument of national purpose.

At first one refuses to believe that this constitutes a fundamental source of socialization. But an examination of decades of school history texts confirms one's fears. In the texts there is some pity but little self-examination, considerable chauvinism and self-righteousness, and much that conforms to the television version of history. There is some respect for the Indian, but only in his role as a noble savage—an honor denied the Negro, also an excluded group, who suffered another form of violence. The Indians' extermination is accepted as the natural offering to manifest destiny. This destruction of people and of cultures has become the object of public entertainment and children's games. Instead of deriving a sense of tragedy from it, America has institutionalized even its genocide.

The violence which has been practiced against the Indian or the Negro is not genocidal in intent. It is instrumental, political, and ethnocentric. Violence is seen as a natural vehicle for the attainment of societal goals, especially when it involves confrontation with culturally and racially alien groups who are often perceived as inferior and expendable. The belief in the efficacy of violence when reinforced by the feeling of racial superiority augments interventionist tendencies, brutalizes the resulting conflict beyond legal or necessary bounds, and also produces miscalculations regarding the will and tenacity of the enemy. All of these have been true in Vietnam. Asians as alien and colored people are particularly vulnerable, which is one reason why a rapid military disengagement of the United States from Asian countries will be highly desirable.

JOHN KING FAIRBANK: The history of Sino-American relations is also part of the soft background of Vietnam. It involves the American image of China, the assumptions and expectations, the feelings about this area in the public mind.

In essence, I would say, the American image of China grew with the American expansion to the East involving missionaries, overseas trade, etc. This, in turn, produced an American-Chinese style of interaction.

In this regard I would make only two points in relation to recent history. The first is that Vietnam is a continuation of this interaction, at least to some degree. On the American side Vietnam has in its background some relation to American benevolence toward China, fear of China, disappointment about China—the combined love and hate feelings inherited from our nineteenth-century contact. In Vietnam the United States feels that it is perhaps getting back at the Chinese for their going communist, or that it is standing firm against "the evil" that grew up in China. In short, it is a further round in our relationship with China.

Second, in the nature of our relationship with China, cultural conflicts inevitably arose every time Americans and Chinese were in contact because they were operating on different bases. The essence of the whole interaction was that when the cultural conflict became insoluble, the West resorted to force—Americans relied first on British and eventually on American gunboats. In this context, at least until very recently, the Chinese did most of the adjusting.

With the cultural conflict, a meeting on peaceful terms has been impossible. Thus part of the soft background provides a feed-in to the American propensity toward violence. On the Chinese side there is a tradition of Boxerism, as the treaty boys used to call it, which reminds one very much of the Cultural Revolution, destructive both against the established order and the foreigner who is a part of it.

I raise all of this to indicate one of the dimensions of our problem. We are talking about American psychological propensities. The relationship with China is part of the American past which has triggered in Asia the case of Vietnam.

The World of the 1960's

§§ SAMUEL P. HUNTINGTON: For twenty years after World War II the pre-eminent phenomenon of world politics was the expansion of the United States. The fears and expectations in 1945 that the United

States would pull back, if not to interwar isolation at least to a less extensive involvement in world affairs, were decisively proved wrong. Beginning with the Greek-Turk aid program, the United States became progressively involved in the maintenance of international stability in all areas of the world and the promotion of economic development in most countries. The causes of this expansion included: a perceived need by American officials to block the expansion of the Soviet Union, China, and/or "international communism"; the demands and pressures from foreign statesmen, groups, and governments for American action to benefit them; economic, technical, and military developments which made feasible involvement in world politics on a world-wide basis; and the willingness and, indeed, buoyant eagerness of important sectors of American public opinion to support such involvement and to play an active role in it. American involvement in Vietnam was one aspect of this expansion.

§§ JAMES C. THOMSON, JR.: A first and central ingredient in the early years of Vietnam decisions was the legacy of the 1950's. This legacy—the so-called "loss of China," the Korean War, and the Far East policy of Secretary of State Dulles—had an institutional byproduct for the Kennedy Administration: in 1961 the United States government's East Asian establishment was undoubtedly the most rigid and doctrinaire of Washington's regional divisions in foreign affairs. This was especially true at the Department of State, where the incoming Administration found the Bureau of Far Eastern Affairs the hardest nut to crack. It was a bureau that had been purged of its best China experts and of farsighted, dispassionate men as a result of McCarthyism. Its members were generally committed to one policy line: the close containment and isolation of mainland China, the harassment of "neutralist" nations which sought to avoid alignment with either Washington or Peking, and the maintenance of a network of alliances with anticommunist client states on China's periphery.

Another aspect of the legacy was the special vulnerability and sensitivity of the new Democratic Administration to Far East policy issues. The memory of the McCarthy era was still very sharp, and Kennedy's margin of victory was too thin. The 1960 Offshore Islands TV debate between Kennedy and Nixon had shown the President-elect the perils of "fresh thinking." The Administration was inherently leery of moving too fast on Asia. As a result the Far East Bureau (now the Bureau of East Asian and Pacific Affairs) was the last one to be overhauled. Not until Averell Harriman was brought in as Assistant Secretary in December 1961 were significant personnel changes attempted, and it took Harriman several months to make a deep imprint on the bureau because of his necessary preoccupation with the Laos settlement. Once he did so, there was virtually no effort to bring back the purged or exiled East Asia experts.

There were other important by-products of this "legacy of the fifties." The new Administration inherited and somewhat shared in a general perception of "China on the march"—a sense of China's vastness, its numbers, and its belligerence, perhaps a revived sense of the "Golden Horde." This was a perception fed by Chinese intervention in the Korean War (an intervention actually based on appallingly bad communications and mutual miscalculation on the part of Washington and Peking; but the careful unraveling of that tragedy, which scholars have accomplished, had not yet become part of conventional wisdom).

The new Administration inherited and briefly accepted a monolithic conception of the communist bloc. Despite much earlier predictions and reports by outside analysts, policy-makers did not begin to accept the reality and possible finality of the Sino-Soviet split until the first weeks of 1962. The inevitably corrosive impact of competing nationalisms on communism was largely ignored.

The new Administration inherited and to some extent shared the "domino theory" about Asia. This theory resulted from profound ignorance of Asian history and hence ignorance of the radical differences among Asian nations and societies. It resulted from a blindness to the power and resilience of Asian nationalisms. (It may also have resulted from a subconscious sense that since "all Asians look alike," all Asian nations will act alike.) As a theory, the domino fallacy was not merely inaccurate but also insulting to Asian nations; yet it has continued to this day to beguile men who should know better.

In the early 1960's the legacy of the fifties was compounded by an uneasy sense of a worldwide communist challenge to the new Administration after the Bay of Pigs fiasco. A first manifestation was the President's traumatic Vienna meeting with Khrushchev in June

1961; then came the Berlin crisis of that summer. All this created an atmosphere in which President Kennedy undoubtedly felt under special pressure to show the nation's mettle in Vietnam—if the Vietnamese, unlike the people of Laos, were willing to fight. The legacy of the fifties shaped such early moves of the new Administration as the decisions to maintain a high-visibility SEATO (by sending the Secretary of State himself instead of some underling to its first meeting in 1961), to back away from diplomatic recognition of Mongolia in the summer of 1961, and, most important, to expand U.S. military assistance to South Vietnam that winter on the basis of the much more tentative Eisenhower commitment. Finally, the increased commitment to Vietnam was also fueled by a new breed of military strategists and academic social scientists (some of whom had entered the new Administration) who had developed theories of counterguerrilla warfare and were eager to see them put to the test. To some, "counterinsurgency" seemed a new panacea for coping with the world's instability.

§§ ADAM YARMOLINSKY: Why did otherwise intelligent and humane persons persist in error where Vietnam was concerned? No facile analogy (however often repeated) to the commitments assumed under the Eisenhower Administration is particularly illuminating. American intervention in South Vietnam clearly changed not only in degree but in quality at least once and probably more than once during the Kennedy-Johnson Administration. Two observations, however, about the Eisenhower Administration's experiences with respect to Vietnam may be relevant here.

First, the Eisenhower Administration was extraordinarily lucky. Its one critical decision on escalation in Vietnam—the decision not to intervene at Dien Bien Phu—was presented as a major step, not to be disguised as anything less. The representations of the Joint Chiefs as to the likelihood that nuclear weapons might be required were enough by themselves to alert all concerned to the gravity of the choice. Even a true believer in massive retaliation was given pause.

But by the same token the Eisenhower Administration in a sense contributed one of the key elements that went into the make-up of the later decisions to go up rather than down. That was the fundamentalist anticommunism exemplified by John Foster Dulles, an anti-communism that remained as an emotional and political factor long after it had been succeeded by a more sophisticated analysis of relationships within and beyond the communist world.

It must be recognized that a somewhat similar attitude continued to find expression in the views of Dean Rusk, and that the foreign service bureaucracy provides an extraordinary—some might say oppressive—degree of continuity in American foreign policy. While the propositions of an earlier age are now stated in somewhat more sophisticated terms, there is still a large element in official American thinking about foreign policy that assumes an American monopoly on virtue and wisdom in a wicked world.

The decision to undertake even the limited amount of military assistance provided to the Diem regime immediately after the Geneva Accords was based on three factors. In descending order of importance they were, first, anticommunist solidarity; second, concern about the domination of Southeast Asia by the Chinese communists and their friends; and third, concern about any shift in the locus of the "iron" or "bamboo" curtains accomplished by force.

The significant fact about these three concerns is that between Eisenhower and Kennedy their relative priorities were completely reversed. This reversal suggests the more general shift in concern from a preoccupation with ideology to a preoccupation with influence.

In addition a series of events early in the Kennedy Administration had an important impact on issues associated with intervention in Vietnam. As Jim Thomson has said, the Bay of Pigs, the Kennedy-Khrushchev confrontation in Vienna, and the decision not to intervene in the civil war in Laos—each argued in its way for some countermove to demonstrate American firmness in the face of Soviet or Soviet-backed probes, whether verbal or physical. In some situations timing becomes all important; and if Vietnam was the wrong place to increase our military commitment, it looked like the right time.

Another factor that undoubtedly contributed to the early decision to escalate in Vietnam was, in a negative sense at least, a legacy from Eisenhower and particularly from Foster Dulles. The Kennedy Administration rejected early and with considerable relief the doctrine of massive retaliation. The realization that nuclear weapons could not be brandished as an all-purpose threat made the use of force at the nonnuclear level seem somehow less frightening. There was even a kind of euphoria about the newly expanded Special Forces, who were being trained, it was said, as much in the arts of peace as in the arts of war, and who might reduce the use of force from the level of megaton monstrosity to the level of individual human effort.

The enthusiasm for counterinsurgency as a new technique was a part of the same pattern. What it lacked in specificity, it made up for in energy. A new Administration is likely to be optimistic about new ways of doing things—even of fighting wars—and Vietnam turned out to be a testing ground for these new kinds of forces and techniques. Because they were felt to be both more effective and less dangerous than conventional (or indeed nuclear) military means, it took longer to discover the limits of their effectiveness and the dangers of their use. And because there was still a strong element of paternalism in American foreign policy, the desirability of finding means for forceful intervention was not seriously questioned.

Again, several factors need to be sorted out in this latter phase of decision-making. The primary focus of these decisions seems to have been on shoring up the—or a—Saigon regime rather than on blunting the force—or determination—of Hanoi. When all the arguments advanced in favor of initiating the bombing of the north are critically analyzed, the most persuasive one turns out to have been the effect of the bombing on crumbling morale in the south. There was no enthusiasm, at the level of political decision, about any of the new escalatory moves. But there was at least less disinclination to examine these alternatives than to examine the alternatives on the down side of the scale. Accounts of the period make it clear that there was unanimous agreement within the government that the only course of action no longer available was to continue at the same level of force. But one senses that there was more concern with minimizing necessary escalation than with maximizing feasible de-escalation.

The pause in the decision process because of an intervening Presidential election was also a factor to be reckoned with. The pacific promises of the campaign, however deeply felt, were probably a less significant determinant of policy than the effect of the practical moratorium on decision-making induced by the campaign itself. Decisions that are postponed end up being accelerated by the accumulated pressure of events. The impact of regularly scheduled elections on the conduct of foreign affairs, as in Korea, Suez, and Cuba, is a subject deserving separate study.

After 1965 one enters the Aeschylean stage of United States intervention in Vietnam. The character of the problem changes significantly. It is perhaps more aptly described as a manifestation of *hubris* than as the evolution of rational, if misguided, policy. To reverse our course, as we seem to be doing at long last, called for a change of heart at least as much as a change of mind. It is on the earlier stages, then, that one might focus in order to try to draw lessons for the future conduct of American foreign policy.

§§ THEODORE DRAPER: One of the points made by Professor Yarmolinsky about our progressive involvement in Vietnam is that the decisions of 1961 and 1962 were not of the same order as those of 1964 and 1965. He rejects the notion, as do I, that the latter decisions were predetermined by the earlier ones. In fact, he seems to think that the difference was so great that the later ones were not even the result of a "rational evolution" but were rather a manifestation of *hubris,* which comes close to saying that they were "irrational." As a result, Professor Yarmolinsky says, we can learn more from the earlier stages than from the later ones, and he therefore thinks it is best or more rewarding to focus on the earlier ones.

If all this is true, the trouble we got into is either too hard or too easy for us to get out of. *Hubris* is something you have or you haven't. If you have it, Professor Yarmolinsky implies, your policy no longer evolves rationally, and it does not lend itself, therefore, to rational analysis or treatment. On the other hand, you may pay such a heavy price for your *hubris* that the shock of retribution will knock it out of you. Once it goes away, you will get back on the rational path and the worst part of the problem will be gone.

Isn't this a too easy way out? First, I rather doubt that there was less *hubris* in 1961 than in 1965 or, even farther back, in 1954 than in 1965. American *hubris,* if that is the right word for what we are talking about, strikes me as having been a fairly permanent condition since the end of the last war. It may have gotten us into more serious trouble in February 1965 than in, say, April 1961, but the reason for the difference may be perfectly amenable to rational analysis and treatment.

I do not wish to go into the question of whether President Kennedy would have done in 1965 the same thing that President Johnson did. We can only speculate, and though I see no reason for not speculating on the basis of whatever evidence we have, this is probably not the place for it. Still, the issue arises because, as has so often been pointed out, so many of the key men in both the Kennedy and the Johnson administrations were the same. Were they suddenly overcome with *hubris* in 1965? My own view would be that there *was* a rational evolution of policy in 1964–65 and that in fact the rationale of policy was quite the same throughout this decade. That President Johnson's decisions were not predetermined by President Kennedy's decisions does not mean that the same theoretical premises could not lend themselves, rationally, to different practical conclusions in different circumstances.

You will note that I have just introduced a somewhat different factor: "theoretical premises." I have done so in order to get to my main point. The Vietnam war has brought on a crisis not only of policy but of the theory behind the policy. The theory behind the policy lent itself to a perfectly rational, if misguided, evolution, and I think it also lends itself to what I hope will be a perfectly rational, if necessarily brief, critique.

Professor Yarmolinsky points out what at first glance may appear to be a paradox. "Massive retaliation," that monstrous doctrine of the 1950's, saved us from large-scale intervention in Vietnam in 1954. But its successor, variously known as "limited war," "graduated response," or "flexible response," has not saved us from increasingly large-scale intervention in Vietnam since 1961 and especially since 1965. In fact, the doctrine of "limited war" as it was worked out in the latter half of the 1950's outside the government and taken over by the government in the 1960's must be held partially responsible for pulling us in.

That something was wrong with the theory was impressed on me by reading the book *Arms and Influence* by one of the most brilliant and respected of the new power theorists, Professor Thomas C. Schelling. In this book, published in 1966, Professor Schelling devoted several pages to the "reprisal" action in the Gulf of Tonkin in August 1964. He hailed it as a triumph of "appropriate" response and as a classic example of how to wage a "limited war," a "restrained war."[1] This view was, of course, not limited to Professor Schelling, and I cite his book because he is an eminent figure in the field and because there can be no doubt about his enthusiasm for the Gulf of Tonkin type of operation. Yet I think few today would dispute that this action set off the entire cycle of events which led the United States to sink deeper and deeper into the Vietnam morass. In Professor Schelling's book, however, there are only praise and celebration of the event. Something must be wrong if one of the outstanding theorists of "limited war" could not see, at least a year and possibly two years later, where the Gulf of Tonkin action would or could lead us.

What was wrong?

Professor Thomson, in his recent article in *The Atlantic,* told of the kind of thinking that went into the Gulf of Tonkin operation. In the late autumn of 1964 the "air-strike planners," as he calls them, thought that the North Vietnamese would "come crawling to us for peace talks" after six weeks of bombing. At one of the meetings someone asked, What if they don't? The answer was that another four weeks of bombing would do the trick.[2]

This, in essence, has been the source of American bafflement and frustration in Vietnam. For three years the United States has applied increasing force to end the war on its own terms. According to the doctrine of "limited war," the Vietnamese communists should have realized at some point that the price was too high and therefore "come crawling to us." If the policy based on the theory has failed, it is time to re-examine the theory.

The theorists of "limited war" saw clearly what was wrong with the doctrine of "massive retaliation," which proved to be little more than a massive hoax. They saw that we were, in fact, not fighting the great apocalyptic war against Soviet Russia or Communist China, and that we needed both a military establishment and a strategic doctrine of greater flexibility and gradation for the difficulties we were getting into. The trouble with "massive retaliation," they recognized, was that it was most relevant to one type of war only—a war between

---

[1] Thomas C. Schelling, *Arms and Influence* (New Haven: Yale University Press, 1966), pp. 141–45.
[2] James C. Thomson, Jr., "How Could Vietnam Happen?" *The Atlantic,* April 1968, p. 51.

the "superpowers." It was not so clear to the "limited war" theorists that their recipes of "graduated response" might be self-defeating in a war between a very great power and a very small one.

When a great power confronts a great power, military victory may or may not be "meaningful," depending on one's attitude toward war in general. But when a very great power, possessing weapons of indescribable destruction, confronts a very small power, what does military victory mean? What is gained if the United States proves that it is militarily stronger than the Dominican Republic or even North Vietnam? To make such a conflict meaningful, the great power has to demonstrate how little force it needs to use, not how much force it can use. Paradoxically, a great power can obtain a meaningful victory over a small power only by using a small part of its strength or at least using much less than it is capable of using. But then it loses some or all of its advantages as a great power; it voluntarily abstains from using its most destructive weapons or from using its more conventional weapons most destructively.

This dilemma can be overcome only by assuming that there is a relatively modest level of destruction which will not be "acceptable," as the phrase goes, to the small power. In fact, we seem to assume that a small power cannot or will not take as much punishment as a large power. But this is precisely where great-power thinking goes wrong. Great powers tend to think of "limited wars" in terms of themselves. They think of the "limit" as what it would be, in relative terms, if they were taking the punishment or in relation to the total force they are capable of using. But neither of these senses may seem very limited to a small power. A great power may use only a very limited portion of its power, but it will be enough to make a small power feel that it must fight an unlimited war or not fight at all.[3]

[3] This may be demonstrated by one of the examples given to show how moderate the United States has been in Vietnam. Professor Robert Scalapino, of the University of California at Berkeley, recently argued that "while we certainly have bombed North Vietnam extensively, we have it within our power, and you know this, to eradicate North Vietnam from the map. The fact that we have risked American lives over months and months in an effort to avoid that kind of total mass destruction of this country, is one indication that Goliath has placed certain limitations upon his power" (*The New Leader*, Feb. 26, 1968, p. 14). Presumably this act of self-denial on the part of the United States should have persuaded North Vietnam to place certain limitations

This is especially true if the small power, or rather its people in sufficient numbers, is willing to die for a cause. Death is not limited; and if enough people are willing to die, they are not going to fight a "limited war." This is the imponderable that cannot be accounted for in any theory of "limited war." It takes two to fight a limited war; and if one refuses to play that game, the other has to go from limit to upper limit despite its better judgment that at some limit the game is no longer worth the candle.

In the case of the Vietnam war, victory might have been meaningful as long as it was basically conducted by two small powers, namely, South and North Vietnam or as a civil war in South Vietnam. Until 1965 it was a war by proxies, which is the only way a great power today may engage in a war without pitting either great power against great power or great power against small power. As soon as the United States took over the main function of the war in 1965, it condemned itself to fighting either an unlimited war from the outset —and horrifying the world and its own people—or fighting a "limited war" which it could not win without exceeding the limits that would make the other side fight an unlimited war. This is the contradiction which the theorists of "limited war" never thought through.

I am persuaded that one reason—and not the least important— for our "progressive involvement" in Vietnam has been the theory of "limited war" as expounded for the past ten or a dozen years. The crucial defect of this theory has been the divorce of power and politics. It is no accident, as some people like to say, that the power theorists, limited and unlimited, have had least to say about the three interventions that have done the most damage to the United States in this decade—those in Cuba, the Dominican Republic, and Vietnam—and what they have mostly had to say might better have been left unsaid. These interventions posed a problem in which power and politics were inextricably tangled up, and politics has never been the strong point of power theorists. Another way of saying the same thing, perhaps, is

---

upon its power. Thus "limited war" is defined, in this view, as anything short of eradicating North Vietnam "from the map." There may be some horrible kind of logic to this from the viewpoint of total American power of destruction, but it totally ignores what effect this self-imposed "limitation" would have on North Vietnam. A "limitation" defined as short of what it would take to eradicate North Vietnam from the map would be well within the limits of what would force North Vietnam to fight an unlimited war.

that wars pure and simple and revolutions impure and anything but simple are not the same things, and revolutionary war could not be encompassed by a doctrine of "limited war."

The policy has failed, and so has the theory. We need a new policy; and before we get it, we may have to work out a new theory. The new theory would not take as its point of departure the difference between limited and unlimited wars, both primarily military in character. It would be based on the relationship between politics and power, and thus limit the use of power to what can be usefully achieved politically.

JOHN MCDERMOTT: In Congress a rather different but fairly systematic critique of the theory of limited war has been developed by certain right-wing members, which goes something like this: the theory of limited war involves, in a sense, telegraphing in advance the increment and the successor to that increment so that a potential enemy will at any given stage be aware of the price he will pay for not going along in the direction we desire. This telegraphing, Congressmen argue, has been a major factor in the success of the North Vietnamese in devising and adjusting their defenses to American attacks and in withstanding American escalation. For example, early in 1965 the air defense of Hanoi was not formidable. However, within a year after bombing began, air defenses were such as to make raids on Hanoi a very expensive proposition.

The kinds of ideas that seem likely to replace the early theory of limited war in political discussions within the Congress seem quite dangerous. For example, the theory based on one reading of the case of the Dominican intervention suggests that overwhelming force applied early in a somewhat unpredictable way is a successful alternative to the kind of failures limited war, illustrated in Vietnam, has involved.

The value of the old limited war theories and theories of international relations was that they were in a sense predictable. You did not make huge, rather unpredictable and incalculable jumps in escalation of force. The jumps were small enough so that an adversary could judge them, could see their limit immediately, and therefore could calculate and make a rational response to them.

What is of interest in the alternative—illustrated by our Dominican intervention—is that in a great-power context it introduces unpredictability into the other side's assessment of what we are doing and therefore into the other side's response. For example, if in early 1965 instead of a slow build-up of the Vietnam escalation we had suddenly injected a million American troops and the United States Air Force had begun launching really very heavy attacks against North Vietnam, then the North Vietnamese, Russians, and Chinese might well have been very anxious and edgy as to what this might portend.

ALBERT WOHLSTETTER: Mr. McDermott is quite right in stressing that, besides the left and liberal criticisms of limited war doctrines, there is an intense right-wing attack on such doctrines too. It is represented not only in the Congress but among some of the military, and by some candidates for the presidency, specifically Reagan and Wallace. In a way, I think it is important to put these two sorts of criticism side by side if we are to avoid misreading the history of such strategic doctrines. Both criticisms exhibit a certain nostalgia for policies which seem to eliminate choices in between massive nuclear retaliation and not responding at all to an aggression. They do this, of course, not because they are fond of nuclear war or even the threat of it. Such criticisms presuppose either that a less flexible policy, because it presents grimmer alternatives to an adversary, will discourage aggression, and so will call for few, if any, occasions for our actually intervening; or that, if there is an occasion for intervening, we will avoid it, since the alternatives of using nuclear weapons are so grim for us. The latter prospect, that we will avoid intervening, is what attracts moderates today.

Adam Yarmolinsky notes that massive retaliation saved us from intervening in Vietnam in 1954 but flexible response didn't keep us out in 1961. Ted Draper thinks flexible response or limited war doctrine is partly what got us in. Ted Draper seems to me to regard the threat of massive retaliation too leniently, as "little more than a massive hoax." (In fact, we can't be sure it was a hoax. And if it was, it was a dangerous hoax. Some high officials in the Eisenhower regime have indicated that we did transmit to Ho, just as we had done in Korea, a threat to use nuclear weapons unless some compromise was reached in negotiations to end the war.)

There was a wide variety of mutually incompatible doctrines developed as a counter to the Dulles doctrine of massive retaliation. We shouldn't talk of *the* doctrine of limited war, as if there were only one. There were many. Some stressed the importance of having the ability to answer a conventional ground attack with conventional weapons. Some merely shifted the burden of response from long-range air-delivered nuclear weapons to short-range nuclear ground forces. Many, like Robert Osgood's analysis in 1957, stressed the importance of controlling military force by political purpose. They surely did not offer military response as a substitute for a variety of nonmilitary political measures where those were adequate. It would be quite unfair to represent any of these varied doctrines as advocating war, limited or otherwise. What they stressed was the importance of trying to limit war, if war should come. And they stressed that all-out strategic nuclear threats were too extreme in many likely circumstances, too out of proportion to the provocation, to deter nonnuclear conflicts reliably. This bare-minimum agreement among the varied doctrines of limited war is quite sound. The alternatives are extremely unsound.

First of all, our threat to use nuclear weapons might seem offhand to preclude lesser interventions by us. But in fact it doesn't and didn't. In the heyday of massive retaliation theory we did intervene in Guatemala, in the Philippines, in Iran, in Lebanon. Making irresponsible threats doesn't mean that, in the event, you avoid intervening altogether in order not to perform on the irresponsible promise. It can mean that, when the threat doesn't work, because it was transparently irresponsible, a more appropriate reply, of the kind that should have been indicated in the first place, will actually be made. Or an *in*appropriate nonnuclear response; or a nuclear one.

Second, I think we kid ourselves if we suppose that issuing nuclear threats to discourage nonnuclear provocations is harmless, even if it doesn't do any good. They raise the probability of nuclear war. Many people want to believe that if nonnuclear aggression should take place in spite of attempts to discourage it with the threat of nuclear weapons, there is no harm done, since no one would fulfill such threats. This *has* been true so far. But it only has to be false once to be too often. A nuclear threat, to have any use at all, has to have some significant chance of being fulfilled. If it were absolutely certain that nuclear weapons would not be used, nuclear threats—and massive retaliation doctrine—would be worthless. (The notion that fighting insurgency is terrible and therefore threatening nuclear war isn't so bad should be compared with the odd theory that had a good deal of currency a couple of years ago about Europe: Europe, it was said, has experienced conventional wars and wants no part of them; therefore, they should depend on nuclear threats instead of conventional preparations. However, even if World War II was no delight, a nuclear World War III would be no better.)

Third, I have often wondered recently, "Whatever became of nuclear war?" At this conference, and in much of the recent debate on foreign policy, references to the possibility of a nuclear catastrophe are either nonexistent or perfunctory. That is why people can so easily forget the vital sound element in the varied doctrines of limited war. But the very men who, just a year or two ago, were talking about nuclear war as though it were certain to come within a few years—an apocalyptic view I never shared—have now forgotten about nuclear war altogether. Today it appears that it never was a problem.

However, it was a problem and it is a continuing problem. Neglecting it, in the lessons that we draw for the future, is dangerous. And the neglect also affects our understanding of the past. I believe that the Kennedy and McNamara changes in defense policy are done a great historical injustice when we note only the errors that led us deeply into the mire in Vietnam, and neglect the vital changes that were made in policy on nuclear arms. These changes vastly reduced the vulnerability of our strategic nuclear vehicles and greatly increased the protection and political responsibility of command and control over these forces. McNamara and Kennedy focused on the problem of reducing the chances of nuclear war. Perhaps their close focus on this problem made it easier for them to blunder into what seemed the lesser danger. And they have, of course, to bear the responsibility for that. But was it wrong for them to concentrate their major attention on the problem of nuclear war? Not in my opinion. However tragic our blunders in Vietnam, things might have been ever so much worse. The problem of avoiding a nuclear holocaust is the most serious problem of our times.

Finally, the reconstruction of our strategic policy at the beginning of 1961 involved a vital extension of civilian control, an increase in its sensitivity and rationality, in crucial matters of defense. Victories for civilian control over nuclear policy may actually have predisposed the civilians to let the military have much greater control over policy in

Vietnam. Vietnam, after all, was an on-going war. Unlike nuclear war it was, as high civilians said at the time, an "operational problem"—more the kind of thing in the military's province. Both Congress and the military had chafed under the control exercised by the Whiz Kids. And the Whiz Kids may very well have felt: "You can't win them all." And so, much less political intelligence was exercised on these matters than might have been. The foregoing is an explanation, not an excuse. It is, however, an explanation that runs exactly counter to current attempts to trace our troubles in Vietnam to flexible response doctrine. And on my observation, it is much closer to the truth.

Today, the right-wing attack on flexible response policy is in good part an attack on civilian control over the military means and over the ends toward which military means may be used. Some variants of "flexible response" could stand discerning criticism now, but I doubt that there is anyone in this room who would really trade "flexible response" for massive retaliation. That should be remembered prominently when we draw lessons from Vietnam.

THEODORE DRAPER: There are two points about my previous comment I should like to clarify.

First, the concept of limited war created a kind of strategic climate which, in one way or another, permeated policy-making circles. Massive retaliation tended to make policy-makers conscious of *how much* force they would have to use. Limited war tended to make them conscious of *how little* they might have to use, and if a little was not enough, it could always be increased. Escalation by what has here been called incrementalism was inherent in waging limited war.

This brings me to my second point—that any sane, decent person will prefer limited to unlimited war. The problem, however, is why the war in Vietnam has evidently gone beyond the limits of what is acceptable to many if not most people in the United States. We started out with the assumption that there was some level of destruction that would not be acceptable to North Vietnam; we are ending up questioning what limits of destruction are acceptable to us to prevent a communist "take-over." The reason for the change is essentially that North Vietnam has been fighting an unlimited war. Instead of our limited war dictating their limited war, their unlimited war has forced us to consider whether we wish to fight what to us is a limited war.

In the context of theories of limited war, I should now like to pick up Mr. McDermott's reference to the Dominican revolt and the Dominican intervention. His reference troubles me very much, especially if, as he suggests, we may go from the Vietnam failure to the so-called Dominican success as the precedent for another policy.

Mr. McDermott mentioned that this "success" involved flooding the Dominican Republic with American troops. It may appear that this approach led to success. But we could easily have had another Vietnam in the Dominican Republic in 1965, and if we did not, it was not because of us. We owed our good luck there to our opponent, to the man that we decided to cheat of victory.

I have spent a good deal of time trying to figure out what happened there, and I think I can tell you this with confidence: Juan Bosch told his followers that it was unthinkable for them to fight United States troops. On this point he would not budge, and he had enough influence so that on those occasions—and there were several—when fighting could have broken out, he held back his followers. Since then, however, he has changed his attitude toward the United States; and if the 1965 revolt happened now, we would have a Vietnam in the Dominican Republic. This was the essential reason for our success there, not the flooding of troops; and as I say, we will not be that lucky again.

ADAM YARMOLINSKY: I thought Mr. Draper was going to make the point I wanted to make about the Dominican Republic, but instead he made a different one, one with which I would take issue, except that I am not sure that it is very germane to the discussion.

I do not regard what we did in the Dominican Republic as a repudiation of the doctrine of limited war. I think it was politically unjustified. But it seems to me that the military decisions were in the mainstream of decisions about the use of limited force. After all, what we did was to interpose forces between two warring camps, and in a remarkably effective way.

One of the few things we did right in the Dominican Republic was to follow this procedure. I don't see this as any change in tactics.

DANIEL ELLSBERG: I do not really agree that it was the theory of limited war that encouraged Americans to favor our Vietnam decision in 1965. I think it was something else, some attitudes and expectations associated with the American way of war.

Specifically, there has been in the United States since World War II a widespread belief in the efficacy and acceptability of aerial bombing, in particular, of bombing of a strategic nature, aimed at the will of the opponent via his industrial and population resources. This belief played a critical, if not decisive, role in getting us into Vietnam, in reassuring us, in giving us confidence to stay there, and then in stimulating escalation while keeping us reassured as to ultimate success.

In 1961 the group of men most in favor of an enlarged intervention, including the sending of ground troops, was headed by Maxwell Taylor and Walt Rostow. These two pointed, as early as 1961, to the essential problem of stopping infiltration. They took the point of view, rightly or wrongly, that the problem in the south would be insoluble until we were able to stop infiltration from the north, not as it was then but as it could become.

It was clearly stated by them that we must go in with the recognition, especially if we were successful in the early stages, that we could anticipate a high level of infiltration, which somehow would have to be stopped. These people, both privately and publicly, indicated that there was only one effective way to stop infiltration; that, of course, was through bombing. This, their recommendation for expanded American involvement in Vietnam, rested on the implicit assumptions that bombing would be used against the north when—as was likely—it became necessary and that it would be effective. Kennedy may or may not have accepted this reasoning or conclusion; the record is not clear. However, given attitudes within the defense bureaucracy and the larger American public, it would have been difficult even for the President explicitly to reject this "solution" in advance. Really no other proposal was ever seriously made for dealing with that essential problem.

In 1965, when we felt ourselves in trouble in Vietnam in a number of ways, especially with regard to the need to demonstrate our commitment, Johnson was not prepared immediately to send troops, but one thing that came easy to an American president was a demonstration by bombing. In other ways as well bombing was the natural solution to our problems; it was the key ingredient in our policy that was going, one way or another, to make everything turn out all right. And in 1966 and 1967, despite disappointments, these same hopes persisted and sustained continued and expanded involvement.

Recently a former ambassador to the United States from Vietnam has expressed a plea, despite his deep pessimism about the prospects today in Vietnam, that we should not precipitately withdraw. He said he was against our immediate withdrawal even though he believed life under the communists would be better than the continuation of this war, which since 1965—not since 1961 or 1964, but since the bombings of 1965 in South Vietnam and since we came in there with our troops—has begun to demolish his society, to turn it into a vast zoo, a vast refugee camp. Despite this belief the ambassador could not be for ending the war at the cost of a quick communist victory because he felt that that would encourage the North Vietnamese in their most aggressive aspects. In that case he foresaw that within five years the Vietnamese would be doing things in Thailand which would cause us then totally to destroy Vietnam.

The calling in of Americans and our subsequent bombing in North and South Vietnam has not brought success; hence the bombing in the South has gone on long enough to disrupt the society of South Vietnam enormously and probably permanently. In general, if local governments who call for American aid are in other respects acting effectively, then any bombing we may do need not last very long and the resulting damage will not be permanent. But if these governments face a strong enemy who can frustrate them and the United States and prolong the war, then the damage done by American bombs can be irrevocable.

We are talking here about lessons for us to learn about ourselves and about lessons for *others*—including those who might ask our aid in the future—to learn about us from our experience in Vietnam and elsewhere. The lesson which can be drawn here is one that the rest of the world, I am sure, has drawn more quickly than Americans have: that, to paraphrase H. Rap Brown, *bombing is as American as cherry pie*. If you invite us in to do your hard fighting for you, then you get bombing along with our troops.

Many of us in Vietnam believed that we were there because we should win, and that we could win, though not by the methods we had been using. "Of course we are against bombing." I can hear myself, with others, saying this hundreds and hundreds of times.

I protected myself, I am afraid, from perceiving what should have been easily foreseeable—especially easy, were I not American and terribly reluctant to realize it—namely, that if you bring in Americans like me, as part of a heavy United States *combat* involvement, you are going to get both strategic and widespread tactical bombing along with them, no matter how critical these particular individuals may be of it. If you ask what will happen in Thailand if we go in militarily and have to face prolonged opposition, the answer is bombing. If you ask what would have happened if the Dominican Republic had chosen to oppose us, the answer is that the Dominican Republic would probably have been heavily bombed.

Indeed, a most ominous lesson is there to be drawn by the people of nations whose leaders might call for United States military support: that such a plea, if the national leader knew that the conflict would be long and the American military commitment great, could amount to an act of treachery against his society.

§§ SAMUEL P. HUNTINGTON: I would like to take an entirely different approach to understanding the 1960's and our Vietnam involvement.

For the reasons I gave earlier, it seems unlikely that a situation like that which developed in Vietnam will develop elsewhere in the immediate future. For other reasons, some noted below, it seems even more unlikely that any situation or crisis in the future will produce a response similar to that which the United States made in Vietnam.

"I do not think the American people would be in favor of another one like that," said "Engine Charlie" Wilson in 1953, referring to what social scientists at that time were describing as "the most unpopular war in American history." In comparison with the clean-cut, all-out struggle of World War II, Korea was indeed a nasty, protracted, frustrating, dirty little war. Now, in comparison with Vietnam, Korea looks like a neat, conventional, sensible sort of war which, above all else, was fought along a regular battle front whose progress up and down the map made it easy to judge who was winning and who losing. The frustration of Korea was that the soldiers could win it militarily but the Administration politically would not let them. The frustration of Vietnam is that the soldiers cannot win it militarily and the Administration cannot win it politically. The one produced an intense reaction on the right, the other an even more bitter opposition on the left. If the increases in frustration represented by the progression from World War II to Korea to Vietnam should be extended to a fourth major military involvement, the constitutional structure of the Republic could well be shaken. In any event, the almost unanimous current resolve of "No more Vietnams" appears to have good roots not only in the war itself but also in a more fundamental shift in the American approach to foreign affairs.

While American involvement in Vietnam was one aspect of the broader postwar pattern of American expansion that I previously referred to, the trauma resulting from the war was the product of a fundamental shift in attitudes toward the costs and benefits of American expansion. The type of involvement which in the 1950's could be viewed as desirable and necessary became in the 1960's a highly dubious venture. By 1967, of course, the costs to the United States—in money and troop commitments—of the Vietnamese war exceeded those of the Korean War.

Opposition to the war, however, focused less on these material costs than on the moral and ideological issues. In comparison to the Korean War the Vietnamese war has been a relatively limited and undestructive conflict. In one year of fighting almost every major city in North and South Korea was virtually leveled to the ground. Up to mid-1968 the only major Vietnamese city which has received anything like this treatment was Hue. In Korea somewhere between two and three million civilians were killed directly or indirectly by the war. The civilian suffering in Vietnam, however bad it may be, has been little by comparison. Senator Edward M. Kennedy estimates the civilian casualties in South Vietnam at about 100,000 a year, only some of which were fatalities. At that current rate the Vietnamese war could thus go on for twenty years before the total civilian casualties (killed and wounded) in South Vietnam equaled the minimum estimate of civilians killed in Korea.

Thus American outrage at the war reflected less the war than it did the impact of TV and, more basically, a fundamental change in American attitudes—official and informed—toward American involvement in international affairs. It is, of course, easy to say with hindsight that this change was predictable. It was also in fact, however, predicted. The shift in opinion on foreign policy in the mid 1960's appears to be simply the latest manifestation of a regular alternation of American attitudes toward foreign affairs between introversion and extroversion. Using a variety of indicators, including naval expenditures, annexations, armed expeditions, diplomatic pressures, and attention devoted to foreign affairs in presidential messages and party platforms, Frank L. Klingberg has charted these alternations in mood since the Revolutionary War.[4] Beginning in 1776 American attitudes toward international affairs have gone through eight alternating phases of introversion and extroversion as follows:

INTROVERSION	EXTROVERSION
1776–1798	1798–1824
1824–1844	1844–1871
1871–1891	1891–1919
1919–1940	1940–

The periods of introversion thus averaged twenty-one years, those of extroversion twenty-seven years. Writing in 1951 Klingberg confidently rejected the possibility of the United States then adopting the "Gibraltar" politics advocated by Hoover and Taft, and predicted that the United States was "probably capable of great world leadership for another decade or more." Extroversion still had sixteen years to run. Klingberg also suggested, however, that further in the future it was logical "to expect America to retreat, to some extent at least, from so much world involvement, and perhaps to do so sometime in the 1960's." He was, if anything, a little too unsure of his own theory, for sixteen years later, the swing of introversion came along right on schedule. The prescience of his forecast is, indeed, quite striking. In discussing the beginning of America's "fifth historical cycle" in the 1960's he said: "It is quite possible that the major problem of the coming period will carry heavy moral implications—as in the case of the issue of slavery following the Revolutionary period (1776–1824). The aspirations of the people of Asia and Africa could well furnish the chief issue, along with special repercussions from America's own racial problem." For those of us who are skeptical of statistical analyses, cyclical theories, and historical determinism, Klingberg's forecast in 1951 of what would happen in 1966–67 is somewhat unsettling.

[4] Frank L. Klingberg, "The Historical Alternation of Moods in American Foreign Policy," *World Politics,* IV, Jan. 1952, 239–73.

Obviously the absolute level of involvement changes significantly from one period of introversion (or extroversion) to the next. Yet there are also good reasons for assuming that changes in need, interest, and generations may produce a shift in attention from one arena to another despite outside "objective" determinants. What people think is important is what counts, and the people of one generation may well think domestic policy important because their fathers thought foreign policy so. As one State Department official commented in 1967, "The generation which put together this security system appears to be wearying of the burden, and a new generation is rising which never understood the reasons for it in the first place."[5] The swing to introversion in the Klingberg cycle is clearly a fact, and it is precisely this fact that caused the national trauma over the Vietnamese war. At an earlier point in the cycle such a war would not have caused so much commotion. But not even Lyndon Johnson could successfully buck Frank Klingberg.

Perhaps the symbolic turning point from extroversion to introversion occurred in July 1967, when the Administration dispatched three C-130 transports and 150 American servicemen to support the Mobutu government in the Congo against an uprising of white mercenaries. The reaction in Congress was immediate, intensive, and widespread, encompassing Vietnamese hawks as well as doves. Fulbright and Russell, Morse and Stennis—all attacked this action, warning that "never again" did they want us to take any action which might lead to another Vietnam type of involvement. Given this reaction to the dispatch of three transports, it seems reasonable to conclude that it will probably not be until sometime after 1984, when the Klingberg cycle has gone full circle again, that the United States will again become involved in a military intervention of Vietnamese proportions.

DANIEL ELLSBERG: Professor Huntington says the Vietnam war has led to an unprecedented revulsion in the minds of the American public essentially because of a cyclical change in American attitudes. If true, this would imply that we are in for some twenty years of similar reaction against any sort of involvement, followed by some twenty years of acceptance of any sort of involvement.

This implication is made more specific by saying that the same

[5] Quoted by Don Oberdorfer, "Interventionism, 1967 Style," *The New York Times Magazine,* Sept. 17, 1967, p. 112.

sort of war waged earlier, with the same consequences, would not have evoked this reaction. I believe this is wrong. If we had taken the same action in Indochina in 1954 or in 1961 that we did in 1965, we would have become involved that much sooner in the same kind of war, with the same prospects, and, in turn, would have gotten very much the same reaction in the middle of the Klingberg cycle. Therefore, the notion of a cyclical change in American attitudes as the main explanation for the response is wrong. The revulsion is largely a response to *this* war, including, among other things, the manner in which we got into it, the manner in which we have explained it, the manner in which we are conducting it, and, perhaps above all, our evident lack of lasting progress or prospects of success.

Speaking personally, and frankly, I must say that Professor Huntington's analysis, insofar as it reveals his perceptions of the war and of the public's reaction to it, distresses me very much. However, I don't want to dwell on my reaction to his description of the Vietnam war, which I had the good fortune to witness, at times fairly close up, as a "relatively limited and undestructive" war. What I wish to explore here is the empirical question of when our government should anticipate widespread public reactions against such an involvement.

Huntington's dismissal of the point that it could be the war itself that led to revulsion is based on a comparison with Korea in which he suggests that the relevant differences in the wars themselves should have led to greater acceptance of the Vietnam war than of the Korean war. Therefore, he concludes, the cause of the actual lesser acceptance could not be our acts in Vietnam.

But what is the relevant difference he considers? When we look closely, it is very simple: it is body count. In other words, the analysis here of the moral issue all comes down to the single dimension of body count. I would suggest that this is as inadequate a predictor of the public's feeling of moral revulsion as it is a predictor of progress in the war.

For one thing, the question of the perceived stakes at issue in the war is relevant. Specifically, the Vietnam war simply is not regarded as a war of self-defense, whereas Korea virtually was, especially early in the war, which was when most of the civilian casualties were inflicted. In the summer of 1950 we had a vision of Western Europe being at stake, with satellite armies poised to profit from the example of successful aggression in Korea. This had, I suggest, great bearing on the acceptability of the infliction of damage on people who themselves were not threatening us.

Moreover, the specific operations in Korea that were causing the casualties were regarded as effective and even essential there. These same operations, such as bombing that is not in close support, Sir Robert Thompson tells us—and I feel sure he is correct—have little impact on Viet Cong strength, yet at the same time, by their social and psychological effects within Vietnam, strongly favor the longer-run political prospects of the Viet Cong. Therefore, regrettably, we have the spectacle of noncombatant casualties being inflicted in Vietnam and massive refugee movements imposed by processes which qualified experts tell us are unnecessary, ineffective, and even counterproductive.

Above all else, you have the factor of perceived failure and the very low likelihood of real success in the future. At the point when this is perceived, moral as well as practical issues will surely arise for everybody for whom they did not arise earlier. Here, of course, is the enormous difference from Korea.

It is simply not acceptable, in the eyes of many people, to kill as many people as we are doing in Vietnam—or even a much smaller number—when the process of violence offers as little promise of success in any terms as it does there, and especially when the stakes for the United States are no larger than they seem to be there. To put it simply, a great many people in the country believe that you must have very good reasons for killing innocent people; and the reasons they now perceive for sustaining the kind of operations we are pursuing in Vietnam just do not appear to be good enough. There may be a trend in attitudes here, especially among youth; yet there would have been no lack of such people, making the same judgment, if they had been confronted with the same war ten years ago.

THEODORE DRAPER: I would like to pursue this point. When we went into Vietnam and for a long period thereafter, the justification for the intervention had very little to do with problems of social or political reform that have occupied some of us here. The justification was that we were faced with an aggression from the north which was an extension of communist power and/or Russian power. In other words, the aggression made the war into a quasi–great power war, and as long as the war could be interpreted as such, we were fighting not only Vietnamese but also Chinese and Russians—and the latter were the real enemies.

This reasoning was once persuasive to a good many Americans and a good many people outside of America. Now, the reason the war has lost much of its persuasiveness is that its original justification in terms of the great-power conflict has been eroded.

There is in the air a pervasive conviction or feeling that an era has come to an end. We are not so sure about the kind of era we are going into. But somehow there have taken place the retrenchment of American power, the retreat of Russian power, and the introversion of Chinese power. This threefold process has laid the basis of the era we are going into. As a result, we launched an action in one period but carried it out in another period, and that is where the persuasiveness of this war disappeared.

American Political and Bureaucratic Decision-Making

§§ JAMES C. THOMSON, JR.: Where were the experts, the doubters and the dissenters who could warn of the dangers of an open-ended commitment to the Vietnam quagmire? Were they there at all? And if so, what had happened to them? The answer is complex but instructive.

In the first place, the American government was sorely lacking in real Vietnam or Indochina expertise. Originally treated as an adjunct of Embassy Paris, our Saigon embassy and the Vietnam Desk at State were largely staffed from 1954 onward by French-speaking Foreign Service personnel of narrowly European experience. Such diplomats were even more closely restricted than the normal embassy officer—by cast of mind as well as language—to contacts wth Vietnam's French-speaking urban elites. For instance, Foreign Service linguists in Portugal are able to speak with the peasantry if they get out of Lisbon and choose to do so; not so the French speakers of Embassy Saigon.

In addition, the shadow of the "loss of China" distorted Vietnam reporting. Career officers in the Department, and especially those in the field, had not forgotten the fate of their World War II colleagues who wrote in frankness from China and were later pilloried by Senate committees for critical comments on the Chinese Nationalists. Candid reporting on the strengths of the Viet Cong and the weaknesses of the Diem government was inhibited by the memory. It was also inhibited by some higher officials, notably Ambassador Nolting in Saigon, who refused to sign off on such cables.

In due course, to be sure, some Vietnam talent was discovered or developed. But a recurrent and increasingly important factor in the decision-making process was the banishment of real expertise. Here the underlying cause was the "closed politics" of policy-making as issues became hot: the more sensitive the issue, and the higher it rises in the bureaucracy, the more completely the experts are excluded while the harassed senior generalists take over (that is, the Secretaries, Undersecretaries, and Presidential Assistants).

Despite the banishment of the experts, internal doubters and dissenters did indeed appear and persist. Yet as I watched the process, such men were effectively neutralized by a subtle dynamic: the domestication of dissenters. Such "domestication" arose out of a twofold clubbish need: on the one hand, the dissenter's desire to stay aboard, and on the other hand, the nondissenter's conscience. Simply stated, dissent, when recognized, was made to feel at home. On the lowest possible scale of importance, I must confess my own considerable sense of dignity and acceptance (both vital) when my senior White House employer would refer to me as his "favorite dove." Far more significant was the case of the former Undersecretary of State, George Ball. Once Mr. Ball began to express doubts, he was warmly institutionalized: he was encouraged to become the in-house devil's advocate on Vietnam. The upshot was inevitable: the process of escalation allowed for periodic requests to Mr. Ball to speak his piece; Ball felt good, I assume (he had fought for righteousness); the others felt good (they had given a full hearing to the dovish option); and there was minimal unpleasantness. The club remained intact; and it is of course possible that matters would have gotten worse faster if Mr. Ball had kept silent or had left earlier than his departure in the fall of 1966.

A related point—and crucial, I suppose, to government at all times —was the "effectiveness" trap, the trap that keeps men within the government from speaking out as clearly or as often as they might. And it is the trap that keeps men from resigning in protest and airing their dissent outside the government. The most important asset that a man brings to bureaucratic life is his "effectiveness," a mysterious combination of training, style, and connections. The most ominous complaint that can be whispered of a bureaucrat is: "I'm afraid Charlie is beginning to lose his effectiveness." To preserve your effectiveness, you must decide where and when to fight the mainstream of policy; the opportunities range from pillow talk with your wife, to private drinks with your friends, to meetings with the Secretary of State or the President. The inclination to remain silent or to acquiesce in the presence of the great men—to live to fight another day, to give on this issue so that you can be "effective" on later issues—is overwhelming. Nor is it the tendency of youth alone; some of our most senior officials, men of wealth and fame, whose place in history is secure, have remained silent lest their connection with power be terminated. As for the disinclination to resign in protest: while not necessarily a Washington or even American specialty, it seems truer of a government in which ministers have no parliamentary backbench to which to retreat. In the absence of such a refuge, it is easy to rationalize the decision to stay aboard. By doing so, one may be able to prevent a few bad things from happening and perhaps even make a few good things happen. To exit is to lose even those marginal chances for "effectiveness."

Another factor must be noted: as the Vietnam controversy escalated at home, there developed a *preoccupation with Vietnam public relations as opposed to Vietnam policy-making.* And here, ironically, internal doubters and dissenters were heavily employed. For such men, by virtue of their own doubts, were often deemed best able to "massage" the doubting intelligentsia.

Through a variety of procedures, both institutional and personal, doubt, dissent, and expertise were effectively neutralized in the making of policy. But what can be said of the men "in charge"? It is patently absurd to suggest that they produced such tragedy by intention and calculation. But it is neither absurd nor difficult to discern certain forces at work that caused decent and honorable men to do great harm.

Here I would stress the paramount role of executive fatigue. No factor seems to me more crucial and underrated in the making of foreign policy. The physical and emotional toll of executive responsibility in State, the Pentagon, the White House, and other executive agencies is enormous; that toll is of course compounded by extended service. Many of today's Vietnam policy-makers have been on the job from four to seven years. Complaints may be few, and physical health may remain unimpaired, though emotional health is far harder to gauge. But what is most seriously eroded in the deadening process of fatigue is freshness of thought, imagination, a sense of possibility, a sense of priorities and perspective—those rare assets of a new Administration in its first year or two of office. The tired policy-maker becomes a prisoner of his own narrowed view of the world and his own clichéd rhetoric. He becomes irritable and defensive—short on sleep, short on family ties, short on patience. Such men make bad policy and then compound it. They have neither the time nor the temperament for new ideas or preventive diplomacy.

Below the level of the fatigued executives in the making of Vietnam policy was a widespread phenomenon: the curator mentality in the Department of State. By this I mean the collective inertia produced by the bureaucrat's view of his job. At State the average "desk officer" inherits from his predecessor our policy toward country X; he regards it as his function to keep that policy intact—under glass, untampered with, and dusted—so that he may pass it on in two to four years to his successor. And such curatorial service generally merits promotion within the system. (Maintain the status quo, and you will stay out of trouble.) In some circumstances the inertia bred by such an outlook can act as a brake against rash innovation. But concerning many issues this inertia sustains the momentum of bad policy and unwise commitments—momentum that might otherwise have been resisted within the ranks. Clearly Vietnam is such an issue.

To fatigue and inertia must be added the factor of internal confusion. Even among the "architects" of our Vietnam commitment there has been persistent confusion as to what type of war we were fighting and, as a direct consequence, confusion as to how to end that war. (The "credibility gap" is in part a reflection of such internal confusion.) Was it, for instance, a civil war, in which case counterinsurgency might suffice? Or was it a war of international aggression? (This might invoke a SEATO or UN commitment.) Who was the aggressor—and the "real enemy"? The Viet Cong? Hanoi? Peking? Moscow? International communism? Or maybe "Asian communism"? Differing enemies dictated differing strategies and tactics. And confused throughout, in like fashion, was the question of American objectives; your objectives depended on whom you were fighting and why. I shall not forget my assignment from an Assistant Secretary of State in March 1964 to draft a speech for Secretary McNamara which would, *inter alia,* once and for all dispose of the canard that the Vietnam conflict was a civil war. "But in some ways, of course," I mused, "it *is* a civil war." "Don't play word games with me!" snapped the Assistant Secretary.

As a further influence on policy-makers I would cite the factor of bureaucratic detachment. By this I mean what at best might be termed the professional callousness of the surgeon (and indeed, medical lingo—the "surgical strike," for instance—seemed to crop up in the euphemisms of the times).

In Washington the semantics of the military muted the reality of war for the civilian policy-makers. In quiet, air-conditioned, thick-carpeted rooms such terms as "systematic pressure," "armed reconnaissance," "targets of opportunity," and even "body count" seemed to breed a sort of games-theory detachment. Most memorable to me was a moment in the target planning during late 1964 when the question, at some midpoint in the projected pattern of systematic pressure, was how heavy our bombing should be and how extensive our strafing. An Assistant Secretary of State resolved the point in the following words: "It seems to me that our orchestration should be mainly violins, but with periodic touches of brass." Perhaps the biggest shock of my return to Cambridge, Massachusetts, was the realization that the young men, the flesh and blood I taught and saw on these university streets, were potentially some of the numbers on the charts of those faraway planners. In a curious sense Cambridge is closer to this war than Washington.

There is an unprovable factor that relates to bureaucratic detachment: the ingredient of crypto-racism. I do not mean to imply any conscious contempt for Asian loss of life on the part of Washington officials. But I do mean to imply that bureaucratic detachment may well be compounded by a traditional Western sense that there are so many Asians, after all, that Asians have a fatalism about life and a disregard for its loss, that they are cruel and barbaric to their own people, and that they are very different from us (and all look alike?). To put the matter another way: would we have pursued quite such policies—and quite such military tactics—if the Vietnamese were white?

Crucial throughout the process of Vietnam decision-making was a conviction among many policy-makers that Vietnam posed a fundamental test of America's national will. Time and again I was told by men reared in the tradition of Henry L. Stimson that all we needed was the will, and we would then prevail. Implicit in such a view, it seemed to me, was a curious assumption that Asians lacked will, or at least that in a contest between Asian and Anglo-Saxon wills the non-Asians must prevail. A corollary to the persistent belief in will was a fascination with power and an awe in the face of the power America possessed as no nation or civilization ever before. Those who doubted our role in Vietnam were said to shrink from the burdens of power, the obligations of power, the uses of power, the responsibility of power. By implication such men were soft-headed and effete.

Finally, no discussion of the factors and forces at work on Vietnam policy-makers can ignore the central fact of human ego investment. Men who have participated in a decision develop a stake in that decision. As they participate in further, related decisions, their stake increases. It might have been possible to dissuade a man of strong self-confidence at an early stage on the ladder of decision; but it is infinitely harder at later stages since a change of mind there usually involves implicit or explicit repudiation of a chain of previous decisions. To put it bluntly, at the heart of the Vietnam calamity is a group of able, dedicated men who have been regularly and repeatedly wrong—and whose standing with their contemporaries and, more important, with history depends, as they see it, on being proved right. These are not men who can be asked to extricate themselves from error.

Throughout the conflict there have been missed opportunities, large and small, to disengage ourselves from Vietnam on increasingly unpleasant but still acceptable terms. Of the many moments from 1961 onward I shall cite only one, the last and most important opportunity that was lost: in the summer of 1964 the President instructed his chief advisors to prepare for him as wide a range of Vietnam options as possible for postelection consideration and decision. He explicitly asked that all options be laid out. What happened next was, in effect, Lyndon Johnson's slow-motion Bay of Pigs. For the advisors so effectively converged on one single option—juxtaposed against two other, phony options (in effect, blowing up the world or scuttle and run)—that the President was confronted with unanimity for bombing the north from all his trusted counselors. Had he been more confident in foreign affairs, had he been deeply informed on Vietnam and Southeast Asia, and had he raised some hard questions that unanimity had submerged, this President could have used the largest electoral mandate in history to de-escalate in Vietnam in the clear expectation that at the worst a neutralist government would come to power in Saigon and politely invite us out. Today, many lives and dollars later, such an alternative has become an elusive and infiinitely more expensive possibility.

There is a result of our Vietnam policy which holds potential danger for the future of American foreign policy: *the rise of a new breed of American ideologues who see Vietnam as the ultimate test of their doctrine.* I have in mind those men in Washington who have given a new life to the missionary impulse in American foreign relations, who believe that this nation in this era has received a threefold endowment that can transform the world. As they see it, that endowment is composed of, first, our unsurpassed military might; second, our clear technological supremacy; and third, our allegedly invincible benevolence (our "altruism," our affluence, our lack of territorial aspirations). Together, it is argued, this threefold endowment provides us with the opportunity and the obligations to ease the nations of the earth toward modernization and stability, toward a full-fleged *Pax Americana technocratica.* In reaching toward this goal, Vietnam is viewed as the last and crucial test. Once we have succeeded there, the road ahead is clear. In a sense, these men are our counterpart to the visionaries of communism's radical left: they are technocracy's own Maoists. They do not govern Washington today—but their doctrine rides high.

§§ RICHARD J. BARNET: The roots of the Vietnam failure lie more in the structure and organization of the national security bureaucracy than in the personality of the President or the idiosyncrasies of the particular group of foundation executives, military commanders,

Rhodes Scholars, and businessmen who have been the President's principal advisors during the escalation of the Vietnam commitment into the Vietnam war. As Tom Wicker's recent study makes clear, the President's personal role is crucial, but he operates within limits set by the vast foreign-policy machinery of government. The President may decide, but the bureaucracy structures the decisions by setting out the choices. If the basis of the American commitment to take on revolutionary movements around the world is institutional, then we cannot hope to avoid future Vietnam-like adventures in other places merely by shifts in personnel or even by changes in general policy pronouncements. We could write a National Security Council directive to avoid large-scale military interventions in the future; but if we do not change the character and direction of the institutions which push us toward intervention, such a paper will have as much effect in keeping us out of future Vietnams as our United Nations commitments have had on the present involvement.

The interventionist thrust of postwar American foreign policy, from Greece in 1947 to the Dominican Republic and Vietnam in the 1960's, has been its most striking characteristic. On an average of once every eighteen months the United States has sent military and paramilitary forces into other countries either to fight guerrilla movements or to overthrow governments considered to be communist or communist-leaning. In addition to the major campaigns in such places as Iran, Guatemala, Dominican Republic, British Guiana, and Cuba, the United States maintains counterinsurgency forces and intelligence operations for manipulating internal politics in most of the other underdeveloped countries of the world. The intervention in Vietnam is not an aberration. It is part of a continuing pattern.

It is not my purpose to argue the merits of an interventionist policy. I have discussed elsewhere why America's arrogation of a "responsibility" to suppress revolutionary movements in the name of anticommunism brutalizes and corrupts not only the societies which we are attempting to set right but our own. My starting point is that the "overmilitarization" of our foreign policy, as George Kennan calls it, combined with the interventionist itch is our greatest national problem.

Another premise is that national policy cannot be defended simply by pointing to official characterizations of foreign threats. It is foolish to deny that the world is in fact a dangerous and anarchic place or that other nations behave in revolting ways—although because of their limited resources not usually to the same extent as the United States does. But threats in international politics can be apprehended not by revelation but by judgment. The threats which are triggers of national policy are intellectual constructs developed by bureaucracies whose function is to discover and deal with threats. Neither the Secretary of State nor the Chief of Staff of the Air Force has the gift of infallible political insight. They must guess. Over the past twenty years there has been a marked tendency to guess in certain ways rather than in others about the nature of the threats facing the United States and what should be done about them.

Put simply, the official world view provides an ideological justification for the ever-growing use of force as an instrument of national policy. The intelligence bureaucracies knowingly err on the "conservative" side in discovering enemies and estimating their intentions. If they do not turn out to have the vast armies and limitless guile which are attributed to them, then, so these bureaucracies argue, no harm is done. It's better to be prepared for the worst, and this means taking on new military "requirements." Sometimes, it is true, threats are minimized in order to justify a seemingly rational policy based primarily on the use of military power. Thus North Vietnam can be beaten in a few months, the advocates of military intervention argued. China, according to the disciples of victory through air power, can be eliminated as a world power by simply "taking out" her atomic installations.

It must be said that many of the threats to which we have responded have been consistently exaggerated. The Soviet invasion of western Europe of the 1940's, the missile gap of the 1950's, and the worldwide campaign for wars of national liberation orchestrated in Moscow are all examples of threats discovered by the national security bureaucracy which in retrospect we know were nothing like what the national security bureaucracy proclaimed them to be at the time. Yet each was the inspiration for major decisions to increase military commitments and interventionary behavior. What are the characteristics of the national security bureaucracy which lead it to identify threats in the way they do and to influence United States policy in the direction of intervention?

The Vietnam experience illustrates the crucial role of bureaucratic momentum. When President Kennedy was considering putting sixteen thousand troops in Vietnam in 1963, George Ball is reported to have told him that it would take three hundred thousand to get them out. The President himself completely understood that deployments are themselves commitments and that a military presence must be protected by a greater presence. "The troops will march in; the bands will play," he told his advisors, "then we will be told to send in more troops. It's like taking a drink. The effect wears off, and you have to take another." Yet he was unable to resist stepping onto the escalator. Once troops are committed and some are killed, then those who advocate escalation can use the irresistible rhetoric of redemption. We must commit more to justify what we committed already.

Each stage of the commitment is looked upon as an experiment. Each bureaucracy specializing in a different technique for controlling the internal development of South Vietnam asks for the chance to show what it can do. The Special Forces argue that six months of pacification efforts will break the back of the insurgency. A few thousand troops are sent. But the political situation in Saigon has come close to collapse. Therefore, the Air Force argues, let us make a dramatic commitment of our overwhelming air power and bomb the North. The Navy has its solution, and the Army also. Because of the variety of military and paramilitary techniques at the disposal of the United States, the apparent weakness of the enemy, and the low risk of massive intervention by the Soviet Union and China, the proponents of escalation can argue that the costs of experimentation are low.

Unlike a major war where the United States itself is endangered, the consequences of failure of any particular military operation against a distant underdeveloped country appear limited. The bureaucracy falls prey to the illusion that they are able to control events because they are free of the fear of retaliation. They feel that they have all the options and they can try them one by one. The great preponderance of power of the United States also relieves them of any responsibility to think through the process of escalation to the end and attempt to calculate the final costs and benefits. They are convinced that the United States is willing and able to "pay any price" or "bear any burden" to carry through what it started. As the commitment increases, so of course does the psychological investment in the objective for which the commitment is presumably made. The preservation of an American sphere of influence in Vietnam looks far more crucial *after* the massive installations at Cam Ran Bay and Danang are built than before.

The "national interest" in small countries where Americans have few ethnic ties or business interests is determined by the national security bureaucracies themselves. They define both the tasks and the techniques to be employed. They are, understandably, not prone to underestimate the importance of what they are doing, nor are they reticent in calculating the support they need. If they are operating a base, it is the most important bastion of the "free world," to be protected at all costs. It matters little that the base was built before the present intercontinental weapons systems and in purely military terms is obsolete. To lose it, the interested bureaucrats argue, would be a political defeat. To them the "national interest" and the Air Force's "interest" are identical, despite the fact that most Americans have never heard of the irrelevant base and would sleep no less soundly if it were gone.

Once an American presence is established in another country, experience suggests that it is unlikely that the United States will limit that presence in either size or character to its original commitment. In Greece, Lebanon, and the Dominican Republic as well as in Vietnam nonmilitary interventions escalated into major military efforts. In each case American soldiers were sent because the nonmilitary bureaucracies were inadequate to maintain American interests as they had been defined. In Greece, United States officers under General Van Fleet ended up running the war for the Greek government, despite explicit assurances to Congress to the contrary. In Lebanon the Marines landed to extricate the United States from a disastrous involvement, largely engineered by the CIA, in internal Lebanese politics.

The progression from aid missions, to counterinsurgency "advisors," to expeditionary forces takes on a kind of Parkinsonian inevitability. This is not true everywhere, to be sure. There is evidence that the United States would not have resorted to a military invasion to keep Indonesia from going communist simply because the task was so obviously formidable. But where the resources of the United States appear adequate to suppress insurgent movements, the result is reasonably predictable. In Latin American countries, for example, where the United States maintains a "little America" with the familiar Military Advisory Group, the contingent from the Office of Public Safety to train and equip the police, and an array of agricultural and educational specialists, we have been ready to expand the national commitment to meet the threat as these bureaucracies define it. In Guatemala the role of the Special Forces has dramatically increased to keep pace with the rising insurgency.

Given the assumptions underlying the original intervention—the necessity to prevent leftist insurgent movements from taking power—the decision whether to escalate the effort from nonmilitary to para-military to overtly military means depends generally on the adversary's toughness, not on American self-restraint. It may be logically possible to impose upon ourselves limits on the scale of intervention in a particular country, but it is usually not politically possible. Because the increments in the scale are small—"What's the matter with send-ing a few more advisors?"—they are hard to resist. Since insurgent movements are growing in both numbers and strength in Asia, Africa, and Latin America, the present bureaucratic entities, which owe their existence to an ideological commitment to oppose such move-ments, have little incentive to resist new occasions for testing the "national will" in exotic places.

The dynamism of the myriad bureaucratic empires dealing in national security assures not only the escalation of United States commitments but their progressive militarization as well. While the responsibility is his, President Johnson should not be judged too harshly for choosing in late 1964 two drastic military techniques to solve the Vietnam problem, for there were only military alternatives proposed to him. The national security bureaucracies were divided as to the specific techniques to use. The Air Force promised good results from bombing. The Army recommended an expeditionary force. Roger Hilsman reports that he wanted to send in Rangers to act as counterguerrillas. The Chemical Corps suggested certain chemical agents. From the idea men in the Pentagon, the CIA, and the State Department, there was funneled up toward the White House a steady stream of proposals for burning, bombing, blasting, and poisoning the Vietnamese enemy. Most of the proposals were turned aside by the civilian leadership, but a certain percentage were of course accepted.

Virtually no energy was spent in those crucial days on finding a political solution to the Vietnamese crisis, so convinced was the whole national security establishment—especially the State Department— that only a military solution was possible. Roger Hilsman notes that as early as 1961 Secretary Rusk "regarded Vietnam as essentially a military problem." Proposals for settlement by U Thant, the Soviet Union, and de Gaulle and peace feelers from Hanoi in 1964 were all dismissed. "We do not believe in conferences to ratify terror, so our policy is unchanged," the President announced. The national security bureaucracy was unready to take the risks of peace-making because they knew so little about the process. The classic political arts of negotiation and compromise, which are far harder to master than even the logistical skill entailed in moving a half million men into battle positions ten thousand miles away, were not in high demand in the State Department.

Thus, while the Pentagon bureaucracy churned out dozens of recommendations for making the life of the Vietnamese more miserable in imaginative new ways, no comparable energy was spent on thinking through the national interests of the United States in the area, other than how we could impose our will on the Viet Cong and North Vietnam. No staff work of any consequence was devoted to the kind of peace settlement we ultimately wanted or had reasons to expect, and to how we could get it. There was no thought given to how the United States might relate peacefully to Southeast Asia. The alternatives were seen simply as "losing Southeast Asia" or crushing the Viet Cong. There were contingency plans on file with the Chiefs of Staff on what to do in the event of war with Cambodia or Brazil, but no body of bureaucratic wisdom on how to obtain a peace settlement in Vietnam by political means.

Knowing that negotiation would produce a result considerably short of a United States victory, the leaders of the Pentagon and State Department sought to avoid the personal risk of association with what political opponents would be sure to call a "sellout." Thus they beguiled themselves with the thought that they could end the war by the application of military power alone. "The guerrillas will simply fade away," an Undersecretary of State told me in early 1966. The failure to treat Vietnam as a political rather than a military problem has been extremely costly for the United States.

Once again the "national security managers"—those in charge of the State Department, the Pentagon, and the White House staff—had reduced a complex political reality to a test of the American will, a symbol of a larger struggle. Because they had neither sufficient knowledge of Vietnamese history nor empathy with the tragedy of that land or its politics, they saw it only as a symbol of a larger struggle. The war in Vietnam was another of the great confrontations that the communists have arranged, as Walt Rostow has put it, to challenge "the nerve and will of the West." Along with Korea and Berlin it was another "test case." In this egocentric view of the universe other nations exist to serve as sparring partners for the United States. So fascinated by the confrontation model of world politics are the national security bureaucrats that they see even relatively minor procedural issues in the same heroic terms. One official greeted the preliminary skirmish over a site for "contacts" with North Vietnam as if it were Armageddon. "There we were right off the bat—eyeball to eyeball," he told a *New York Times* reporter, "on a question of prestige as well as procedure. And they're the ones who blinked. Now we're one up."

Because the national security bureaucracy tends to squeeze political problems into the confrontation mold, it favors using instruments of violence to solve them. Even where the essentially political nature of the problem is recognized, as in Vietnam, where for years official analyses have stated that the war was primarily one for "hearts and minds" that had to be won on the "political battlefront," the military effort completely engulfed the nonmilitary strategies. When the American expeditionary force overran villages and the Air Force obliterated them through bombing, Special Forces pacification teams found the campaign to win their political support by being nice to children and old people somewhat compromised. The national security bureaucrats explain the familiar phenomenon of military strategy overtaking and rendering ineffective nonmilitary strategies by noting "that's the way the world is."

The official view that guerrillas are part of a world-wide army intent on humiliating and defeating the United States rather than political rebels reacting to local political conditions cannot, however, be explained by reference to an "objective" reality. Again and again the State Department has misread the politics of guerrilla movements in order to make them fit the preconceived military model. Thus the Greek guerrillas in 1947 were Stalin's agents carrying on, as Ambassador Loy Henderson put it at the time, "the red tide of invasion." In fact, Stalin was trying to stop the insurgency. According to William Bullitt, who was influential in setting United States Vietnam policy in 1947, Ho Chi Minh was a Chinese agent. And in 1951, in his oft-quoted analysis, Dean Rusk pronounced Mao's China to be a "Russian Manchukuo."

These are not random "mistakes"; they are part of a consistent official ideology which cannot be explained by stupidity, for the national security elite are on the whole a group that excels in law school examinations. This ideology provides rationalizations for committing America's military power. The peculiar mental set of the national security bureaucrat is the product of certain biases which, I would contend, are inherent in the bureaucratic structure itself. Put simply, for almost thirty years the United States government has been organized for war. Since 1940 we have spent from 50 per cent to 75 per cent of the national budget on military and paramilitary bureaucracies. We have staffed them with bright, energetic people who define their goals in the traditional terms of *Machtpolitik* and use military means to achieve them. The impact of World War II on the subsequent militarization of American policy is so crucial that we must look at it in some detail.

Under the impact of war, the position of the federal bureaucracy in American society changed radically in two ways. First, government agencies came to control the creation and disposition of a significant share of the national wealth. Second, the balance of power within the federal bureaucracy shifted decisively to those agencies which concerned themselves with foreign and military affairs. In 1939 the federal government had about eight hundred thousand civilian employees, about 10 per cent of whom worked for national security agencies. At the end of the war the figure approached four million, of which more than 75 per cent were in national security activities. The last premobilization defense budget represented about 1.4 per cent of the Gross National Product. The lowest postwar defense budget, an interlude of about eighteen months between demobilization and remobilization for the Cold War, took 4.7 per cent of the Gross National Product. Defense spending alone for fiscal year 1948 (the year of the lowest postwar defense budget) exceeded by more than 1 billion dollars the entire budget of the federal government for the last prewar year. Once postwar remobilization was underway, defense spending seldom dipped below 8 per cent of the GNP.

The phenomenal increase in the size and importance of the national security bureaucracies was accompanied by major transformations in their character. The State Department and the military agencies came out of the war with views of their functions and roles that differed substantially from their prewar self-images. In large part this metamorphosis was attributable to a generation of new men, schooled in war, who now stood ready to take over the swollen machinery of government.

Only for a few fleeting moments in her history had the United States attached high importance to the diplomacy of negotiation or awarded more than ceremonial status to the men who practiced it. In the earliest days of the Republic, Jefferson, Jay, and Franklin, the political and intellectual leaders of the United States, had shrewdly carved a place for the new nation as an adjunct of the European state system. In the weakness of infancy the United States relied heavily on persuasion and political maneuver to protect herself. But the Monroe Doctrine, which marked the divorce of America from European politics, also marked the shift of American diplomacy from cosmopolitanism to parochialism. The focus of the State Department turned from negotiating with equal or stronger powers to servicing the process of expansion. In most of the world the American ambassador limited his role to that of a reporter or a scout for commercial opportunities. The Department in Washington devoted its energies principally to economic, consular, and trade matters. The diplomatic career was a pleasant life for the rich man's son, the dilettante, or the retired financier who did not mind being outside the mainstream of politics and commerce. It hardly taxed one's intellect or initiative, and the salary Congress was prepared to appropriate for the diplomat reflected the value it placed on his services. In the late nineteenth century the top ambassadorial posts began to go to prominent businessmen. The embassy, like the honorary degree, had become a ritualized reward for commercial success.

The alternative conception of diplomacy was imperialism. From the Monroe Doctrine to the Truman Doctrine, American diplomats spent much of their time helping the army to wrest control of the continent from the Indians and extending the United States' sphere of influence to Latin America and the island prizes of the Spanish-American war. While he was a passive agent of American interests in the great courts of Europe, the American diplomat was an active and vigorous defender of American business interests among more backward peoples and an engineer of territorial expansion through purchase and war.

Nothing American diplomats had done in the prewar period equipped them to deal with the fantastic problems and opportunities that faced America across the ruins of Warld War II. The situation in the world was unprecedented: one nation had been restored and strengthened by the war that had ravaged most of the rest. How the United States should relate to a starving, seething planet was a task for which the diffident socialites who had graced the European embassies and the proconsuls who had managed the United States' interests in Latin America were equally ill fitted. Most of the prewar generation of diplomats soon disappeared from the scene. A generation of career ambassadors, like Norman Davis, as well as the leading administrators of the State Department in the New Deal period, Cordell Hull and Sumner Welles, did not survive the war in office. Despite repeated reorganizations during the war, the State Department's staff continued to reflect the prewar conception of its function. It was far stronger in economic, trade, and consular matters than in the practice of international politics. Even three years after the war the Department had a total of only 336 officers supposedly dealing with political questions out of a total complement of 5,906.

Franklin D. Roosevelt, who loved to play both the soldier and the diplomat, helped finish off the feeble prewar foreign policy bureaucracy with a series of blows. First, he appointed as Secretary of State a decent, old-fashioned moralist who bored him utterly. When he felt compelled to communicate with the State Department at all, he usually did so privately through Sumner Welles, the old schoolmate he had appointed as Undersecretary. Throughout his memoirs Hull complains about being left in the dark on the great issues. With the outbreak of war, communication between the White House and the State Department broke down almost entirely. "Don't tell anybody in the State Department about this," the President told Robert Murphy, then a junior foreign service officer about to leave on a presidential mission to North Africa. "That place is a sieve." To ensure against State Department interference in his foreign policy, Roosevelt carried on his most important correspondence in Navy Department codes.

The State Department's prestige and power in government declined in other ways as well. Many foreign service officers were drafted. It was not considered an essential occupation. Thus while the officer corps of the military services grew astronomically, the ranks of the professional diplomatic service were depleted. At the same time the professionalism of the foreign service was further challenged. New foreign policy bureaucracies responsible to other, more powerful agencies, such as the Departments of Agriculture, Treasury, and Commerce as well as the emergency agencies, came increasingly to overshadow the State Department. At the height of the war forty-four separate government agencies had representatives stationed at the American embassy in London. At the end of the war the Manpower Act of 1946 encouraged the "lateral entry" of military officers into the top foreign service grades, thus diluting the old club atmosphere and bringing in a new breed of diplomat fresh from the war. Veteran diplomats mourned the passing of the good old days when a half dozen men would gather in the Secretary's office and talk over the state of the world.

The early postwar spy scandals further weakened the prestige of the older foreign affairs bureaucracy. Then, before McCarthy, came McCarthyism. Alger Hiss, the old China hands, the Poland losers, the Czechoslovakia losers, and the other "vendors of compromise" in the State Department, as Senator John F. Kennedy would later call them, became tabloid celebrities before Senator McCarthy produced the blank piece of paper that supposedly listed 205 known communists in the State Department. The Army eventually triumphed over McCarthy, but the State Department suffered further casualties in the war. Scott McLeod, a former police reporter, FBI agent, and administrative aid to Senator Styles Bridges, believed generally to be a McCarthy man, took over as the Security Officer of the State Department, bringing with him an Elbert Hubbard motto for his desk: "An ounce of loyalty is worth more than a pound of brains." Full field investigations were conducted on veteran foreign service officers all over the world. Dulles encouraged the house cleaning, demanding "positive loyalty" from his diplomats. John Paton Davies, who years earlier had come up with so unpopular a prediction as Mao's victory in China, was found to be "lacking in judgment" and was dismissed despite repeated clearances from various loyalty boards.

In the war years the President turned increasingly to his generals and admirals for foreign policy advice, not only because his primary focus was on winning the war but, perhaps more important, because Marshall and his associates inspired confidence, as Hull did not. The Joint Chiefs, not Hull, attended the Big Three meetings at Cairo, Teheran, and Casablanca. At Yalta, Roosevelt threw aside the voluminous briefing books the State Department had provided him because he thought they were, in general, too equivocal on the future of the British, French, and Dutch empires and too hostile to the Soviet Union. When the subject came to China, he banished the State Department representatives from the room. At the outset of the war Hull himself accelerated the State Department's decline by renouncing interest in vital political matters on the grounds that they sounded like "technical military" affairs. He refused even to look at the "ABC" papers, the strategic directives drafted by American and British military leaders in the months preceding Pearl Harbor. On November 27, 1941, Hull "washed his hands" of the Japanese negotiations and turned the problem over to Stimson and Knox—the Army and the Navy. The Joint Chiefs of Staff were the most resourceful agency in the government in obtaining information. They received copies of the Roosevelt-Churchill correspondence "on a strictly personal basis" from the top British general in Washington, Sir John Dill. The military aide in the map room at the White House also smuggled out for his colleagues in the Pentagon memoranda prepared by F.D.R. All of these were of course quite unavailable to the State Department.

The power of the military services had grown swiftly once the President turned his major attention from economic recovery to preparation for war. In December 1941, shortly after his first wartime meeting with Churchill, Roosevelt created the Joint Chiefs of Staff. This bureaucratic innovation, which was based on neither Congressional legislation nor an executive order, greatly strengthened the position of the uniformed military and profoundly affected the future course of American diplomacy. The purpose of the decision was to create a counterpart to the British Chiefs of Staff who sat with the American officers on combined planning boards, and to discourage interservice rivalry. The effect was to create the most efficient structure in the government for the planning and implementation of national security policy. The Joint Chiefs acquired a huge staff and drew also on the Operations Division of the War Department, which for a while was headed by General Dwight Eisenhower. They had direct access to the President, a relationship strengthened by Admiral William Leahy, who had an office in the White House and served as ambassador between the military chiefs and the President. The military leaders saw the President far more frequently in the war than did their civilian superiors. F.D.R., who had enormous respect for General Marshall—"I feel I could not sleep at night with you out of the country"—rejected the advice of JCS no more than two or three times.

Perhaps most important, the military supplied to the rest of the government the conceptual framework for thinking about foreign relations. Walter Millis has summarized this major development in these words:

Because the State Department was so effectively sidetracked, because the military establishment had such a dominant institutional position, and because American experience furnished so little in the way of precedents for guidance, the inherited and ingrained American military doctrines about war and the functions of force in national policy became unusually important.

Thus the major decisions of the war with the greatest obvious political impact were made by the President, the Joint Chiefs of Staff, and Harry Hopkins. The Chiefs prepared for diplomatic conferences, negotiated with the Allies, and in the war theaters the commanders, Eisenhower and MacArthur, were supreme. Each obtained the power to pass on all civilians sent to his theater and to censor their dispatches. "Through these controls of overseas communications," Millis observes, "JCS was in a position to be informed, forewarned, and therefore, forearmed, to a degree no civilian agency could match."

Not only did the war radically shift the balance of power in the federal bureaucracy, catapulting the military from a marginal institution without a constituency to a position of command over the resources of a whole society, but it also redefined the traditional tasks of the military. We have seen how in practice the traditional semantic barriers between "political" and "military" functions were eroded; in the development and execution of strategy the military were deep in politics. As the war ended, the generals and admirals themselves, but more important, the civilian leaders in the Pentagon, were at work on an ideology which would assure a permanent place in American foreign relations for the military outlook, military personnel, and military techniques for achieving international objectives.

In the New Deal days military officers had been brought into a few civilian agencies. Major General Philip Fleming had been Federal Works Administrator. There was usually a military officer on the Maritime Commission. In the diplomatic corps middle grade officers served as military attachés, which were largely ceremonial assignments. But for the most part civilian government was beyond the reach of the Army and the Navy. Indeed, there was a wall of separation between the government of peace and the government of war.

As the war ended, it was unthinkable that the military would ever revert to their former role. They had achieved enormous prestige in the whole country. In public speeches they had taught again and again that weakness invites aggression. The generals made their postwar plans on the assumption that force would continue to be the primary instrument of American diplomacy. "We have tried since the birth of our nation to promote our love of peace by a display of weakness," General George Marshall wrote in his final report as Chief of Staff. "The world does not seriously regard the desires of the weak. . . . We must, if we are to realize the hopes we may dare to have for peace, enforce our will to peace with strength." That principle, as Harry Truman made clear in his first major postwar foreign policy speech as President, had been fully accepted. Speaking from the bow of the nation's mightiest battleship on Navy Day, he reminded the world that the United States was the greatest naval power on the planet and that American strength would enforce the peace.

At a time when Stalingrad was still under siege and it would have taken a lively imagination to conjure up a Soviet threat of world domination, United States military planners had already begun planning a huge postwar military machine. As the war ended, the Army demanded a ground force capable of expanding to 4.5 million men within a year. General Marshall hoped that universal military service would be swiftly enacted to meet this "requirement." The Navy thought it wanted to keep 600,000 men, 371 major combat ships,

THE ROOTS OF MISCONCEPTIONS / 65

5,000 auxiliaries, and a little "air force" of 8,000 planes. The Air Force also had specific plans. It wanted to be a separate service and to have a seventy-group force with 400,000 men. With these plans the top military officers made it clear that they were through being fire fighters called in when the diplomats had failed. From now on they intended to be a continuing influence in United States foreign relations.

Their civilian chiefs in the Pentagon, James V. Forrestal, the Secretary of the Navy, and Robert P. Patterson, who succeeded Stimson as Secretary of War, were the military's advocates. In the fall of 1945 Ferdinand Eberstadt perpared a report for Forrestal urging the creation of a National Security Council which would, as Forrestal put it, "guarantee that this Nation shall be able to act as a unit in terms of its diplomacy, its military policy, its use of scientific knowledge, and finally of course in its moral and political leadership of the world." The military, Forrestal asserted, must be permitted to have its say on all important foreign policy questions. There were no wholly "military" or wholly "political" questions. Since war and peace were part of a continuum, not separate categories, the administrative machinery for conducting foreign relations must reflect that reality. "Our military policy," Harry Truman declared, "should be completely consistent with our foreign policy." While this commendable purpose lay at the heart of the National Security Council proposals, the power of the Pentagon combined with the weakness of the State Department meant that the military often defined the terms of American foreign policy for the diplomats rather than the other way around.

The National Security Council symbolized at the apex of government a development that was taking place throughout the foreign policy machinery. The problems of diplomacy and international relations were becoming redefined as problems of "national security." This meant not only that military criteria for judging policies became more important and the processes of diplomatic adjustment less so, but also that personnel from the military departments, both uniformed and civilian, came to play a much more prominent role.

While the war was still on, some of the key individuals who ran the emergency government that had descended on Washington were planning to integrate it permanently into American life. Under the pressure of war entire new techniques for manipulating the politics of other countries had been developed; those who had put together the bureaucratic structures for operating these techniques fought to preserve their life. In the postwar world, they argued, the United States would need them, whatever the political environment would look like. The world-wide deployment of United States forces at the end of the war represented an opportunity for projecting power that a great country could not be expected to renounce. Thus the Joint Chiefs of Staff argued successfully for retaining most of the network of bases acquired in the war. The Research and Development Program, the Public Relations and Propaganda Networks, the Military Assistance Program, and the Subversion and Intelligence Apparatus, which hardly existed in 1940, continued to be major recipients of government funds after peace returned. The thinking, as peace dawned, of General William Donovan, the creator of the wartime OSS, offers an insight into the indestructibility of bureaucratic instruments. His assistant Robert H. Alcorn has described his views:

With the vision that had characterized his development of OSS, General Donovan had, before leaving the organization, made provision for the future of espionage in our country's way of life. Through both government and private means he had indicated the need for a long-range, built-in espionage network. He saw the postwar years as periods of confusion and readjustment affording the perfect opportunity to establish such networks. We were everywhere already, he argued, and it was only wisdom and good policy to dig in, quietly and efficiently, for the long pull. Overseas branches of large corporations, the expanding business picture, the rebuilding of war areas, Government programs for economic, social, and health aid to foreign lands, all these were made to order for the infiltration of espionage agents.

Thus before the Soviet spy revelations of 1946, before the first clashes of the Cold War, decisions were made to use "for the long pull" the instruments of subversion fashioned in war.

The emergence of a dominant national security bureaucracy was a prime legacy of war. The power which these institutions wield to set national priorities and to define the threats and opportunities facing the nation has a decisive impact on the direction of policy.

It is not surprising that essentially military bureaucracies define the principal threats to national security as the military threats, for these are the only kind they are equipped to handle. We see the same phenomenon in domestic life. If the technology to produce a supersonic transport plane becomes available, a new national goal is suddenly discovered and the machine will be built, regardless of how dubious its ultimate social utility. The forces in command of the technology are able to create a political reality within which it is impossible to say no to "progress."

Similarly the development of techniques for influencing political behavior of other countries accelerates the interventionist thrust of foreign policy. Having come into the possession of esoteric knowledge or esoteric techniques which can give it status and power, a bureaucracy fights to use it. If you can fly over another country or infiltrate its labor unions or destroy its crops, it's not hard to find a convincing reason to do it. The fascination with technique is almost irresistible. According to Stewart Alsop, President Eisenhower agreed to the U-2 flights over the Soviet Union after being shown a photograph of the Augusta golf course. "Every detail of the familiar well-loved course was clear to the President, who delightedly picked out a golf ball on a green." So a new capability spawned a new requirement, and it became necessary to fly over the Soviet Union.

Harold Lasswell once described the bureaucrat as a man with "an infinite capacity for making ends of his means." Robert Merton made the same point when he suggested that for the bureaucrat an "instrumental value becomes a terminal value." James V. Forrestal illustrated this fascination with technique rather than purpose when, as Secretary of the Navy, he learned of the spectacular capture and flag-raising ceremony on Mount Suribachi, Iwo Jima, and exclaimed, "This guarantees the continuation of the Marine Corps for five hundred years!" The authentic experience is the professional activity; the higher purposes, the abstract causes for which the bureaucracy exists, become symbols to be manipulated in pursuing a career. Indeed, the bureaucrat is comfortable only when his choices are instrumental. To challenge the assumptions behind a policy is to challenge the system which is the source of his power and status.

Being "in on the action" is the supreme status symbol in a life where the rewards are measured in the perquisites of office rather than in great differentials in cash. For the career bureaucrat a secretary in the outer office, a water pitcher, a couch, a rug, and especially a title are the currency of success. For the "national security managers" at the top, the goal is making something happen which hopefully history will smile upon but which on no account will lose him the respect of his peers on Wall Street or in Detroit. For the bureaucrat at the top and just below the top, activity of recognized importance is the highest reward.

The running of a bureaucracy is a collective experience. Participation is a goal in itself, and exclusion a bitter punishment. This phenomenon is not limited to the national security bureaucracy or even to government. It is common to all large organizations whose purposes are so complex or obscure that the individual loses grasp of the meaning of his own work. In discussing commercial as well as governmental bureaucracies, Robert Presthus points out that "the acquisition of status and prestige becomes an end in itself rather than a derivative of some significant achievement." The validation of one's efforts is a nod from the bureau chief or the privilege of attending the next meeting with the Secretary. "I'm sorry, he's with the President," the receptionist smiles. For the bureaucrat the invitation to participate is the significant event.

In complex national security issues there are few objective criteria for judging successes and failures. Was the operation in Greece in 1947 a success? Was NATO a success? It depends on what you think the alternatives were and what time frame you use for making the judgment. If, as historians are coming increasingly to believe, Stalin and Malenkov would have settled for a reunified neutralized Germany in 1952 and 1953, then NATO was not, in my judgment, a success. If the contemporary problems of Greece have their roots in the unresolved political issues temporarily obscured by the counterinsurgency campaign in Greece in 1947, then the Truman Doctrine was something less than a success. But bureaucrats for very practical reasons do not concern themselves with long-term results. Twenty years of stability and order is itself, in their view, a great accomplishment—indeed, all that one can expect. They view themselves as custodians rather than problem-solvers because they are conscious of their brief authority. Dean Rusk once said that his personal ambition as Secretary of State was to hand over the major problems to his successor in no worse shape than he found them. The assistant secretary on a two-year tour of duty in Washington or the Foreign Service officer awaiting reassignment is even more susceptible to this "keep the balls bouncing" view of statecraft. The canny bureaucrat is sustained by the faith that, when the policy collapses, he will be somewhere else.

This sort of approach to statecraft itself favors the recommendation of military measures. First, a military move can usually be presented as "buying time." To order in a few troops looks like a way of postponing difficult political decisions, although actually such an act, as the Vietnam experience shows, is itself a critical decision which circumscribes future choices. Second, a military initiative is much easier to arrange than a political initiative. The bureaucracy excels at deployment and logistics. If a man can define his professional responsibilities as moving troops or bombing targets, he is not likely to make an immediate professional blunder. If, however, he sets his goal as reconciling conflicting political interests, he has given himself a thankless task and will probably fail. Ordering the killing of Viet Cong is much easier than attempting to reconstruct Vietnamese society. For a powerful country, fighting comes far more naturally than negotiating.

The self-defined business of a bureaucracy, therefore, is to dispose of means and techniques. The man who questions, not how the techniques are to be used, but whether they should be, makes himself a candidate for reassignment. Audiences roared when the Air Force general in *Dr. Strangelove,* prompted by his pride in the penetration capabilities of the B-52, forgot momentarily that the whole government was trying to prevent an errant bomber from reaching Moscow, and triumphantly assured the President that the plane would get through. The meeting David Lilienthal describes in his diaries at which Secretaries Forrestal and Royall urged President Truman to turn over the atomic bomb to military control is reminiscent of the same inability to look at the larger picture. "You have to understand that this isn't a military weapon," Truman began. "It's used to wipe out women and children and unarmed people, and not for military uses." "But, Mr. President," Forrestal argued, "as an old weaponeer yourself, you know how important it is to get used to handling a new weapon." Yes, agreed the Secretary of the Army, "We have been spending 98 per cent of all the money for atomic energy for weapons. Now if we aren't going to use them, that doesn't make any sense."

The tragic proclivity of a bureaucracy to avert its collective eyes from the consequences and meaning of its acts is illustrated by the history of two of the greatest government-ordered slaughters of the innocent carried out in this century. The Final Solution of the Jewish Problem and the Dropping of the Atomic Bomb. They are distinguishable in magnitude and context, but as examples of the amorality of bureaucracy they are strikingly similar.

At the meeting SS chief Heydrich called at the peaceful Berlin suburb of Wannsee on January 20, 1942, "to clear up the fundamental problems" of the projected genocide, fifteen high-ranking representatives of various ministries and agencies discussed various ways and means of carrying out the job, but not one challenged the effort. Similarly a committee of distinguished Americans temporarily brought into the bureaucracy, including the president of Harvard, the president of the Massachusetts Institute of Technology, the president of one of the largest insurance companies, a former Supreme Court Justice, and a former Secretary of State, recommended unanimously "that the bomb be used against the enemy as soon as it could be done . . . without specific warning and against a target that would clearly show its devastating strength." They were not asked to give an opinion whether the bomb should be used as a terror weapon, nor did they volunteer one.

We are accustomed to thinking of the Nazi bureaucrats as monsters. For this reason Hannah Arendt's argument that Eichmann's evil was "banal" and hence duplicable in other societies was profoundly disturbing to many Americans. But James Conant, Vannevar Bush, William Clayton, Henry Stimson, and, finally, Harry Truman were not monsters nor notably less humane than Dwight Eisenhower, John Foster Dulles, or Pope Pius XII, all of whom subsequently deplored the decision to use the weapon on a population center without first having demonstrated its lethal effect somewhere else. What separated the first group from the second was their bureaucratic responsibility.

The pressure to stay within the accepted framework of policy and to take the premises of policy as given are common to all bureaucracies. In the national security bureaucracy old premises take on a particularly sacred character because proponents of the *status quo* have carefully wrapped them in the flag. For a bureaucrat to suggest in the early nineteen sixties that Diem was something less than a democrat or that torture was a more important instrument of his rule than charisma, was to leave himself open to the charge of "parroting the communist line," a charge that was both true and irrelevant, as well as highly effective in stifling self-criticism.

Robert Presthus has observed that all big organizations "place a high value upon power, status, prestige, order, predictability, easy acceptance of authority, hard work, punctuality, discipline, and conventionality." It is also clear that many of these qualities, so necessary for bureaucratic success, constitute the ideological goals of American foreign policy. Order and stability, however unjust or undemocratic their base, are to be preferred to political turmoil or revolution. It is better to support Trujillos, Batistas, or General Kys than to take a chance on the deluge that might follow them. Nonmilitary intervention is to be preferred to military intervention, but the United States must be prepared to use force rather than lose control over the political development of countries in which we have declared an interest. The bureaucrat with his strong personal commitment to established order and authority believes that the capacity to control the politics of other countries is essential to American national security. An uncontrolled environment is in his view a threatening environment. The politics of liberation frightens him, for a revolution, however spontaneous, leads to chaos and to possible domination by other outside powers. It is an article of faith that if events are allowed to unfold without American interference, they will end up badly for the United States.

The urge to intervene rests as much on psychological anxiety as on hardheaded calculations of economic interest. Indeed, the fear of losing control is more important than the fear of losing resources. Projecting his own hierarchical view of the world, the "national security manager" tends to discount spontaneity in others. Where people act, they are acting under orders. Thus the Greek guerrillas had no motives of their own to seize political power. They were directed by a conspiracy, as were the Guatemalans, the Dominicans, and the Viet Cong. In the bureaucrat's view of the world, conflict itself is distressing, for the continued supremacy of the United States depends upon the maintenance of order.

Early in the Cold War, Walter Lippmann referred to the American "refusal to recognize, to admit, to take as the premise of our thinking the fact that rivalry, strife, and conflict among states, communities and factions are the normal condition of mankind." In the American ideology "the struggle for existence and the rivalry for advantages are held to be wrong, abnormal, and transitory." The Foreign Service officer and the national security bureaucrat are especially troubled when others resort to violence, which they view as disease to be eradicated rather than as a technique of change which throughout history all but the very rich have felt the need to use. Despite extensive travels the national security bureaucrat is peculiarly isolated from political events in other countries. His information comes from the local American bureaucracy or from the client government we may be defending against an insurgency.

Individually the national security bureaucrat knows that life is more complicated than is dreamed of in his White Papers. He does not like napalming villages and knows that "aggression" is not the key to understanding what has happened in Vietnam. But bureaucratic truth is different from personal truth, just as collective morality differs from personal morality. As Harry Stack Sullivan has noted, the value system of the group provides the intellectual and moral framework for the individual. The individual conforms to the group "because of the extremely unpalatable, extremely uncomfortable experience of anxiety" he feels when he thinks or acts in deviant ways.

Becoming a successful bureaucrat involves a learning process not unlike the educational experience of a child. He learns what it takes to become an accepted "team player" and what he must avoid. The bureaucracy socializes and forms basic political attitudes because it is the chief source of rewards and punishments. Membership in the community can bring the individual the prestige and personal satisfaction of important activity and access to important people. It can assure financial and psychological security. But it can also wield the parent's primary weapon: rejection. "Shape up or ship out" is the army's succinct way of expressing the bureaucratic commandment.

Arthur Schlesinger, Jr., offers insight into the anxieties of the bureaucrat and what he does to overcome them. In his account of the decisions leading up to the Bay of Pigs affair, he attempts to explain why, having written lucid memoranda opposing the invasion for the President, he failed to speak up at meetings where the final decisions were taken. Pointing out that he was a "college professor fresh to the government" who found it difficult to oppose the institutional judgment of the State Department, the Defense Department, and the CIA, he went on to make a more fundamental point:

The advocates of the adventure had a rhetorical advantage. They could strike virile poses and talk of tangible things—fire power, air strikes, landing craft, and so on. To oppose the plan, one had to invoke intangibles—the moral position of the United States, the reputation of the President, the response of the United Nations, "world public opinion," and other such odious concepts. These matters were as much the institutional concern of the State Department as military hardware was of Defense. . . . I could not help feeling that the desire to prove to the CIA and the Joint Chiefs that they were not softheaded idealists but were really tough guys, too, influenced State's representatives at the Cabinet table.

If, as Veblen argues, the education of a bureaucracy is a "trained incapacity," the prime instrument of collective self-deception is official rhetoric. We have noted some of the characteristics of the bureaucratic system which make it difficult to correct errors or to ventilate the policy-making process. Language plays an enormously important role in assuaging guilt, suppressing criticism, and otherwise removing impediments to the smooth functioning of a bureaucracy on the move. Hannah Arendt has noted how the affectless language of the Nazi bureaucrat made it easier for him to accept the fact that he was in the genocide business. In the same way the rhetoric of "pacification" or the "surgical strike," evoking the images of a Quaker meeting or the operating room, served the purpose of rescuing the Vietnam policy-maker from a human confrontation with the consequences of his acts. Bureaucratic detachment, as James Thomson has called it, feeds on the "sanitized" truth of the mimeographed page, and such emotional disengagement makes it easier to treat other nations and their people as objects rather than neighbors.

Another characteristic of bureaucratic language is its abstraction and lack of concrete referents. The use of such terms as "power vacuum," "stability," or "balance" draws heavily from concepts of Newtonian physics. They are good for describing rather simple mechanical models like a see-saw but quite inadequate in the era of post-Newtonian physics to describe the physical environment, much less the political environment. The use of such metaphor helps to avoid a difficult discussion of the relationship of ends and means. How do you decide whether there is or is not a "power vacuum" in the Indian Ocean as Paul Nitze discovered a few days after becoming

Secretary of the Navy? The term "power vacuum," when applied to a country, as it often is in the national security bureaucracy, conceals a crucial political premise: there is a "vacuum" when the local government is in effective control of the country and is not a client of one great power or another. By using the term a bureaucrat writes off the possibility of national independence without even being aware of it.

The structure of language itself thus influences bureaucratic choices by reinforcing a particular view of the world political environment. Bureaucratic language is a ready-made instrument for perpetuating error because the realm of discourse is so far removed from the ordinary life experience of the human beings who make up a bureaucracy. Official truths cannot be validated or invalidated by personal experience. The global canvas which the national security bureaucrat confronts is so vast and psychologically so separate from his own life that his analysis is dependent upon metaphor and historical analogy. But making "grand designs" for other nations when you have neither personal loyalties nor indeed personal relationships of any kind with them puts an unbearable strain on the processes of human judgment. This inherent limitation in the capacity of human organizations to govern at a distance offers a clue as to why empires eventually fail.

As long as the business of foreign policy is seen essentially as a game in which the objective, "security," is defined as making sure that the rest of the world is sufficiently intimidated and that other countries do not develop in ways we do not like, military interventions will continue. As long as the legitimacy of unilateral military intervention is accepted, the only restraint on the commitment of American power to future Vietnams is the national security bureaucracy's own assessment of the limits of our national power. Because the national security bureaucrat has in many ways been a stranger in his own country, he is likely once again to misunderstand and misuse the strengths of the nation. If the national security institutions themselves continue to define our national purpose, we will be taught once again that what is good for the Air Force or the CIA is not necessarily good for America.

§§ ALBERT WOHLSTETTER: I have my doubts about Mr. Barnet's diagnosis, but that does not imply that I believe there is nothing to diagnose. Mr. Barnet asserts many points without elaboration and sometimes quite ambiguously. He rejects explanations of Vietnam as a series of mistakes or the fault of individuals like Dean Rusk, Walt Rostow, Maxwell Taylor, William Bundy, and Robert McNamara. There were mistakes, and he would have fired all of the individuals listed. But his own thesis is: "the roots of the Vietnam failure lie more in the structure and organization of the national security bureaucracy" which makes the United States "take on revolutionary movements around the world."

He doesn't define the U.S. failure in Vietnam. It is not that the United States failed to achieve its goals there. Rather it was intervention itself. Or so it seems. He does not make clear whether what is bad is (a) all intervention, or (b) military intervention, or (c) large-scale military intervention, or (d) unilateral military intervention, or (e) intervention by force against any movement that styles itself "revolutionary," or (f) any nonmilitary opposition to any revolution, or (g) any support for any government faced with rebellion, or (h) any opposition to communist rebellion, or (i) any opposition to rebellion that grounds itself merely on the fact that they are communist or communist-leaning.

However the failure is defined, its root is the "national security bureaucracy." While the latter, too, is undefined, it seems to include all those who manage our foreign or military affairs. At least, the State and Defense Departments and the White House staff, but also, evidently, the CIA, AEC, NSA, and the international divisions of Commerce, Treasury, Agriculture, etc. And in talking of "roots" most of the time Mr. Barnet appears to mean that such intervention is an unavoidable result of the characteristics of the national security bureaucracy. "Bureaucratic momentum" makes inevitable the escalation of a small use of military force to larger and larger amounts and makes inevitable escalation even from economic aid to military intervention: "The dynamism of the myriad bureaucratic empires dealing in national security assures not only the escalation of United States commitments but their progressive militarization as well." And "the progression from aid missions to counterinsurgency 'advisors' to expeditionary forces takes on a kind of Parkinsonian inevitability."

The national security bureaucracy "consistently" exaggerates threats. (The supposed missile gap of the late 1950's and the Soviet invasion threat in Western Europe in the 1940's are offered as examples.) This leads to increased military commitments and is indeed a rationalization for them. In fact, the United States' national security bureaucrats "favor using instruments of violence to solve" political problems. American bureaucrats seem worse in this respect than Maoist or Soviet ones. Elsewhere[6] Mr. Barnet has said that Soviet and Chinese communists do not scruple at the use of violence but normally prefer other means. American bureaucrats, it seems, *prefer* violence.

Mr. Barnet doesn't deny that the world is "dangerous and anarchic." Other nations are dangerous, too. However, they are less dangerous than the United States (even if they also should prefer violence) because they are less powerful.

But the deadly trouble with the American national security bureaucracy seems much more general than its American or even its national security character. It has to do with the basic characteristics of bureaucracy. And not simply governmental bureaucracies. Nongovernmental ones as well, e.g., commercial bureaucracies. Bureaucracies inevitably must convert means into ends. A particularly important example of this has to do with technology, both military and civilian. So the supersonic transport in the commercial aviation field: "If the technology to produce a supersonic transport plane becomes available, a new national goal is suddenly discovered and the machine will be built, regardless of how dubious its ultimate social utility." And the U-2 in the military field: "A new capability spawned a new requirement, and it became necessary to overfly the Soviet Union."

For a bureaucrat "to challenge the assumptions behind a policy is to take on the system which is the source of his power and status." Bureaucrats are conformists. They use unemotional language. This itself makes it easier to commit genocide. In fact, Barnet equates Truman's decision to use the A-bomb to end the war with Japan with Hitler's genocide, the "Final Solution" for the Jews.

Mr. Barnet sweeps over and touches on many other matters. He hints, for example, that national interests are a function of ethnic ties and a linear function of distance. And he closes with a geopolitical view rather like that of Mr. Kennan, who has held that "the effectiveness of power radiated from any national center decreases in propor-

[6] Richard J. Barnet, *Who Wants Disarmament?* p. 76.

tion to the distance involved." "The global canvas," Mr. Barnet says, "is too vast. Making 'grand designs' for other nations when you have neither personal loyalties nor indeed personal relationships of any kind with them puts an unbearable strain on the processes of human judgment. This inherent limitation in the capacity of human organizations to govern at a distance offers a clue as to why empires eventually fail."

I hope it will be plain from my later comments that I put a great deal of store in reflecting on ends as well as means, and that I feel there was not nearly enough of that in Vietnam. I have frequently written in other connections on the need in systems analysis for searching critiques of the accepted objectives. So I am sympathetic with Mr. Barnet's stress on the dangers of neglecting ends. Moreover, I have spent much of my professional life appraising technologies, several times showing the negative utility of some major technical innovations—sometimes persuasively. Further, I am not at all fond of bureaucracies and I dislike bureaucratic jargon (also social science jargon, hippie jargon, and a number of other jargons). Nonetheless—with all this going for it—Mr. Barnet's argument leaves me unsatisfied. It seems to me to be expressive rather than analytic; it conveys a mood, not an explanation.

And perhaps this is fortunate. Taken literally, Mr. Barnet's main argument seems to leave us almost no hope. If the general characteristics of bureaucracy or any large organization lead us so directly to genocide, nothing remains except a prayer that the world can be broken up into very small self-subsistent units in which contacts are face to face. Perhaps something like the Greek city-states, not counting the slaves. But then they *did* get into quite a few quarrels. And it seems hardly likely that we can manage our foreign and military affairs today in city sizes or in smaller units than commercial enterprises, which, we are told, also have the fatal bureaucratic traits.

But Mr. Barnet's argument cannot be taken literally. It is less downright than it generally sounds. On major points he frequently softens or contradicts it. Thus on "bureaucratic momentum" it seems that the Parkinsonian inevitability is not ineluctable after all. Perhaps "Parkinsonian" should read "Pickwickian." For he follows one such statement immediately with "this is not true everywhere . . . but where the resources of the United States appear adequate to suppress insurgent movements, the result is predictable." But even this is not true. The "resources of the United States" are not that constraining. And the United States has plainly not undertaken a good many actions for which it has resources. If one proceeds beyond the very broad constraints of general resources to an analysis showing that a particular military action would have been a *poor* use of our resources, in the sense that it would have meant surrendering something more important, then one says something very uncontroversial: we will act wisely whenever we do not undertake such an action. Almost no one will disagree.

Or take "threats"—an important matter. *Has* the national security bureaucracy consistently exaggerated threats and so led us into intervention? Mr. Barnet qualifies this. The bureaucracy "consistently" exaggerates "*many*" threats (100 per cent to a certain extent). And in fact it turns out that he doesn't think that having the threat appear large always encourages intervention: "Sometimes . . . threats are minimized in order to justify a seemingly rational policy based primarily on the use of military power. Thus North Vietnam can be beaten in a few months, the advocates of military intervention argued." And "the bureaucracy falls prey to the illusion that they are able to control events because they are free of the fear of retaliation."

It is not hard to multiply cases where the military greatly overestimated enemy forces and as a result did not intervene. For example, at the time of our decision not to intervene on behalf of the Chinese Nationalists at the end of the 1940's, General Marshall estimated the number of Russian divisions to be 260.[7] He neglected the con-

[7] "General Marshall told an audience in the Pentagon in November 1950: '. . . when I was Secretary of State, I was being pressed constantly . . . by radio message after radio message to give the Russians hell. . . . When I got back, I was getting the same appeal in relation to the Far East and China. At the time, my facilities for giving them hell . . . was 1⅓ divisions over the entire United States. This is quite a proposition when you deal with somebody with *over 260* and you have 1⅓.'

"With reference to the situation in China in 1947 and 1948, General Marshall testified: '. . . There, the issue in my mind, as Secretary of State, was to what extent this government could commit itself to a possible involvement of a very heavy nature in regard to operations in China itself. . . .

'We would have to make a very considerable initial contribution and we would be involved in the possibility of very extensive continuing responsibilities in a very large area.

siderable Russian demobilization (revealed later by Khrushchev) that had taken place since the war, ignored differences in size, manning, and equipment of these divisions (analyzed later by assistants to Robert McNamara, in particular Alain Enthoven), and compared them with categories of American force that were not strictly comparable. And we did not intervene.

That the military nearly always exaggerate enemy capabilities and that this leads to intervention is a cliché and a vast exaggeration. It isn't so. The truth is that they sometimes overestimate and sometimes underestimate—and sometimes even get it right—and that either sort of mistake may in various circumstances lead toward or away from intervention, or may be largely irrelevant. It is hard to see what we can conclude—except that it's nice to have better estimates of threats and to consider concretely a good many other things besides threats in deciding on whether, where, and when to commit ourselves.

Mr. Barnet's reference to the "missile gap" indicates a very popular misunderstanding. In the first place, the "missile gap" was not an issue raised by the "ins"—the top managers of national security under Eisenhower. It was a political gambit of the "outs"—the Democrats. President Eisenhower's top bureaucrats stoutly defended themselves against the charge: they said that we might have fewer missiles but we had and would have more bombers, that in any case there was no deterrent gap. Second, during the Eisenhower regime the strategic force was genuinely and dangerously vulnerable, but this vulnerability had nothing essential to do with the hypothetical "missile gap." It had to do with the fact that the strategic force in the 1950's had no adequate warning or other protection against even a small manned

---

'At that time, our own military position was extraordinarily weak. I think I mentioned the other day that my recollection is . . . we had one and a third divisions in the entire United States.

'As I recall General Wedemeyer's estimates, about 10,000 officers and others would be necessary to oversee and direct those various operations.

'In view of our general world situation, our own military weakness, and the global reaction to this situation, and my own knowledge out of that brief contact of mine in China, we could not afford to commit this government to such a procedure.

'Therefore, I was not in agreement with undertaking that, nor were . . . the chiefs of staff.' "

Tang Tsou, *America's Failure in China, 1941–1950* (Chicago: University of Chicago Press, 1963), pp. 366–67.

bomber attack. Moreover, the essential major changes made in the strategic force by President Kennedy and Secretary McNamara had to do with substituting less vulnerable strategic vehicles and a more responsible and protected control of this strategic force. This drastic set of changes was indicated in any case and had been proposed in classified form *before* the Kennedy Administration and *before* a hypothetical "missile gap." The proposed changes had been accumulated by analysts, many of whom took great pains to separate the problems of deterrence, of responsible control against "accidents," and of reducing the vulnerability of strategic forces from the problem of matching forces in number.

The mythology of the "gap" includes not only the potential gap that turned out not to be actual but also the myths about the role the gap played. I am quite familiar with them, since I began writing analyses to demonstrate the essential irrelevance of bomber gaps, missile gaps, engineer gaps, and the like beginning in the early 1950's, and as late as 1960 I sent a lengthy explanation to the man who was writing John Kennedy's main campaign speech on defense, specifically to suggest why the "missile gap" was not only a theoretical and operational misunderstanding of the problem but also one that was very likely to kick back politically. It did, but only after the election.[8]

The Russian invasion potential in the late forties is the other example cited by Mr. Barnet. It would take quite a lot of space to evidence why, but I believe that his judgment about what was wrong with our various estimates at the time and what role our erroneous estimates played in our commitments is itself in error. A study of the quotations from General Marshall suggests why. Let me simply register my disagreement.

On technologies it seems to me Mr. Barnet greatly overstates his case and gets some of the historical record quite wrong. On the historical record the U-2's existence did not create the requirement for

[8] Mr. Barnet is in error in suggesting that basic changes in the strategic force made in the early years of the Kennedy Administration depended on the existence of a "missile gap." The gap was strictly inessential. On the other hand, his own comments in *Twenty Years After* on the recent state of the missile gap and its future suggest the need for caution about not merely the significance of gaps but their possible future existence and direction. He was confident two or three years ago that the Russians were quite willing to put up with a large gap favoring the Americans. The evidence since suggests that they are not.

overflight. On the contrary, the U-2 was an unusually clear-cut case of a rather precisely defined lack generating a technology. The need at the time for better estimates of Russian forces might be suggested by the troubles I have discussed with early estimates of Russian capabilities. In fact, some of our early knowledge seems to have come from German data and Russian documents captured by the Germans during World War II. These were quite a bit out of date by the early 1950's. And our information then was quite incomplete. In any case, the need for better information was felt in the administration. And according to public accounts, a variety of government officials and advisors explored the possibilities of gaining reconnaissance at extremely high and hopefully safe altitudes. The crash project at Lockheed to develop the U-2 was in response to this perceived need—quite the reverse of Mr. Barnet's description that flying over the Soviet Union was decided on because we had the plane. In fact the desire for information about Soviet military forces appears to have generated not one but several technologically distinct modes of fulfilling the same need.[9] The relationship between technology and aims is usually much more complex. I doubt that there are many examples as clear as this.

Yet Mr. Barnet suggests that the creation of national goals regardless of ultimate social utility is automatic. If this were so, it would be impossible to explain the fact that a great many technological developments have been sharply limited or canceled altogether—military developments such as the Navaho ramjet missile, the B-70 manned bomber, the Skybolt missile, the nuclear-propelled aircraft, and a great many others. The world would have been knee-deep long ago in a wide variety of military hardware, most of which has never seen the light of day.

The same may be said for civilian technology. Our choices here, as in the military case, are frequently misguided, and often we are too fascinated by techniques, but it is fortunately not the case that every technology feasible is made actual. There are many in which there is little argument, and there are some, like the development of the nuclear merchant marine, in which arguments against have so far

[9] The magazine *Air Force*, March 1968, p. 53, states that satellites for reconnaissance were studied before as well as after Sputnik. And Soviet accounts report reconnaissance over Russia, not only by the U-2 manned aircraft, but also by balloons (*The New York Times*, Feb. 6 and 12, 1956, and Oct. 12, 1958).

prevailed, and some, like Mr. Barnet's own example of the supersonic transport, in which there has been a great deal of argument pro and con with the pros winning but under much severer restraints than had been proposed. It has not been anything like as automatic as Mr. Barnet suggests. Moreover, the most potent arguments against supersonic transport, perhaps to Mr. Barnet's surprise, have been made by systems analysts borrowed from the Defense Department (Dr. Stephen Enke, for example; see his paper in the *American Economic Review,* May 1967).

In fact, Mr. Barnet's description of the automatic coming into operation of any new technologies is excluded by the fact that there are resource constraints. Choice is not only possible, but necessary. To develop one alternative precludes developing some others. Mr. Barnet's nightmare of bureaucracies automatically sponsoring every technology would simply be too crowded. It is a logical impossibility. This does not, of course, mean that *good* choices will be made. But *choices* will be made. What are we to conclude from this? Only that we should keep working at improving our methods of selection— recalling always that our choice of means is related to our choice of ends.

On the matter of ends and means, once again Mr. Barnet seems to me to have greatly overstated the problem, made it appear in fact insoluble. I quite agree with him that bureaucrats tend to forget about their ends. They frequently, as Santayana remarked about fanatics, redouble their efforts as they lose sight of their goal. On the other hand, as the context of Santayana's remark suggests, this is hardly limited to government bureaucrats or bureaucrats in commercial enterprise. It can be true in political parties, and had obvious illustrations in the party bureaucracies of the left, which Robert Michels analyzed. But it is also true, sad to say, of violently antibureaucratic movements. The anarchists, as is familiar, have frequently taken revolutionary violence as an end in itself. There is a great deal of romanticism current on this subject. And much of the discussion of whether one should support revolution or counterinsurgency proceeds on these sentimental terms. But whether a revolution is worth supporting or opposing should surely depend on what it is a revolution to as well as what it is a revolution from, and what the human costs are of the revolutionary process, and what other alternatives for change there are. Reflection on ends as well as means seems quite as rare among insurgents as among counterinsurgents.

In sum, I do not see that Mr. Barnet shows it to be impossible for men who manage foreign and military affairs to reflect on goals as well as means. And if this is rarer among military men and statesmen than we would like, so is reflective behavior almost any place.

On Mr. Barnet's opposition to intervention, I will not try to select for comment one or two out of the nine or ten possible meanings that I have listed. I will note only that he does relent a little on his indictment of the national security bureaucrats. Although at one point he indicated that they actually prefer the use of violence, at another he said that they preferred nonmilitary intervention but will use force rather than lose control where we have an interest. My own views in this respect are quite close to those of my colleague, Professor Morgenthau:[10] one cannot decide whether it is good or bad to intervene at a given time or place without a great deal of concrete empirical analysis. It is not clear to me that Mr. Barnet agrees.

I will not comment at length here about the bare suggestion in Mr. Barnet's paper of a geopolitical view that relates national interests to ethnic ties and linearly to distance. I have written extensively about the limitations of such views elsewhere.[11] On the ethnic argument let me say only that I think it particularly incongruous today when voiced by those who want to turn from foreign concerns to the problems of domestic, racial, and ethnic inequities. I'm afraid we'll have to deal with both.

ARTHUR SCHLESINGER, JR.: I think there is a certain amount of insight mingled with a great deal of extravagance and error in Mr. Barnet's argument. I would sharply distinguish the remarks I made earlier regarding the growth of a warrior caste in the United States from Barnet's general thesis.

[10] "To Intervene or Not To Intervene," *Foreign Affairs,* April 1967.

[11] "Technology, Prediction and Disorder," in *Dispersion of Nuclear Weapons,* ed. Richard Rosencrance (Columbia University Press, 1964); "Illusions of Distance," *Foreign Affairs,* January 1968; "Strength, Interest, and New Technologies," in Adelphi Paper No. 46 (London: Institute of Strategic Studies, 1968); "Theory and Opposed Systems Design," to be published in *New Approaches to International Relations,* ed. Morton Kaplan, in the fall of 1968; "Distant Wars and Far Out Estimates," with Richard Rainey, to be published.

I previously suggested that a great factor in the momentum which led us into the Vietnam situation is the warrior group inside our government. This group, because of its own internal needs, constantly presses for more and more military involvement. It is one dynamic and irrational element within the government, operating in amorphous situations. But it does not *inevitably* determine United States policy.

I would like to make three brief points about Barnet's thesis. First, despite the impact of this warrior caste, American foreign policy since World War II has not been, in my judgment, predominantly military in its conception or execution. Mr. Barnet vastly overrates this role of the National Security Council as an agency of decision. The National Security Council, as far as I know, made no important decisions on anything in these years. It was occasionally a ratifier of decisions, but at no time that I am acquainted with did it play a serious role, in that odious term of the political scientist, in the decision-making process.

I would say that military conceptions, far from determining our policy, predominated only in certain areas and at certain moments, and often as a matter of last resort. True, Vietnam is a case in point. But Mr. Barnet, I believe, has taken Vietnam as the model for every decision in foreign policy made since World War II, whereas Vietnam represents a kind of culmination of error. It is not typical. In fact, one reason for the dominance of the military in Vietnam is the deliberate abdication in 1962 by the Secretary of State of any concern with Vietnam. Most of the important things we have done in foreign policy since World War II have been political and economic rather than military in nature.

Second, the national security bureaucracy is portrayed in Barnet's argument as being a unified monolith, which, of course, it is not. The national security bureaucracy has been, not only in general but also in its military component, sharply divided. For example, in the 1950's there were the arguments between General Ridgway and General Gavin and the Army, on the one hand, and Admiral Radford and the Air Force, on the other, on such questions as intervention in Vietnam; there was the argument in 1960 over the Cuban missile crisis, when most of the Joint Chiefs were in favor of taking out the nuclear bases in Cuba by surprise attack, but were opposed by General Shoup, of the Marine Corps, who because of his superior common sense differed from his colleagues on many issues. The Joint Chiefs during the Kennedy Administration usually did not get their way. President Kennedy paid serious attention to the Joint Chiefs on a major decision only once, in the Bay of Pigs intervention. In connection with Laos, the Cuban missile crisis, Berlin, the test ban treaty, etc., he listened courteously to their recommendations, but he then disregarded them, though, of course, he believed they had some usefulness in organizing their own services.

In 1966 and 1967 the national security bureaucracy was far from acting as a unit. Indeed, the champion of the political approach to Vietnam was the Secretary of Defense—a curious exchange of roles, where the Secretary of Defense became champion of political interests and the Secretary of State became champion of military interests. Robert McNamara wanted to talk about possibilities of negotiation, while the Secretary of State, sitting in the State Department, knocked down possibilities of negotiation and picked out bombing targets.

McNamara's initiative led to preliminary secret discussions, which in turn led to the negotiations in Paris. All of this was done in the face of skepticism and resistance on the part of the Secretary of State. Even today, the CIA, which is not regarded very highly by Barnet, has for some time been leading the challenge to Rusk and the Joint Chiefs on the question of the effectiveness of what we are doing in Vietnam. The CIA has provided realistic reporting in relation to bombing assessments and in relation to the political situation in Vietnam, and their evaluations have been opposed by other elements in the military and diplomatic bureaucracy. This tends to show that Mr. Barnet's monolith theory does not correspond at all to the realities of the national security bureaucracy.

Third, I would say that the elements of militarization and escalation, which Barnet thinks are inherent in the bureaucracy, do not inevitably win out. The great trouble with his argument is that it concentrates on those who give the advice rather than on those who take it. Kennedy did not escalate at the time of the Bay of Pigs, and after the Bay of Pigs he never again took the advice of the Joint Chiefs of Staff on a serious issue. At best, all those who give advice can do is to give it, but the decisions are made by—and the responsibility rests on—those who take the advice. The useful area of concern for us is who makes the decisions, who takes the advice, and why. This is an area which transfers discussion from the organizational problem, which is really a phony issue and an escape from the serious difficulty, to the actual intellectual problem.

Essentially it is the acceptance on the part of the President and Secretary of State of such advice that makes it significant rather than the fact that elements of the bureaucracy generate it. Of course, the military are going to make these recommendations. I don't see why anyone should be surprised by this. What Barnet exaggerates is both the unity and the force of the kind of advice the military gives. And, in my judgment, he leaves out the basic thing, which is why anyone listens to what they have to say.

CHESTER COOPER: One of the real problems I have with Mr. Barnet's argument is his obsession with the insidious plans of President Roosevelt and his principal advisors to strengthen the hand of the military at the expense of the political bureaucracy. His arguments are so slanted that many of them fall down. He conveniently ignores the fact that despite military planning for a "huge postwar military machine," the United States virtually demobilized its armed forces within months after V-J Day. We rearmed only after the Soviet Union had proved the generals' point that "weakness invites aggression." Nor does he mention that despite the strong pressures of the military to control our atomic energy establishment, control was actually given to the civilians. Mr. Barnet mentions neither of these. Mr. Barnet balances off these and other sins of omission in the historical section by a profound sin of commission: he puts such men as James Conant and Vannevar Bush in the same company as the leading Nazis because, when advising President Truman, they recommended using the atomic bomb against Japan. His monstrous charge hangs on this statement: "They were not asked to give an opinion whether the bomb should be used as a terror weapon, nor did they volunteer one." So, in Mr. Barnet's eyes, they join the ranks of Heydrich and Eichmann.

Barnet argues that "if we do not change the institutions of the United States government which push us toward intervention," we will be confronting future Vietnams. This may or may not be true, but Barnet offers no hint as to what particular institutions he would change or how he would go about changing them. He points out that firing the top level of the government would do no good since "it is wildly optimistic to think that the overdue retirement of a group of individuals will in itself produce a change in policy"—there is apparently need for much more drastic surgery. Presumably we have to get rid of a wide swath of policy-makers, advisors, and technicians which we must assume comprises the "bureaucracy" Barnet is worried about. But beyond the matter of pointing to such villains of the peace as the "bureaucracy," the reader will find no prescriptions, no antidotes, no solutions, no alternatives.

His specific references to some of the developments of the past several years are so plainly wrong or so obviously subjective as to make one suspect much of what Mr. Barnet says. For example, he feels that the "most striking characteristic of American postwar foreign policy" has been its "interventionist thrust." He cites "our major campaigns" in Iran, Guatemala, the Dominican Republic, British Guiana, and Cuba and links these with the intervention in Vietnam as part of the "continuing pattern." If we fought a "major campaign" in Iran or British Guiana, it will come as quite a surprise to the Pentagon. But even if one accepts that these instances represent American attempts to intervene in situations abroad which it found unpalatable, this is a far cry from saying that the United States has institutional commitments "to take on revolutionary movements around the world." In recent years we have stood aside in Indonesia (as Mr. Barnet himself admits), but in the early postwar period we assisted the forces of revolution against the Dutch (which Mr. Barnet ignores). We have watched anxiously but have remained pretty much aloof from "revolutionary" threats in such places as Bolivia, Burma, Venezuela, Aden, the Sudan, and black Africa. In Yemen we sided with the "revolutionists" (to our sorrow).

Or again, Mr. Barnet says "there are more United States counterinsurgency forces in Thailand today than there were in Vietnam early in 1965." He is wrong by a factor of approximately twenty. As a matter of fact, we can number the American military officers actually in the field with Thai military forces against the insurgents in northeast Thailand on the fingers on one hand. By far the major part of the American forces there are Air Force personnel in support of our military in Vietnam.

In commenting on the American assessment of the world situation, Mr. Barnet deals very lightly with the threats we confront. For example, he seems to feel that we should regard Soviet espionage activities as a harmless spectator sport. He also seems uncertain as to where to place blame with respect to our experience in Vietnam. In one place he cites our "failure" in Vietnam as being the fault of our "bureaucracy"; a few paragraphs later we learn that "for a variety of historical reasons mainly concerned with the fact that Ho Chi Minh has gained a certain proficiency through practice . . . the Vietnamese intervention is a failure." Finally, according to Mr. Barnet, "the intelligence bureaucracies knowingly err on the 'conservative side' in discovering enemies." But "sometimes threats are minimized." He has it both ways here, but neglects to mention one quite recent, critical event in which the "intelligence bureaucracy" guessed right— the Soviet missiles in Cuba.

I would agree with Mr. Barnet in his complaint that insufficient attention has been paid to the political problems in Vietnam. But having spent, together with many other "bureaucrats," some of the best years of my life on "how to obtain a peace settlement in Vietnam by political means," I can state with some authority that Mr. Barnet's discussion of negotiations is just plain incorrect.

RICHARD M. PFEFFER: I would like to defend Mr. Barnet's paper, which in his absence has hardly been given its due, to say the least. What we have done here is in style the polar opposite of what Robert Kennedy reportedly did when, during the Cuban missile crisis, the United States received two notes from Khrushchev. Rather than pursuing the fruitful interpretation, as he is said to have done, we have gleefully interpreted Barnet in a way which makes his position almost asinine. We have not tried to understand what he is saying.

There are problems in his presentation with respect to his mode of expression which may facilitate this abusive interpretation. Barnet is an easy target. His arguments, phrased in terms of monolith and inevitability, are susceptible to being made into straw men, easy to knock down. This is what Professors Schlesinger and Wohlstetter have done. Nobody has attempted to see whether there is much truth in Barnet.

The extreme vulnerability of his argument about inevitability is equaled only by the vulnerability of arguments on the other side— that a situation remains always fluid. I seem to perceive that that is the suggestion being made by some of his critics.

Barnet is in the tradition of C. Wright Mills—he is talking about and expressing an awareness of the drastic change that occurred in the American government since World War II. At this level, at the very least, he is useful because he starkly describes the drastic changes and sets out the kind of framework that might be used for understanding the structural differences between the prior and the subsequent situations. In considering statements of Adam Yarmolinsky and Jim Thomson, I find suggestions which are very similar to those of Barnet. The major difference between them is perhaps that Barnet bit off more than one can chew. He tried to present structurally what others have presented as situational arguments. Right or wrong, there is a need for this kind of analysis.

The focus of our discussion here has been on decision-making. In the argument with Barnet we are back once again to the old confrontation between the power elite theorists and the pluralists, who focus on different things and therefore come up with different conclusions. Barnet focused only partly on specific decision-making, and I agree that he is weakest on that point. He is more convincing when he deals with the issue of the variety of alternatives considered by decision-makers and with one of the resulting patterns of American foreign policy. The range of alternatives frequently has been circumscribed, and that is, of course, very important.

Barnet's use of structural analysis to explain a trend makes his citing of specific individual decisions primarily useful to his critics, who can focus on rebutting individual cases.

ARTHUR SCHLESINGER, JR.: The point I tried to make earlier is that one great new element in the situation, the basic element in the enlargement of our commitment in Vietnam, has been a series of pressures that have been generated in an irrational way by the military establishment. To say this, however, is commonplace; and if that were the point Barnet was making, it is one which, I imagine, three quarters of the people in this room would instantly accept. The point he is making, I take it, is a very different point, that is, that everything we have done in foreign policy since World War II has been determined by monolithic military viewpoints which inevitably produced certain results. This is something I find hard to accept.

Obviously one of the greatest dangers facing this country is militarization of life and thought. When you get a liberal mayor of New York faced with a garbage strike and he cannot think of anything better to do than call up the National Guard, this suggests how far the infection has gone. But if that is Barnet's point, then he should make that point. He shouldn't say that *everything* is determined by unified national security bureaucracies, which I gather was his point.

WILLIAM R. POLK: I agree that it is a mistake to talk about bureaucracy as though it were a unit. Things look very different from different places in the functioning bureaucracy. It is interesting that Mr. Barnet, for example, was himself in the Disarmament Agency and was particularly conscious of the fact that the Pentagon was heavily represented.

JAMES C. THOMSON, JR.: On this point Barnet gives us a monolithic bureaucracy and a conspiracy theory. My own impression is that ours is a pluralistic bureaucracy, and my theory of its operation is a theory of disorder. From my experience I would give much more importance to the role of the individual and the role of the irrational in the process of tragedy over the past seven years.

Nevertheless Barnet is trying to put his finger on something important: the cumulative momentum of the past, the inherited baggage of the past in terms of people and ideas. I have reference, of course, to some of the people Professor Schlesinger referred to earlier.

§§ RICHARD J. BARNET:[12] Messrs. Wohlstetter, Schlesinger, and Cooper apparently cannot resist the temptation to mount search-and-destroy missions against straw men. They came to my paper armed with a barrage of nonspecific and undocumented charges of error and exaggeration as well as an impressive collection of internally inconsistent arguments. It is difficult to defend against Mr. Wohlstetter's twin charge that I am guilty of exaggeration and excessive qualification, and I shall not try, for I should like to move the discussion away from paper grading and back to substance.

[12] Since Mr. Barnet was unable to attend the conference, he has been given the opportunity to rebut here in writing the criticism of his paper.

Let me start by restating what the paper is not about. It is neither an analysis nor a critique of American intervention policy (I have attempted this in *Intervention and Revolution: The United States in the Third World,* which has just been published). Mr. Wohlstetter and I have very different views on the wisdom and the legitimacy of United States policy on intervention. To debate those issues would have taken another paper if not a volume. I started with what I thought was a common recognition of failure in the Vietnam policy, and I focused my inquiry on some of the causes and conditions of that failure. Nor did the paper promise the recommendations Mr. Cooper says he wants to see about reconstructing the national security bureaucracy.

What I tried to do in the paper was to ask why the United States government has developed its taste for intervention; specifically, what is there about our governmental machinery that favors a certain kind of analysis of the contemporary world and a certain pattern of response for dealing with it? I do not know how to convince Mr. Cooper that the interventionist thrust has indeed been the principal characteristic of our policy. From his service in the CIA he must know at least as well as I the dimensions of our efforts to prevent undesirable governments from coming to power and, where possible, to overthrow them if they do. That we did not intervene everywhere is quite beside the point. Nor does it make our policy less interventionist if we are able to succeed by subsidizing a band of about 120 refugees (as in Guatemala in 1954) or a handful of agents (as in Iran in 1946) or a selected group of hooligans (as in British Guiana in 1964). In each case the objective was "major": the overthrow of the legitimate government. In each case the amount of force employed was sufficient to the task.

My starting point is that the general direction of policy is a product of the organization and structure of the institutions that generate it. It seems that if our policy is a problem, we ought to look hard at the men who make it and particularly at the institutional pressures under which they operate. It is useful to identify some of the characteristics of the bureaucracy, such as Mr. Thomson has listed, like fatigue or detachment, but these insights do not really get at the roots of the problem. They do not explain much. I am interested in exploring why the misperceptions, errors of judgment, and faulty analyses happened. This strikes me as an essential inquiry if we are to try to regain control of the foreign policy machinery and restore some rationality to national security policy.

I have sufficient respect for the difficulties of the problem and the vast amount of careful analytical work that still needs to be done not to offer a "grand theory" that promises to explain everything about American foreign policy or even American interventionism. I think what I have called "bureaucratic momentum" is an enormous national problem. I never said and do not believe that the bureaucratic process is ineluctable. I was talking about what I take to be strong tendencies arising out of certain identifiable factors, among them the system of rewards and punishment in the bureaucracy, the historical development of that bureaucracy, and the relationship of the bureaucracy to the democratic process.

Far from believing the zany theory of bureaucratic determinism which several of the commentators ascribed to me, I still cherish the rationalist faith that we do not have to be slaves to our institutions. We can make them serve rational and moral purposes. But to do this we must understand them. We must go through a process of painful self-analysis before we can grow up as a nation. It is a clinical process that can succeed only if we avoid the twin dangers of defensiveness and self-hate. When I compared Nazi deliberations on the "Final Solution" and the Truman Administration deliberations on dropping the atomic bomb, I was making the point that good men frequently behave like bad men when they act on behalf of bureaucratic entities. This may well be a "monstrous charge," as Mr. Cooper contends, but it is a problem of our national life which is now manifesting itself in the systematic destruction of Vietnam.

The attempt to avoid discussion of what I said in the paper by pointing to alleged errors of fact could be fully answered only by a compendious rebuttal as pedantic and irrelevant as the criticism. To take for example, however, Mr. Cooper's arithmetic on Thailand, I must conclude either that he is uninformed or that, although he is no longer in the government, he still feels compelled to contribute to the credibility gap. According to the Pentagon, there were 23,300 American military personnel in Vietnam in January 1965. There are now 45,000 in Thailand, all with a counterinsurgency mission.

Two observations of the commentators, however, which recur rather frequently, deserve some clarification. I am supposed to believe in a "conspiracy theory" to explain American foreign policy. I also learn with some surprise that I believe that the national security bureaucracy is another incarnation of that dangerous animal "the monolith." I learned in law school that a conspiracy is a "meeting of the minds," a planning or a plotting together to do something unlawful. Where members of the administration have planned military operations in Vietnam which they knew violated the laws of war and the Geneva Conventions, I think "conspiracy" is an appropriate word to describe their conduct. But it is a word I would never use to describe the ordinary operations of government.

I was saddened to read that Mr. Cooper had taken my paper to be an indictment of President Roosevelt as the archconspirator of the bunch. The comment is particularly ironic, not only because I happen to think F.D.R. was the greatest President of the century, but, more particularly, because President Roosevelt himself recognized precisely what I was talking about in the paper. Like Woodrow Wilson before him, he worried about the militarization of our institutions as a consequence of total war. It is hard to argue against militarizing the country in time of war, and I never suggested that the great power of the Chiefs of Staff in wartime was anything but a necessary development. But human institutions have a strong instinct for survival and growth, and the incredible concentration of power in the national security bureaucracies in World War II transformed the face of this nation. The war educated a whole generation of policy-makers in the assumptions and techniques of war, and we have not yet faced the implications of what happened to us almost thirty years ago.

I do not understand why those who are made nervous by attempts to analyze the groups of individuals who make decisions—the "power structure," "power elite," or "establishment," "ruling circles," or whatever you want to call them—insist on characterizing such analytical efforts as conspiracy-mongering. There is a suggestion that an analysis that looks at what motivates men is the equivalent of a criminal indictment. Of course there is a power elite in charge of national security policy. Since 1940, 398 individuals have held the top national security positions in the United States. They are an elite by definition, and few would deny that they have had great power. We ought to be able to look coldly at them—where they come from, who picks them, what pressures operate on them, where they go when they leave government service—so that we can identify the problems inherent in the system of recruitment and education of our leaders and try to correct them.

Our intellectual and political task is magnified exactly because the "national security managers" do not constitute either a Mafia or what I think Mr. Schlesinger means by a "warrior caste." The principal source of energy for America's interventionist policy has been, not the professional military, but the top civilian leadership of the national security bureaucracy, the Secretaries, Undersecretaries, and Assistant Secretaries or their equivalents in the Departments of State and Defense and in the Central Intelligence Agency. By almost any conventional standard these have been the best educated, the most intelligent, and the most endowed men in the country. If we had a real warrior caste, a group of easily identifiable Junkers, our problem would be relatively simple. We would try to keep the government out of such dangerous hands. But what are we to do when professors who become "national security managers" turn out to be old-fashioned militarists who habitually recommend bombing as the solution to difficult political problems? This suggests to me that the problem may lie in institutional structures which generate pressures that influence men toward militarist analyses and militarist solutions. We need to understand much better the way in which the personal career interests of individuals and the interests of such bureaucratic structures as the Air Force or the CIA influence and shape national purpose. My paper was an attempt to begin on such an effort.

As to "the monolith," that is another extraneous issue. I served in the State Department. I am well aware that there are conflicts among bureaus, between the Air Force and the Army, between the Joint Chiefs of Staff on the one hand and the Secretary of Defense on the other. It is also true that the CIA and the State Department sometimes find themselves on different sides in foreign interventions, as in Laos in 1960. Sometimes they have different policy approaches, as has often been the case in Vietnam. But what is the significance of this for the problem under consideration, the interventionist character of American foreign policy? The general effect of these conflicts is not to restrain the use of force or the acquisition of weaponry, but rather to bid up the price or duplicate the effort.

When the acquisition of a new weapons system is successfully resisted, say, because a Defense Department systems analyst together with the Navy is able to block a major Air Force procurement program, this does not mean that the defense budget as a whole comes down or that the bureaucracy as a whole shifts emphasis. It usually means that some other weapons system will be built in its stead. The assumption underlying the often acrimonious fights over the defense budget pie is that the pie will get bigger year by year and everyone will continue to be served. There may be, as Charles Hitch has asserted, no single "military-industrial complex" but rather a host of competing military-industrial complexes; but all this activity within the national security system does not change its general direction. There is nowhere in the national security establishment a countervailing power for the promotion of peace through arms control or political negotiation. The balance of power within the government has been decisively on the side of those bureaucracies whose function is to manipulate military power. It is not very reassuring to assert, as does Mr. Wohlstetter, that we have not built every conceivable weapons system that somebody has thought of. The point is that the general thrust of our policy has been to stockpile or make use of in some way in the pursuit of national security every major technological innovation.

Mr. Wohlstetter has a point when he criticizes my reference to the U-2 incident. My elliptical treatment of that episode did not do it justice. There is no doubt that the Air Force decided there was a "military requirement" to overfly the Soviet Union. Those were the days when the Air Force generals were much taken with "first strike," "preemptive war," and "counterforce" strategies. But the decisive appeal to Eisenhower to make the final decision to commit American military power in this unprecedented and highly dangerous way was based, not on an assessment of the political benefits and costs, but on technical virtuosity.

I should like to close with a remark about one of Mr. Schlesinger's comments. Mr. Schlesinger says that "most of the important things we have done in foreign policy since World War II have been political and economic rather than military in nature." I wonder what measure he uses for that. Not the budget, surely. Not the aid program, which except for the Marshall Plan has been overwhelmingly weighted in favor of military and paramilitary aid (AID furnished me with charts, which I have appended to my recent book, that demonstrate this).

The Truman Doctrine, perhaps? Or the succession of military interventions that followed it? He can't be talking about the system of military alliances which absorbed most of John Foster Dulles's energies. Nor can he be referring to how the President spends his time, for he could consult the entries on foreign policy in *A Thousand Days*. What he asserts I would like to believe, and I hope that the chroniclers of the next thirty years will be able to say it in truth.

JOHN MCDERMOTT: I would like to be an archivist and review the years in which major decisions were made on the American escalation in Vietnam. For example, in 1947, 1949, 1950, 1951, three times in 1954, 1956, 1959, 1961, 1963, 1964, and in 1965 critical decisions were made on escalation in the Vietnamese war. They were both military and political, each one.

ARTHUR SCHLESINGER, JR.: There was no military escalation involved in the 1950's.

JOHN MCDERMOTT: You are quite wrong, Professor Schlesinger. For example, in 1950 President Truman signed the order sending our troops to Korea, and in that same order, as a separate business, he assigned a military or advisory mission to Vietnam. That mission became a critical factor with regard to opening up southern Indochina as a major front against China at the conclusion of the major fighting in Korea in 1951. Each of these decisions bears an important, if not determinative, causal relationship to the next decision.

I think, if in examining the history of the process, one can see concrete empirical ways in which previous decisions contributed to the next and so forth through the chain, then the interesting point is that the series of decisions stretches across four administrations and, I guess, several generations of policy officials and several generations of desk men in the government. Therefore, whatever may be the individual defects of this or that explanation of Barnet, a theory which attempts to unite this data is needed. Barnet, at least, has found the problem that has to be formulated.

To ascribe the Vietnamese problem to the changing whims of a Presbyterian Secretary of State or a non-Presbyterian Secretary of State, while interesting, does not have the latent predictive value that a successful Barnet theory might have.

THEODORE DRAPER: We have had a series of decisions, as Mr. Mc-Dermott mentions, between 1947 and 1965 on the Vietnam war. The problem is whether we should consider this series as a whole, put all of the decisions in the same box and beat them all with the same stick, or whether we should draw distinctions between decisions. Were they all of the same order?

My impression is that a distinction must be made between what might be called quantitative decisions and qualitative ones. A series of quantitative increases may at some point result in a qualitative leap. My impression is that the qualitative leap in this case came in 1964–65 and that the decisions before that point may be considered quantitative ones.

The fundamental difference is that the pre-1965 decisions were still based on the premise that this was primarily a South Vietnamese war and we would help the South Vietnamese to win it. In 1965, however, the decisions implied that we were taking over responsibility for the war, and then by the end of 1966 the full implications were spelled out publicly. But my impression is that the 1964–65 decisions were not bureaucratic decisions and cannot be ascribed merely to the cumulative momentum of the bureaucracy.

The qualitative decision was the responsibility primarily of the President and his advisors, and what impresses me at this kind of turning point is the awful responsibility of the President. Another example of this is the Bay of Pigs. If cumulative momentum were all that was involved, then President Kennedy should have sent in American troops to retrieve the loss suffered by the American proxies, the Cuban exile troops. However, he did not. At this point he drew back from taking a qualitative leap.

The trouble may very well be that until Vietnam, or until this stage of the Vietnam war, our policy-makers have simply not taken the risks and costs of intervention seriously. In fact, this "we can do no wrong" type of military intervention is so risky, so costly that, as I tried to say earlier, it must be considered as a last resort in a situation of extreme peril.

Perhaps we are now again facing a situation where a Presidential decision will make or break us. Do we have a Presidential candidate in sight who can say to the American people, "We have suffered a failure in Vietnam; it is costly to get out; it is more costly to persist."

I fear that unless this is said now and said clearly, we will not get out of this morass.

JOHN MCDERMOTT: In dealing with these matters I think it is important that a diagnostic approach be taken. Obviously there is no such thing as complete description, and in dealing with phenomena like this the building of a model is well-nigh impossible. Barnet, nevertheless, provides the interesting diagnostic idea that one should examine the bureaucracy to see what system defects there may have been which may partly have led into this impasse. This is the first step in understanding before one can make radical adjustments in the bureaucracy.

There was a certain frankness about Barnet's presentation that opens the way. It is really a much more interesting diagnostic idea than others presented.

STANLEY HOFFMANN: It only happens to be wrong.

JOHN MCDERMOTT: Perhaps I find it intellectually more interesting now. The role of theory, even if wrong, in determining how we set up our categories of relevance is crucial.

ARTHUR SCHLESINGER, JR.: I had always supposed the function of theory was to explain facts.

JOHN MCDERMOTT: However, what does "explain" mean in relation to being able to predict?

ARTHUR SCHLESINGER, JR.: To explain what happened. This doesn't explain what happened. The facts invoked in its behalf are wrong, and it really doesn't explain at all. It vastly exaggerates what we all concede to be an important element.

JOHN MCDERMOTT: I would like to emphasize more strongly a point Mr. Pfeffer brought out and which you made, I believe, in good humor.

I think the response to Barnet's presentation was a bad one because it was not taken as a serious effort by a colleague who is trying to make some sense intellectually out of the very difficult facts. Obviously our Vietnam policy is clanging about our ears, and our responses should be commensurate with the problem we acknowledge.

The kind of crisis, intellectual and otherwise, Vietnam has brought on is terribly serious. I would ten times rather be wrong with Barnet than just dismiss the crisis as a problem, saying, "Well, we should be wiser, more relevant, and not make mistakes."

ADAM YARMOLINSKY: My principal criticism of Barnet is that he has not generalized sufficiently, that he talks about the evils of the American bureaucracy and the military bureaucracy as if the evils were peculiar to those institutions rather than general to bureaucracies at most times and places. This does not mean that we should not seek to loosen up our own bureaucracies. I believe we should. Nor does it mean that we should not seek to find ways to exert more effective political control through, in the first instance, seeking to have more accurate and complete information reach the level of political decision-makers.

I believe, however, we ought to do so in light of a very acute realization that problems of bureaucracy are not the result of any tendency to original sin which is peculiarly American or peculiarly military. These are human characteristics, and they are characteristics of all large human institutions.

STANLEY HOFFMANN: Barnet's presentation, it seems to me, was a hyperbolic killing of a very good point. This kind of kill and the kind of conspiracy theory on which it rests seem to be the symmetrical opposites of the Administration presentation. This is what I resent about a position with which, on the whole, I sympathize. It carries a good thing so far that it becomes the mirror image of the very thing he condemns.

When one talks about the role of bureaucracy, a very important subject, one has to distinguish between two kinds of issues. On the one hand, there is bureaucracy as merely the carrier of certain basic American intellectual styles and attitudes, applied to a new situation. What is new is that the scene of action has now become the world. The whole world can now be the victim of propensities of which, before, we were the only or main beneficiaries. The lower bureaucracy, especially, acts as the carrier of those American attitudes Mr. Schlesinger mentioned earlier. I would mention two others particularly. One is a certain general American orientation toward force. Here I would support Mr. Ahmad's earlier remarks. The other attitude is our engineering approach to solving problems, especially our tendency to predominantly military engineering once a situation is perceived primarily in military terms.

On the other hand, however, there are also areas in which the bureaucratic machinery itself contributes to our dilemmas of intervention. One finds, first of all, that given the nature of the bureaucracy, its way is very sinuous, very complex, and very protracted. Much time has to be spent achieving some kind of working consensus within the bureaucracy, and the terms on which the consensus finally jells may not at all be those which are required by the external situation. Thus the internal needs for building bureaucratic consensus may detract from the external needs for decision.

Second, because it is painful to build this consensus, once it has been reached it tends in normal times to be very difficult to reverse. Therefore there is a built-in momentum, or inertia.

Third, this consensus is particularly easy or relatively easy to build or to reverse when there is a crisis. Therefore there is a tendency to wait for a crisis, at which point it may be too late to deal with the issues in terms other than military. This problem, incidentally, is not limited to American bureaucracy.

Finally, once one is launching a military operation (because one hasn't been able to do anything else before), then and only then do the pressures from the military become very important and tend to drown out the other considerations. From then on there is a certain logic of military operation which almost naturally takes over and which it takes a determined and unlikely combined over-all effort of the other agencies, including sometimes the Pentagon, to reverse.

Therefore what Barnet would tend to describe in terms of conspiracy theory, or built-in militarism, I would take largely to be a result of these two kinds of bureaucratic problems.

A final point about bureaucracy: are bureaucratic problems ones about which we can do very much? I am not convinced. It seems to me this is one of the areas in the American political make-up on which we have little leverage. If there is a lesson to be learned from this, it is, perhaps, that very little can be done to change it. We should therefore know how to avoid the kinds of situations in which the momentum of the bureaucracy will carry us further and further.

LUIGI EINAUDI: Two additional points have proved in my limited experience to be important institutional constraints on ways in which the bureaucracy functions in dealing with the question of intervention. The first of these is a factor I would call shortness of institutional memory. This is caused, in large part, by personnel turnover and secrecy, both characteristics of bureaucracy.

The shortness of institutional memory has, I think, two effects. One frequently runs into government officials who know only what took place during their current tour and perhaps during their predecessor's tour (if they happened to overlap), but know very little about what happened before that because, being good bureaucrats, they were concerned at that time with other problems elsewhere. This means, in the first place, that we unnecessarily limit our knowledge of local situations, knowledge which might enable us to intervene in an intelligent and informed fashion. Secondly, the shortness of institutional memory increases the momentum of incrementalism: new people come in; they don't know what was being done previously, and they are therefore all the more prone to take a "fix it" attitude, to try to do a little bit more of what in the general atmosphere one is expected to try more of. These institutional forms tend to compound the general cultural misinterpretation of events, which has been one of the themes of our discussion.

A second characteristic of bureaucracy is the routinization of language into a sort of lowest common denominator. The phraseology we all must use to communicate our perceptions, especially in the Washington atmosphere, adds enormously to the difficulties of communicating the realities of a different culture, of a significantly different environment.

I had this strongly drawn to my attention by one senior reporting official in Brazil who found that at a crucial period he simply was unable to find within bureaucratic language the flexibility the situation demanded. Because of this difficulty he felt that he was unable to communicate an adequate picture of the environment which he saw every day about him and that, as a result, his superiors could not properly evaluate alternative policies and their effects.

These two aspects of bureaucracy affect the likelihood of intervention because they set up a dynamic, first of ignorance and then of self-deception, which I think is fundamental to prolonged unsuccessful intervention.

§§ ADAM YARMOLINSKY: I would like to see us go on to think about ways in which we can generate alternative techniques within the bureaucracy to deal with these problems. After all, the United States, as a great power, is going to want to go on dealing with these problems to some extent. If we can find new and imaginative ways to deal with them other than by military force, we can develop bureaucracies able to compete with the military bureaucracy.

Otherwise, so long as the present military means are available, situations like Vietnam are going to recur. As it is, because we have the means and also because we are as big and strong and rich as we are, we likewise have to have a bureaucracy to go with the means, and the bureaucracy, in turn, is going to push itself on others. The sad truth is that it can be held back by political leadership only to the extent that political leadership exercises superhuman qualities.

The natural tendency of the use of force to feed on itself, the size and weight of the national security establishment, the relatively greater sizes and weights of the components of that establishment directly concerned with military solutions to national security problems, the distance that ideas and information have to travel from the bottom to the top, the constraints placed on policy-makers by domestic political considerations, and the difficulty of securing a minimum basis for common understanding and communication without antagonizing—all have contributed to the momentum of American policy in Vietnam.

Minimizing all these factors may be one of the great tasks of our foreign policy in the post-Vietnam period. In other words, we ought to find ways to make it harder to get in and easier to get out. One can identify three elements that can help to make the process of gradual involvement more conscious and more controllable. These are: the collection of comprehensive and sophisticated intelligence about the arena of possible involvement, the prompt communication of that intelligence to the responsible policy-makers, and the preservation, by a variety of means, of maximum flexibility in the face of domestic political constraints—constraints imposed both by political pressures on the government and by internal pressures within the government.

Collecting intelligence, like playing a musical instrument, is not a matter of volume but of quality. In fact, as Roberta Wohlstetter has pointed out, the more noise, the more likelihood that no one will hear the tune. The failures of intelligence in the war in Vietnam are not attributable to any dearth of statistics. A few critical insights may be worth more than any amount of routine information. The problem of obtaining these insights is not primarily a problem of getting better people. Of course there is no substitute for brains. But the general level of people in the intelligence service—including the reporting services of the Department of State—is remarkably good for a bureaucracy, which is what any permanent service has to be. It could be enhanced by more free lateral entry and career movement back and forth between government and academia at the professional level. But one can't always have the best people in the most important place at the critical time. The personnel assigned to United States embassies at times when acute crises have developed have not always been men at the top of their profession. But it would be unreasonable to suppose that the foreign and military services should assign their very best people to such posts, given all the other demands that were being made on them at the time.

One device that might be tried to loosen up some of the inhibitions on judgment imposed by the communal sense of the intelligence community would be to apply the adversary system to the collection of intelligence on critical issues so that one team would be assigned to attempt to prove a particular proposition, while another team would be assigned to attempt to disprove it. If this method proved too artificial, it might be worthwhile to bring in outsiders to examine particular situations—as the Foreign Intelligence Advisory Board examines the over-all picture—but on an *ad hoc* basis so that these advisors did not in their own minds become identified with the establishment. If these *ad hoc* advisors created a security problem by including too large a group in the need-to-know class, they might be given a mixture of real and hypothetical raw material, without identifying which was which but asking them to make alternative judgments, eliminating one or another set of facts.

But even the best intelligence is no good unless it reaches the decision-makers—and reaches them without so many other miscellaneous sounds that it is drowned out in the general noise level. Here the principal problem is to eliminate layering. Information almost always looks better, the farther away you are from the source. It is less flawed, less ambiguous, and it tends more to conform to your original premises. One of the great sources of Robert McNamara's strength as Secretary of Defense was his ability and determination to penetrate more deeply into the factual bases of decisions than any of his predecessors or, indeed, of his associates. Cultivation of this faculty is essential for policy-makers who would avoid being misled into untenable positions.

At the same time it is important that decision-makers not cut themselves off from essential information by restricting access to information about their own plans and intentions so that people who should advise—or criticize—what they are proposing to do, have the opportunity to do so. It is an unhappy paradox that the more crucial the decision, the less likely it is to be exposed in advance to the cross fire of critical comment.

Finally, flexibility is a matter of concern even for policy-makers who have avoided an obsessive compulsion to keep their options open. The President of the United States has very considerable latitude in shaping issues in public debate, particularly issues of foreign policy.

The reasons why the American public and its opinion leaders regarded the tension between Libya and Egypt or between Ethiopia and Somaliland with relative indifference had less to do with objective reality than with the public posture of the United States government. Both of these situations involved Soviet interests, potential East-West confrontations, and a danger of internal subversion. But they have attracted the attention of only a few area specialists. If, on the other hand, the President says that the war in Vietnam is a test of American commitments to its allies around the world, then the Vietnamese war does indeed become such a test. If he suggests that our reasons for being in Vietnam are peculiar to the local situation, then it will be rather differently regarded, both around the world and back home. If the President describes Cuba as a major source of subversion in Latin America, he will be under greater (domestic) pressure to take positive action against Cuba than he might be otherwise. It takes two parties to maintain a bipartisan foreign policy, and if the President treats a particular issue of foreign policy as a partisan issue, he cannot continue to rely on bipartisanship in that connection.

Whatever the President says, of course, has endless reverberations. Issues of foreign policy are generally less touchy, politically, than issues of domestic policy; but within the area of foreign policy, issues directly affecting national security are particularly difficult to defuse and treat dispassionately, as President Kennedy discovered to his sorrow in the civil-defense-shelter crisis in 1961. The American people were willing to accept accommodation in Laos with relative equanimity. They are emotionally involved over the prospects of accommodation in Vietnam because large numbers of American lives have been lost in pursuit of goals now recognized to be unattainable.

Flexibility must be maintained, not only in the face of popular pressures, but of bureaucratic pressures as well. In this connection the political influence of the United States military establishment in these realms seems somewhat overstated. The military make themselves heard on the conduct of military operations, although even this close to home they are increasingly and remarkably responsive to civilian direction and control. On the crucial issue of the initiation of military operations, however, the military respond to requests for proposals, but they are disinclined to press their proposals. It is in the nature of military bureaucracy, as of any bureaucracy, that it tends to offer solutions to problems in its own terms, which are military terms. But as suggested earlier, the political leadership retains the option, until that option is deliberately or negligently abandoned, not to pick up the military solution.

Where the military bureaucracy is more likely to impose limits on the civilian desire for flexibility is in the conduct of military operations. The analytical review of military development, procurement, and organizational policies and practices simply has not been extended to military operations. Perhaps in the nature of things it cannot be extended. But in its absence the political authorities find it more difficult, as perhaps they should, to assert control over specific military operations—the choice, for example, between search-and-destroy and clear-and-hold—in order to avoid deepening political commitments. This fact of politico-military life only underlines the critical importance of the first stages of involvement in a potential intervention situation.

A more complex problem is presented to the political leadership of the country by other elements in what has been called the "military-industrial complex." The military-industrial complex, to the extent that it exists at all, is surely not a conscious conspiracy of like-minded groups and persons but rather a fortuitous coincidence of interests of military professionals, industrialists, labor leaders, local and national political representatives of domestic areas affected by military activity, and a supporting cast of characters providing professional services to their principals and expressing their principals' views in the media. The fact of this coincidence of interest does, however, bring a concentrated set of influences to bear on the choice between more or less active, more or less military responses to particular situations. The influences are brought to bear not so much at the moment of crisis as pervasively and continuously over time. The virtues of military power are extolled, albeit in a context of its peaceful and defensive employment. The potential of particular weapons and techniques is discussed. The need for even greater effort is stressed. The dangers of relaxing vigilance are scored. And the net effect is to create a climate somewhat less hostile to military adventure and perhaps also somewhat less receptive to nonmilitary alternatives than might otherwise exist.

Quite apart from the influence of the military-industrial complex, there is a paradoxical problem for political leadership seeking to maintain a flexible posture in the aftermath of unhappy episodes of military intervention. This is the possibility that a nonmilitary but activist response to a foreign crisis may be resisted on the ground that it may result in a dangerous foreign entanglement, leading eventually to a sacrifice of American blood as well as American treasure. The resistance to the Congo airlift and to economic sanctions against Rhodesia are cases in point. The resistance is probably reinforced by recent efforts to equate the Eisenhower Administration's commitment in Vietnam to the Kennedy and Johnson commitments. Still, this antiactivist resistance may serve a salutary purpose if it does not paralyze foreign policy but rather raises fundamental questions about the propriety of any nation's attempts to impose its views on the conduct of another nation's internal affairs. It seems we have taken too much for granted, not simply the old fashioned Dulles position of United States opposition to monolithic communism, but even the propriety of United States intervention, at least occasionally, in the affairs of other nations.

One of the significant limits on flexibility to terminate involvements is the reaction of the antagonist to efforts to terminate the intervention on some mutually satisfactory basis. Settling a military conflict by mutual agreement is never easy, but here the methods and techniques of modern warfare make it even more difficult. The first major obstacle to negotiations in Vietnam was the strategic bombing of North Vietnamese territory. In retrospect this was probably a step that should never have been taken, since it produced no military advantages except for its putative favorable impact on morale in the south. But it was taken, at least in part, because it was one of the things that the United States military forces were best prepared to do.

Perhaps the second most serious obstacle to terminating the Vietnam intervention by negotiations has been Hanoi's concern that the United States would not willingly abandon its enormous physical investment in South Vietnam—the acres of concrete, the rows of barracks, the square miles of bulldozed land. It is extraordinarily difficult to convey the idea, particularly to the leaders of an underdeveloped country, that this kind of investment is considered expendable and that the United States is prepared to abandon it. Perhaps if negotiations go well over the months to come, this proposition will be demonstrated in fact; but even when actually demonstrated on one occasion, it may not be readily accepted on another occasion. The fact that the United States retains foreign bases from Okinawa to Guantanamo Bay gives some substance to this continuing concern. An intervention based on "forward floating logistics depots" may be more credibly terminated than an intervention based on (even temporarily) occupied territory.

A third obstacle to successful negotiations in Vietnam is the fact that Hanoi feels it was fooled twice, by the French in 1945 and by the allied powers in 1954, and it doesn't propose to be fooled again. The importance of the appearance (as well as the reality) of fair dealing in order to ease the process of extrication is perhaps only a secondary lesson in Vietnam. But without making any assumptions about the probity of its antagonists, the United States can achieve greater flexibility by maintaining its reputation for integrity in its dealings with them.

The problem of maintaining one's integrity in the face of an antagonist who may have quite different procedural standards for his own behavior is only a special case of the general problem of reciprocity in international relations. It is easy to justify an escalating intervention by pointing out that you are only matching force with force and greater force with greater force. But what looks to one side only like an application of Newton's first law, may look to the other side like a disproportionate escalation. The same argument applies to the conduct of a mayor in bloodily suppressing a ghetto riot or the conduct of a university president in calling in the police to end a sit-in. In each case the use of force to counter force may be justifiable in reciprocal terms, as seen by the person initiating the counterforce, but in human terms it may only result in avoidable tragedy. Where other courses of action are available to reach the same end, the use of force is seldom if ever a properly justifiable alternative. If the question is asked whether previous events justify the use of force in response, one may be tempted to reply in the affirmative; but if the question is put, rather, as to whether the alternative involving the use of force is the best one available in light of all the facts and circumstances, the answer may be quite different. And if the question of alternatives is raised, not only at the outset of a course of action involving the use of force, but at every stage of potential escalation as well, it may result in a process of involvement that will indeed be more cautious and more controlled than some of our recent involvements in other countries' problems.

If the United States is to increase the breadth and intensity of the dialogue between the governed and the governors on which peaceful change and progress depend, it must find new ways to avoid being drawn into an escalating contest of force with those who question its legal or its moral authority. It is not enough to make it easier for the United States to slow down or stop after choosing the alternative of violence. The alternative of violence is simply not available to great powers today in a wide range of situations without risking Armageddon. Therefore it behooves us to find other means to influence the course of human events, and indeed to be open to the influence of new events and new ideas on ourselves.

CHESTER L. COOPER: Let me pursue this. First, I agree with Mr. Yarmolinsky that a major bureaucratic problem is that by the time lower-level judgments, sometimes provided by the intelligence community and sometimes by political means, reach top decision-makers, many of the qualifications and many of the differences of approach get washed out, partly because the desire, and sometimes the necessity, to reduce problems to a page or two becomes a governing factor— mainly because busy men feel unable to read the facts.

Intelligence judgments tend to be communicated upward in the decision-maker's terms and in response to requests by decision-makers. The fact of the matter is that most of these judgments, in the last analysis, are basically "gut" feelings. There is not much hard evidence you can bring to bear. The judgments primarily reflect the consensus of men who, however well informed and conscientious, have only a limited amount of information.

What is washed out in most of this are the consequences of what happens if the predicted seventy–thirty probability does not in fact take place. What happens if one is wrong? The consequences of being wrong, especially the consequences of the worst possible case, are very horrendous at times. On the basis of predicted probabilities one can proceed with a fair amount of confidence on a given task; but if the consequences of being wrong are horrendous, then even low odds of being wrong should be looked at very carefully.

However, political papers that come out of NSA or State tend in their estimates and judgments to wash this out. Basically there is a feeling that one has done one's duty by simply indicating that there is an area of doubt that is probable but not certain. But such qualifications don't help a decision-maker very much.

It seems to me that it would be useful if at points we could inject into the decision-making process a technique I would call the "consequences of the worst case." If the Russians had used this technique in connection with putting missiles in Cuba, if they had looked at the consequences of the worst case, perhaps they would not have made the decision that they did.

STANLEY HOFFMANN: Was there within the government something like an adversary procedure? Sometimes I have had the impression from what I read that there *were* systematically selected devil's advocates; and if this is what happened to them, what can we expect?

ADAM YARMOLINSKY: The adversary procedure was used too rarely and then on an *ad hoc* basis.

CHESTER COOPER: In point of fact, some of the devil's advocates were not really hurt. For example, George Ball was frequently brought to a meeting to put on his dog-and-monkey act of being a devil's advocate; but as Jim Thomson has said, once having listened to the devil's advocate, you felt that you had done your duty. He got his hearing, and you proceeded. The technique I suggest is not quite the same thing as this.

DANIEL ELLSBERG: Surely the term "devil's advocate" itself was a protective euphemism for Ball. I feel sure that he was saying what he believed and that he had to be called a "devil's advocate" because it would have been too dangerous and unacceptable to admit that he believed what he was actually saying. This is not a nice commentary on the language necessary within our bureaucracy.

CHESTER COOPER: The standard form for a man confronted with some of these problems is to say "if I can play the devil's advocate for a moment." In that way you cover your rear, flanks, etc. It is a good way of saying "I think you are all wet" without resigning from the club.

SAMUEL P. HUNTINGTON: I have three rather pedestrian points to make dealing with the problem of the operation of bureaucracies, which lead me at least in part to come down on Mr. Barnet's side.

First, obviously you have to have some sort of institutionalized checks and balances in a bureaucracy in order to make error confront error. I think the only way, by and large, in which we really have been able to do this is by making operators and promoters check each other. This has been of some consequence. Barnet suggests that everybody has a solution they try to push and develop a rationale for, and so you have the Army, the CIA, and State, all pushing their solutions, and as a result we tend to end up adopting all of them. What is crucial in the face of this mechanism toward expansion and further intervention is to devise some sort of system of checks and balances which does not have this expansion dynamic built into it.

I would suggest, to the extent that it is possible in our system, that we create an institutional arrangement whereby people will be assigned to check up and report on, but not to advocate or become involved in, operations. The failure to observe such limits, of course, has been a recurring problem with the CIA, illustrated most clearly by the Bay of Pigs incident. However, more generally this is a characteristic of our bureaucracy: units in it tend to become multifunctional and to develop a variety of operating characteristics. Consequently it is very hard to devise a unit which will perform a purely collecting, reporting, criticizing type of function.

The one instance I saw where a group did simply carry out these functions, and reasonably well, was actually in Vietnam. There I was struck by the across-the-board differences in attitudes, assessments, and evaluations between the operators in the AID structure, who were committed to programs and achieving objectives, and the staff in the embassy—particularly in the political section of the embassy—whose only job was to report and who by and large did just report. As a result they gave a much more critical assessment of the situation.

Second, as Adam Yarmolinsky suggests, it is vital to eliminate the filtering process that occurs in the communication of information up the hierarchy. Here I am struck by the problem of what I would call the overcommitted middle.

Think of the structure of the government as involving political administrators at the summit, the top civil servants in the middle, and the lower civil servants down at the bottom. There appears to be a major problem in the middle, with the very competent, in many respects, very expert people who become much more committed to existing policy, insofar as I can see, than either the people at the bottom, who have their own sorts of problems to worry about and therefore are not that much involved with policy, or the people at the top, who have a variety of other pressures—political considerations—influencing them.

Finally and very briefly, there is the problem of rotation of personnel, already referred to. In Vietnam we have a perfect case: civilians are over there for eighteen months and the military for twelve months. This results in a continuous turnover and influx of new people which, in turn, give our operation there a tremendous dynamism. On the other hand, it also ensures that each generation will repeat at a higher level the errors of the previous one.

We have devised a unique sort of bureaucratic machine which ensures or tends to ensure that our operation in Vietnam will always be vigorous, will never grow tired, but also will never grow wiser.

DANIEL ELLSBERG: There is no question the bureaucracy must bear substantial responsibility for our failure in Vietnam. The bureaucracy, of which I was formerly a part, finds it peculiarly difficult to learn from failure, in large part because, for both bureaucratic and political reasons, failure can be neither recognized nor admitted. But if one is to learn lessons at all from Vietnam, one must be prepared to draw lessons from failure, for that has been our dominant experience there. I am talking about the situation as it looks today and last year, and and that, of course, defines failure. Our experience there to date involves failures upon failures.

"Bureaucracy," I want it clearly understood—more clearly than in Barnet's discussion—includes here the participants at the highest levels of the United States government. I am really tempted to include as well the establishment, from which many of the top cabinet people were drawn. The performance of this "bureaucracy" in connection with Vietnam policy has been very bad, so bad that it is very hard to characterize it simply as an aberration or bad luck.

We could have foreseen that the enemy—probably the most finely trained guerrilla organization in history—would perform as well as it did and that our bureaucracy and military would perform as inadequately as they did. Some people did foresee this. For example, Stanley Hoffmann attacked my defense of our expanded involvement on just these grounds in 1965 when, representing the Administration, I confronted him at a teach-in. Therefore, in this sense it was foreseeable. But not by our "bureaucracy."

There was ignorance about the problems, about the area, about the people, about ourselves. But there is another related factor just as important: the fact that the ignorance persisted, that it diminished scarcely at all over time. Important United States decisions on Vietnam have been made since 1950 and especially since 1961. I participated in a small way in decisions in Washington in 1964–65 and in Vietnam in 1965–67. I have now had occasion to study both 1961 and 1963 in great detail. I believe that I at least know what was going on in these years.

The bureaucracy was raising the same problems then—starting in the earliest years—that we raise today, though in a different context. And some of these problems have been understood clearly, then and now. Yet the actual performance of our system for exerting influence and for deciding about and operating in Vietnam reveals not only ignorance at every stage but also the persistence of ignorance, the inability of the system in this particular sphere to learn from a very long record of experience. I don't believe the bureaucracy is any smarter about this problem in 1968 than it was in 1965 or 1961 or 1954.

As a result of being in Vietnam, I became aware, over a long period, of some of the sources of willful ignorance, what one might call "antilearning mechanisms" in the United States government. I think one can only appreciate this by viewing the performance up close. Newspaper readers cannot really get it. You have to be close to the decision-making apparatus to know how inexcusable some of these things are, month after month and year after year. I draw from this not only a lesson about the limited ability of our system to learn and adapt, our inability, at least on some important occasions, to reduce our initial ignorance. I also draw a general policy indication concerning the prospects for United States intervention in areas and problems of which initially we know little.

The "limitations of power" many people are talking about are really, I think, identifiable in many cases as limitations due to ignorance and the inadequate ability of the system as it now exists to learn from experience and especially from failure.

We have a tendency to deny failures or to disguise failures by a process of self-deceit. Now, this might be viable if we were not also troubled by a tendency to activist intervention in large parts of the world about which we do not know much to start with.

I infer that we should be especially cautious about any policy that calls for activist intervention in these areas. There is no use jumping in, no matter how important the problems seem to be, with the objective of on-the-job training, because it just doesn't work. Moreover, however nice it might be in Huntington's framework to have a super CIA to facilitate more appropriate political intervention in these parts of the world, we do not now have any agency adequate to this role, and we could not have it next year or, in my opinion, in five years or even longer. Therefore, it seems to me, one lesson we should draw concerns situations we should stay away from.

EDWIN REISCHAUER: I think we are back to the discussion of whether our problem has been basically one of institutional or conceptual failures. I think it could be both.

We are very much aware of the limitations and weaknesses of bureaucracy. We all recognize that the bigger bureaucracy gets, the greater are its limitations and weaknesses and also the greater is the problem of reversing errors once made.

We are also aware that "hard facts" are usually given more weight within the bureaucracy than what are called the "soft facts," and the hardest facts are military ones. The second hardest ones are economic, and the softest ones are political, psychological, etc. My own experience indicates that the latter probably are most important, but they get the least consideration. When we get into a war situation, the hard facts of the military are given even greater weight.

I think we are all aware of this, but this still does not change the possibility that our long-persistent error in connection with Vietnam or Asian policy is basically a conceptual error.

I believe Mr. McDermott suggests that inasmuch as we have persisted in these errors over long periods of time, the explanation must be something else than wrong ideas. But wrong ideas are persistent in human minds. You can go back into history and find nations doing stupid things for practically centuries at a time because they could not get rid of wrong and bad ideas.

If we all came to these problems as children, with completely open minds, we would probably learn quickly. However, we do not examine them that way. We come to Asian problems, for example, with wrong conceptions. It therefore takes a long time to relearn.

I don't think, in relation to Mr. Ellsberg's terms of willful ignorance, that we have to try to perpetuate ignorance. The human mind tends to operate in this way. It is human nature.

With regard to Asia and what we have pointed out here, I am rather surprised that we have managed to learn within twenty years that we are on the wrong track. This is pretty good for man.

Vietnam:
III Misconceptions in Action

The Intellectual Failure

§§ STANLEY HOFFMANN: The immediately preceding discussion centered on aspects of our Vietnam policy which illuminate the weaknesses of our decision-making process. Those weaknesses were important. But we should not turn the machinery into a scapegoat.

A theory of bureaucratic determinism fails to account for three important facts: one, the crucial decisions were not imposed by the bureaucratic apparatus (although it may have slanted the process) but were reached by the political leaders or made by the public; two, the notion of a generalized responsibility of bureaucrats does not help (they may have been far more responsible for not learning than for intervening); three, whereas the machinery has exhibited rigidities and shortsightedness characteristic of most modern bureaucratic establishments, the perceptions, conceptions, and criteria of the bureaucrats can be explained only if we look beyond the institutions into the American political style as it has been shaped by American history—if we move from the organization to the minds. The kind of changes we may want to introduce into the machinery in order to avoid future Vietnams depends on whether one believes the heart of the trouble is mechanical, or whether one thinks, as I do, that the reasons go much deeper and that neither administrative reform nor a romantic revolt against the national security bureaucracy is a substitute for a re-examination of the very substance of our policies in terms of our national style.

115

The central problem does not lie in the *nature* of America's objectives. The idea that a majority of the South Vietnamese people does not want to live under communist rule and ought to be allowed to choose its form of government, the goal of a united and stable regime in South Vietnam, the objective of proving that an armed minority, using the ideology and techniques of "national liberation wars" and supplied from outside the limits of the country it tries to seize, can be defeated—so as both to protect the majority in the country and to prevent the diffusion of the movement—the goal of assuring other Asian governments of America's concern for their security, the idea of preserving a balance of power in Asia, of "buying time" for the countries situated around China—these were all worthy ends.

The central problem of American policy—of any policy—is the relevance of its ends to specific cases: the more ambitious or ideological a policy, the more indispensable it is to analyze the realities of each case with critical rigor before applying to it one's concepts or preconceptions, for otherwise the statesman will trip into the pitfalls of irrelevance, "adventurism," or unreality. Our own policy was of necessity ambitious because of our very role as a superpower; and it has, if not an ideology, at least a set of principles and dogmas such as resistance to aggression, attachment to self-determination, opposition to forceful communist takeovers, etc. . . . *The tragedy of our course in Vietnam lies in our refusal to come to grips with those realities in South Vietnam that happened to be decisive from the viewpoint of politics.*

What was determining, or operational, was not the inchoate and unorganized opposition of a majority of its people to a communist takeover. It was and remains the inability of this majority to pull itself together sufficiently to resist the Viet Cong's determined attempt to seize power in a conflict which simultaneously involves both a social revolution—in a society whose traditional order is crumbling—and the completion of a movement of national unification undertaken over twenty years ago against the French and interrupted in 1954. It is the failure of the leadership in South Vietnam to establish a new legitimate and authoritative government capable of rallying and mobilizing the energies of the people, of appealing to the villagers' desire for security, of providing the citizens with the incentives and means of self-defense, of establishing procedures for the redress of grievances. The root of the tragedy is the demonstrated absence in Saigon of the capacity for sustained self-government, for which there is no substitute. In its absence the controlling factor is not that the Viet Cong constitutes only a minority, but that it constitutes the only national movement that cuts across religious and social lines. We have refused to recognize the uniqueness of this situation by comparison with the other guerrilla or revolutionary wars we have known intimately. We have also refused to recognize the similarity of our predicament as the outside power in such a situation with that of the French both in Indochina and in Algeria. If we want in the future to avoid new Vietnams, we must find out why we have refused to recognize, ever since the beginning of our involvement, what I for one have felt to be the decisive and blindingly obvious facts about Vietnam.

Part of the answer lies in our fear of the consequences of recognizing reality. To acknowledge South Vietnam's inability to provide for its own, noncommunist "political development" would have meant resigning oneself to a communist takeover either by force or after a face-saving negotiation. In the eyes of our policy-makers this would have meant a betrayal of the noncommunist majority, a victory for the most militant part of the world communist movement, a demoralization of the other noncommunist governments of Asia, an encouragement to armed minorities, etc.

Two points should be stressed in this connection. First, instead of trying to attenuate the unpleasant or disastrous consequences of the reality we feared, we tried to deny and reverse reality so as to avoid those effects. Second, in our vision of those results we overestimated the "domino effect" and underestimated the purely domestic reasons for the potential triumph of a communist movement in South Vietnam —reasons that do not exist to any comparable degree elsewhere and that make of this case a perfectly unsuitable model for other "national liberation movements" in Asia or, as Regis Debray has recognized, in Latin America. In other words, our fear of the consequences was magnified by our very tendency to misinterpret reality; had we understood it correctly, then the effects would have appeared to us less catastrophic. Thus, we must look beyond and behind that fear.

Another deeper part of the answer lies in a certain form of ignorance that I would call the shock of nonrecognition. Our understanding of South Vietnamese society was poor, the expertise at our disposal limited. In such circumstances we tended to distort our analysis by reducing South Vietnam's uniqueness to elements that seemed familiar and reassuring, to features that we had met and managed elsewhere. All those traits were indeed present in the picture, and we have been clinging to them mentally. Yet in the total picture they have turned out to be far less important than all the other disturbing traits, whose ominous meanings we have tried to deny by repeated rhetorical exorcisms. What made Vietnam unique was the simultaneous and intertwined presence in one area of the weaknesses we had been able to overcome before only when we had met each one in a different place.

We have exaggerated the possibility of reaching our final objectives by invoking two analogies. One has been the Korean analogy; to be sure, in both cases we have a mixture of civil war (one was a war among Koreans, the other a war among Vietnamese) and aggression (the North Korean crossing of the 38th parallel and, despite the 1954 Geneva agreements, infiltrations into Laos and South Vietnam, first by returning Southerners who had gone north after Geneva, later by North Vietnamese supplies and units).

But these similarities were quite superficial. The war in Korea was a conventional war. Pyong Yang tried to dominate Seoul by way of invasion. The fragmentation of South Korean politics, the backwardness of the South Korean economy, the authoritarianism of Syngman Rhee might have eventually provided the communists with opportunities for insurgency in the south; but their very resort to invasion threw those chances away and consolidated a regime and a society that showed at once their aptitude to rally under attack and later showed a remarkable capacity for self-government, change, and growth. One reason why the Korean communists resorted to invasion and found no help in the south was that the cause of nationalism, the appeal of self-determination, had been clearly captured by the South Korean regime. In those days it was Pyong Yang that looked like a puppet. In Vietnam, Diem in the early years had a claim on nationalism and did a superficially effective job of governing at a time when Hanoi's efforts at total control in the north were producing revolts and refugees. But Diem's social policies, his police, his methods, his entourage, and his aloofness paved the road to insurgency. After him the whirlwind of shaky governments and the growing involvement of the United States gave a kind of monopoly of the nationalist image to Ho Chi Minh, who could hardly be called anyone's puppet.

The other analogy invoked was that of countries in which communist insurrections had been defeated: Greece, the Philippines, Malaysia—all of which had shown that a determined and well-organized minority can be brought under control by a divided society riddled with hates, corruption, and factional strife. However, the analogy was misleading in one decisive respect: in none of these cases had the insurgency reached such levels of cohesion and organization and the threatened regime fallen to such depths that the minority appeared defeatable only by a colossal foreign intervention. Yet our emphasis on superficial similarities made us neglect a quantitative difference that amounts to a qualitative one: the difference between, on the one side, a society and polity that manage, with limited foreign help and with domestic means that may be rough but are effective, to pull itself together and to meet the challenge and, on the other side, a society and polity that literally have to entrust their survival to a foreign trustee. We forgot that in the cases we pointed to for hope, the threatened regime finally won because it was able to appeal to the population's national consciousness, to provide it with security, and to present the communists as agents of outside powers. In the Philippines, Magsaysay also stole much of the communists' appeal as social reformers. In Greece the insurrection fell apart after Tito's defection, both because it had remained so deeply dependent on outside aid and because this defection heightened its own internal divisions.

We have blundered through failure to analyze rigorously enough the conditions for large-scale insurrection. We were used to seeing in communist movements mere branches of a central trunk. We refused to believe that large masses of people could willingly embrace communism for essentially local reasons, i.e., we had refused to learn from the Chinese precedent. We did not want to admit that the fusion of communism and nationalism achieved by Ho Chi Minh had survived the phase of the fight against the French. We mistook the presence in the south of distinguished but unorganized noncommunist nationalists for evidence of the good nationalist standing, and therefore the representative character, of the Saigon regimes. We failed to distinguish a sect from a party, a clique from an organization, a group of intellectuals or politicians with tiny clienteles from a political movement, a police force, officer corps, and set of rich merchants from a political class. We tended to attribute South Vietnamese chaos to a combination of communist disruptiveness and reversible South Vietnamese mistakes (such as Diem's way of applying the strategic hamlet idea). We failed to realize that those "mistakes" were, so to speak, doubly of the essence. They were the inevitable product of a narrowly based, unrepresentative, insecure, and artificial regime deeply suspicious of or removed from its own people. And they provided the communists with a cause and opportunities for disruption that allowed them to reach proportions unknown in all the other cases.

The proper analogy ought to have been Chiang's China—but Chiang's China was too huge for us to have had any illusion about our capacity to "save" it from Mao. Yet the very precedent of China must have somehow led our officials to want to do for Saigon what we could not do for Chiang, something that turned out not to be feasible here either. What has defeated us in Vietnam is not the physical size of the area (our consolation in the case of China) but the very nature of the issue. Our "loss of Cuba" made us move into the Dominican revolution; there we "prevailed," in the sense of reaching our immediate objective (this implies no approval of our intervention and of its goal), because the insurgents preferred a peaceful solution unfavorable to them to a bloody battle between them and us. Our "loss of China" made us step into South Vietnam, and we have not prevailed.

At the time when we were faced with the choice between letting South Vietnam fall to communist subversion and massive intervention to "save" the Saigon regime, the very terms in which we saw the alternatives indicate that the chances the South Vietnamese regime had of defeating the insurgents on its own (or with minimal help) were gone. The rules of successful counterinsurgency laid down by Sir Robert Thompson were violated by Saigon.[1] The goals of a "clear political aim," respect for the law, good administration, priority to the defeat of political subversion (rather than the guerrillas), close contact with the people, destruction of the enemy's infrastructure, building the ability to protect the population and look after its needs, avoidance of a large conventional army whose operations would be

[1] See his book *Defeating Communist Insurgency* and his article in *Foreign Affairs* (April 1968).

self-defeating—all were neglected or played down.

We failed to recognize how all these errors differentiated the case of Saigon from those we had invoked. We also failed to recognize that these errors resulted not from ignorance or blunders but from that very inability which the various regimes in Saigon had demonstrated (in sharp contrast with Hanoi) to provide South Vietnam with the rudiments of nationhood. The long-term interest of the Saigon leadership may have been reform for survival. But its nature was such that drastic reform would have eliminated it as surely as a communist sweep: this, too, had not been the case in Athens or in Manila, although it was true in the case of the Batista and Chiang regimes. In the short run Saigon's interest was not to reform but to let us fight for its survival. By misreading reality, we were led to believe that our intervention could somehow bring to South Vietnam all that had failed to grow there in the years of our mere "advice."

Thus we come to the other great failing of our policy. An optimistic and simplified reading of reality served as the basis for our *hubris*. If the situation in South Vietnam was serious mainly for the very reason that triggered our intervention, i.e., communist mischief, it was easier to believe in our capacity to save South Vietnam; for we saw our task hopefully as saving it from its enemies instead of hopelessly as saving it from itself.

Our misreading of reality and our self-confidence have fed one another in a vicious circle of ever-increasing delusions. What the South Vietnamese could not do for themselves, we could not do for them. But our self-confidence has misled us into thinking both that we could and that they would do it with us; and our need to cling to our illusions has led us for years to analyze the evolution of the war with an optimism that sprang from our initial misreading, an optimism it took the Tet offensive to begin to shatter. The Korean analogy helped us misjudge the Viet Cong's strategy (and call enemy defeats his failure to reach objectives he did not have); the Greek or Filipino analogy helped us misjudge the "progress" of South Vietnamese political and economic development.

Our *hubris* is that old "illusion of omnipotence" denounced by Brogan, which I have analyzed elsewhere in some detail.[2] In South Vietnam our faith in our talent for "fixing" has taken several forms.

[2] *Gulliver's Troubles, Part II; The State of War* (Praeger, 1965), ch. vi.

One has been our belief in the possibility of bringing insurgency into control and its North Vietnamese directors to their knees by the massive exertion of mechanical power. We did not realize that, short of invasion and occupation, air power alone was not likely to defeat North Vietnam or that the degree of guerrilla "immunity to the direct application" of our military power was high and that we were indeed up against the "Asian birthrate" in a Sisyphean contest (search-and-destroy) with the manifestations of insurgency that left its roots intact. This has been pointed out so often and so frequently cited as an example of our fondness for military, or "hardware," solutions to complex problems—our "engineering" approach to politics—that one would feel almost ashamed of mentioning it again, were it not both the most blatant demonstration of our misreading of reality and a symptom of another, deeper form of our *hubris*.

We acted as if our massive dispatch of troops and our air war could turn what was essentially a colossal insurgency into something more manageable by us—a conventional war that we would win through what Herman Kahn has called an "attrition-pressure-ouch" strategy[3] aimed at breaking Hanoi's will and at forcing the enemy in the south into increasingly costly battles. We attempted to change reality by acting as if it did not exist, as if we could both impose our rules of the game on our enemy on the ground and turn into a predominantly "northern" war what was still at heart an insurrection in the south (helped, to be sure, by the north, but neither so decisively as to collapse even if the "will of Hanoi" had snapped nor, most importantly, by means easily susceptible to our kinds of pressure). In the process we have not only misjudged our adversary, but we have forgotten the very sobering lessons World War II should have taught us about the efficacy of air bombing.

We had been warned by all kinds of experts about the irrelevance of conventional war machinery to insurgency situations. Yet we thought that we would overcome its tactical disadvantages by ingenious innovations in technological gadgetry which would increase mobility and our fire power. But mobility, while capable of thwarting enemy moves and making enemy bases insecure, is no substitute for pacification (seize-and-hold). Moreover, both mobility and fire power increase destructiveness and disruption. Yet we let ourselves be swayed by the

[3] *Can We Win in Vietnam?* ch. vi.

advantages rather than by the disadvantages of our kind of might. We have shown again the combination of a wishful reading of reality (e.g., a permanent underestimation of the damage we do, a refusal to see the fundamentally political character of the struggle) with a conviction that the people would, so to speak, forgive us our destructiveness—by contrast with, say, that of the French in Indochina and Algeria—because they would realize that it was a necessary evil inflicted upon them for the sake of their protection, as in the case of our bombings of France in 1943–44.

This is the *hubris* of believing that others will interpret our deeds as we interpret them and that our intentions cancel out our acts. It matches our illusion that the South Vietnamese intention of remaining noncommunist amounts both to the willingness and the capacity to organize and to the acceptance of any act of war against communism. Whether we could ever have made the South Vietnamese people look at us as their defenders against insurgents who are, after all, their kin is a big question, although one could argue that different tactics and a less obtrusive presence might have helped us put all the blame for disruption on the Viet Cong and Hanoi. But the very scale of our operations has made this a moot point—and a smaller scale might have proved ineffective sooner.

Another form of *hubris* shows in our belief that we could do what no other nation has done—build someone else's nation, create a stable society and polity elsewhere, in the midst of a large-scale war. "Pacification" is, of course, not only compatible with counterinsurgency operations, but an indispensable complement to them and their ultimate target. But pacification is in any case very difficult to achieve once the military operations reach a certain level: the clash between search-and-destroy and hold-and-protect becomes unbearable when, say, relocation for greater security gives way to the mass production of refugees. Moreover, Moshe Dayan has written, pacification must be undertaken by the native country; indeed, it must be an undertaking of the villagers themselves, under the protection of the military and with the help of the government. *Pace* Herman Kahn, there is more to pacification than good administration. Out of *hubris* we failed to understand that as Americans we simply could not play this role, being, to quote Dayan again, not merely foreigners but strangers whose very presence undermines the standing of the people we came to defend.[4] Indeed, the more we tried to be the "pacifiers," the more we undermined any capacity the South Vietnamese people and government might have had in this connection, as well as their self-respect.

True, we paid lip service to the notion that pacification was their affair. But misunderstanding reality, we failed to see that the South Vietnamese regime and military both could not and would not be the right agent for this. They could not because the people lacked confidence in a regime that had too often proved ineffective or repressive or corrupt, and they would not because they never showed enough confidence in their own people to entrust the villagers with the authority and the means (military and financial) to provide for their self-defense. The Viet Cong, in zones under its control, has replaced the old village structures by a mass movement, substituting the politics of mass involvement for the politics of traditional society. Saigon has been unable either to compete with the Viet Cong or to strengthen traditional village autonomy and solidarity: it has undermined the legitimacy of village rulers but provided no substitute. The villagers were thus left in a kind of physical, administrative, and emotional no man's land, torn between identification with the Viet Cong which they respect but fear and identification with a regime for which they have no respect. And whatever normalization of local life could be achieved in this no man's land in the absence of any self-identification with the regime is regularly disrupted by the Americans, whether they come as temporary administrators or as warriors.

Our faith in omnipotence has expressed itself further in our conviction that we could "win" this war, not merely with, but, to an increasing extent, for the South Vietnamese—without a true understanding of what "winning" means in such a context. Our first instinct, or reflex, has been to look for victory in military terms—with the help of body counts and "victories" won ever closer to and recently in Saigon. Over the years we have learned that this is not the only or the most significant index, and we have spoken of "winning the hearts and minds" of the people. But our power to raid has always been greater than our power to hold, and our lack of experience in this sort of a war has deprived us of handles, tools, techniques, and organizations which would have been effective anyhow only if they had been used by the South Vietnamese. We have been too easily satisfied with the fragile appearances of pacification without asking ourselves whether

4 Unpublished article.

the schools built would stay open or whether the population under control was truly loyal. Our *hubris* has consisted of not taking seriously, or not applying to us, Raymond Aron's warning that in a revolutionary war the insurgents win if they do not lose, the defenders lose if they fail to win. We have interpreted our failure to lose as a victory and their failure to win as a defeat. In the process we have misread not only the realities of South Vietnam but our own.

If there was ever any chance of success after our decision to intervene more massively than we had prior to 1963, it depended on two factors. One was our capacity to incite the South Vietnamese regime to broaden its base to include all those anticommunist leaders with respectable nationalist pasts who served as our alibi (in our belief that their country really wanted to be saved from communism) and to reform ARVN so as to make it truly a national army. But here we have been inhibited both by that merciless reality we had tried to ignore and by ourselves.

On the one hand, we always wondered whether any reform and re-equipment of ARVN would not ultimately benefit our enemies rather than improve ARVN's will and ability to fight. We wondered whether any significant broadening of the Saigon regime would not weaken its own determination, whether the anticommunist majority was truly resolved to do battle with the communist minority, and would not prefer to deal with it in negotiations that we feared would ultimately lead to a communist takeover because of superior communist cohesion and resolve. We wondered whether there was really more than a militant but unpopular and narrow (hence necessarily unstable or dependent) minority that wanted to do battle.

On the other hand, we were also deterred by an American quality which both tempers our *hubris* and makes it even less justified: our reluctance, when we intervene, to act as if we had the right to push our protégés around and do more than advise them. Somehow we realize our limitations and become humble when faced with the stark need to take extensive measures of political and social reform in friendly territory. We are stopped less by our ignorance (*vide* our extensive interventions in defeated Germany and Japan) than by our credo and principles: respect for self-determination in the country that we come to defend, even when only shallow, indeed self-defeating, *forms* of self-determination exist there.

In the countries we occupied (advanced industrial nations) our confidence was enhanced by our sense of legitimacy: we felt that we could make a new bottle as well as pour in the wine of our experience. In Vietnam we try to pour an irrelevant wine into the misshapen bottle that we found there. Thus our pride of omnipotence stops, so to speak, at our client's doorstep, which makes our conviction that we could clean house for him even more extravagant. We end up having all the disadvantages of colonialism and none of the advantages. We have approached the South Vietnamese with one hand tied behind our back and the other holding inappropriate tools.

Another condition for improbable success was time—time to convince (if one would not coerce) the South Vietnamese establishment to change its course, time to relegate the insurgency to certain areas while the rest of the country convalesces from the war and its awful side effects, time to instill in the villagers a sense of confidence and identification with Saigon and in the city dwellers a sense of being the citizens of a genuine nation. But once more our lack of experience in these realms buttressed our somewhat hectic approach to world affairs. However often the frustrations of the years brought to our leaders' lips the litany of calls to patience and fortitude, the frenzied need for quick results to reassure a nation that reacts badly to defeats and uneasily to protracted, inconclusive conflicts brought on our officials in South Vietnam a constant pressure for quick results. That need also brought to our briefings and communiqués a constant flow of comforting statistics, thoroughly devoid of meaning in the context of a long-term operation. Our impatience both fed our *hubris* and defeated it.

In our sense of omnipotence our whole policy and the terms in which it has been presented made sense *only* if we achieved that final victory on the battlefield or in a negotiation to save our enemies' faces. Everything was predicated on success. We failed, in so tricky an operation, to protect ourselves against possible failure. We left ourselves no room for maneuver or for the sort of elegant retreat that does not look like an admission of failure. We have repeatedly burned—or let the South Vietnamese regimes burn—bridges behind us: by destroying or jailing their political opponents who could have been of help to us had we wanted to change our course, by discarding possibilities of negotiation at a time when the military balance was more favorable to us. We have encouraged other Asian regimes to stake their safety on our presence in Vietnam, without realizing that this way of buying time for them could easily become an alibi for their neglect of those domestic factors that could kindle an insurgency on their soil far more surely than a victory of Ho Chi Minh on his. We failed to realize that their taking seriously our conviction that we were their main shield could lead them to revulsion against us if we did not succeed. In the meantime it serves as an excuse for us to persist in trying to do the impossible, because "other Asians" want us to stay on. By trumpeting the cosmic importance of Vietnam, we made the consequences of eventual failure far more critical than they might have been had we understated the general significance of Vietnam. But the more we have needed success to justify our investment, the more we have exaggerated the effects of failure and the resort to false analogies: oversell was not a salesman's trick but a trapped man's need.

Above all, we have constantly rationalized the damage and disruption we inflicted on the country and explained away the corruption and mismanagement of the Saigon regime by the argument that our final victory would prove the ruins worthwhile, allow the scars to heal, and cure the traditional diseases of Vietnamese society. It is indeed true, alas, that in many other cases, as in Korea, success retroactively vindicated horrors and inequities. But in Vietnam the more atrocious the evils, the more we have had to put all our hopes on success, which became the only justification for an intolerable process. The more success became the only tolerable outcome, the higher the price one has had to pay (or inflict) in order to try to succeed. The two great extenuating circumstances of war's moral outrages—final success and a certain appropriateness and proportionality of means to ends—have both been war casualties here.

In a conventional war, providing security to the population one comes to protect—i.e., pacification—is less essential and indeed depends on the prior defeat of the enemy; destruction, alas, may be the prelude to security and the price of protection. However, even great destruction ordinarily leaves the government and society capable of recovery. In Vietnam not only have we failed to "win" (under any definition of winning), but our means have undermined the society we wanted to defend and the frail legitimacy of the regime we wanted to save. Here security should have been the means of defeating the enemy, and protection required that destruction be minimal. We have made ourselves at least as unattractive as our enemies to the South Vietnamese. The worst aspect of our *hubris* has been our assumption of the right to "destroy in order to save" in conditions where "salvation" was never likely to begin with and where it has been made even less likely by our presence and methods.

It is becoming fashionable among men who at one time or another supported the American effort in Vietnam to assert that a different strategy could have produced better results. It is my contention that this is not the case: this was never a "winnable" contest. A limited intervention would have—indeed, has—been ineffective; a massive one has been counterproductive; the longer our involvement, the more we could only prove either the former or the latter.

As long as our presence was small, conditions in South Vietnam—first, Diem's neglect and distortion of the requirements of counterinsurgency; later, the chaos that followed his assassination—brought the insurgents very close to victory. Our intervention on the ground made sense in the perspective of thwarting an impending *forcible* communist takeover and negotiating rapidly a *political* solution that would have given to the noncommunist South Vietnamese a last chance and framework to prove their worth and to the communists a chance to win by means of the ballot.[5] But this "scenario"—which has finally become our last resort, except that officially we continue to look for ways so to sweeten the pill as to change its nature—would have required a deliberate effort to reform the Saigon regime; and it would have been far more credible if it had come before instead of after America's failure to achieve a military victory—the failure to "pacify" the countryside, the demonstration of domestic disunity, and the systematic attempt to strengthen and legitimize the Thieu-Ky regime. In any event such a political solution could never have been more than a framework within which the noncommunist South Vietnamese, with their backs to the wall, might have *tried* to save their country from communist rule.

But there is a great difference between "intervention for extrication" and the kind of "intervention for victory" that we chose. Failure

[5] To argue now that a peaceful communist victory through elections was always an acceptable solution to us makes one wonder why we did not try to negotiate on such a basis sooner—and why we remain so ambivalent about any communist participation in a post-cease fire, interim government.

in the latter case makes the costs of extrication higher and, in my opinion, worsens the chances of survival of a noncommunist South Vietnam. Why? Because the disruption which the war has inflicted, far from providing the noncommunists with belated opportunities for organization, must have laid the groundwork for the totalitarian *encadrement* of sullen and destitute masses, ready for revolution but alienated from anything Saigon stood for. Also the possibility of organizing a coherent coalition of noncommunist leaders after the lacerations of jail or exile and the lassitude of war is pretty slim.

In any case "intervention for victory" ensnared us in a network of traps and dilemmas we were foolish first not to see and later to court. To send a small army—say, up to a hundred thousand men—seemed too little for victory. To send an army capable of holding once and for all the liberated countryside—holding was more important to us than to our foe, given our fundamental need for pacification—would have required an effort we never really contemplated. To send a large army, yet one much less huge than this, was to create insuperable strategic problems. To keep our men in enclaves sacrificed what we deemed our main assets (mobility and firepower) along with the countryside. To send them to fight guerrillas in the countryside would have meant far worse attrition for us than for them and given great opportunities to North Vietnam's main forces. To concentrate on fighting the latter meant focusing most attention on the conventional aspects of the war and neglecting the villages and pacification. In trying a melange of the second and third strategies, we have ended with the worst of all worlds: the North Vietnamese forces have not been broken; the countryside has been lost; and while our mobility has kept us stabbing in the dark, the enemy has succeeded both in preserving most of his sanctuaries and in depriving us of security in ours.

Other sets of dilemmas have affected our policy toward Hanoi. In order to "break Hanoi's will" we would have had to bomb much closer to China, to close Haiphong, perhaps to invade the north. But effectiveness on the spot (besides being of debatable relevance to the final stake: control of the south) collided with the needs of prudence at large. Our larger purpose, allegedly, was to avoid World War III, to contain China, to convince Russia of its interest in such containment—not to destroy the regime in Hanoi, to promote a larger war, to provoke China's entry into it, nor to oblige Russia to demonstrate more militantly its solidarity with a small communist state. Thus we chose prudence at the cost of effectiveness. In our choice, however, we again produced the worst of all worlds: we put enough pressure on Hanoi to make impossible the reintroduction of external restraints on North Vietnam (comparable to Soviet and Chinese pressure at Geneva in 1954) and to reinforce the North Vietnamese national resolve and regime. But a combination of calculations of prudence and miscalculations of strategy (due to the misapplication of concepts derived from mixed-interest conflicts to one that was far closer to a zero-sum game) led us to apply our pressure so gradually as to allow the other side to adjust.

We also got the worst of all worlds in our relations with the South Vietnamese. Too reticent to take over the functions they were mismanaging which we know how to manage (be it garbage collection or health services), reluctant or incompetent to reform areas of blatant corruption or brutality, unwilling to appear in control of the political process, we have nevertheless been saddled in the eyes of many —in South Vietnam and elsewhere—with responsibility for a client who would be swept away without us. At the same time, the Americanization of the war has worsened the client's condition in many ways. It has provided the insurgents with a cause that is now both national and social, that is, by reducing the difference between the second and first Indochina wars and making this one appear as the mere prolongation of the earlier one. It has discouraged many noncommunists (in the villages or in the cities) from actively opposing the communists on the side of the Americans. It has introduced into an old, fragile, and backward society a technological Frankenstein that completed the communists' job of fostering insecurity and disruption of which they hope to be the beneficiaries. Finally, Americanization of the war has brought not merely physical but social destruction to the people we came to protect—and it is no solace to say that this is true in any war, given the special political nature and stakes of this one.

Caught in a lasso from which we could not escape, we could only tighten the noose through our twisting and squirming. If, because of Viet Cong and North Vietnamese mischief, the anticommunist majority failed to organize and unite, the situation was hopeless, since the elimination of this mischief required both the demolition of South Vietnam's society and the political and social success of pacification, which our acts of war precluded. If, on the other hand, this lack of organization was inherent in South Vietnamese society, our task was hopeless because either the reform of that society would fail to take place as long as it was entrusted to its present leadership—the product and beneficiary of its corruption—or else reform would have to be undertaken by us, and we neither knew how nor wanted to take over. We were in a vicious circle: in such a war there can be no genuine pacification without security; but the search for security against so obstinate and omnipresent a foe could not but interfere with pacification, and one ended up with neither pacification nor security.

The verdict is somber. We have fought a war for objectives that were unreachable—the exemplary defeat of a large "national liberation movement," the restoration of our version of the Geneva agreements, a stable South Vietnam with a noncommunist regime, the preservation of international stability by sticking to the partition line agreed upon between the great powers. The more those objectives eluded us, the more we have escalated our means, without realizing that the means we used made our goals even more unreachable and destroyed any chance there might have been of getting near them.

As in previous total wars the escalation of the means has led to an emotional and ideological escalation. The greater the war machine, the losses, the wreckage, the more one had to justify them in terms of the vital importance of the stakes—thus making retreat so much more painful since military de-escalation must be accompanied by a kind of de-escalation of the stakes, an operation that may well leave deep traces both in our public, whose consent to future involvements may be affected by its leaders having cried wolf too often and too loud, and among Asian leaders, whose earlier admiration for our stamina may lead to a mixture of horror for our excesses and distress at our failure to deliver goods we had proclaimed so essential to us and to them. The more we escalated the stakes, the higher (and more erroneous) were the expectations we created at home and abroad.

In this predicament our original mistakes and the need to succeed made us grasp every illusion in the wind and delude ourselves instead of facing the stark realities of South Vietnamese disaster and American *hubris*. Thus, as a way of comforting ourselves about our mission, we pointed to facts that were true yet irrelevant. We have demonstrated Hanoi's grip over the NLF in order to confirm our views about aggression, but we failed to see that the controlling facts were not Hanoi's control but the Viet Cong's achievements and the connection between the civil war and the struggle for national unification. We stressed the totalitarian character of North Vietnam, the post-1954 flow of refugees to the south, and thus justified our commitment to a free government for the south; but we failed to note that in an area where Western democracy is unknown, the efficiency of Hanoi's regime, its sense of purpose, and the remarkable discipline and commitment of its population were the decisive features: in the battle of symbols, we were fighting the steely image of a united and dedicated north with the misty mirage of a future model south. We took solace from the southerners' failure to rally around the Viet Cong. Yet the decisive features here were, first, that the southern politicians who refused to go over to the NLF also refused to lead— or were prevented from leading—the south, and second, that the urban population that did not rise when the Viet Cong came to the cities nevertheless provided the Viet Cong with at least some help in organizing infiltration and with the negative protection of secrecy; even passive support for us would not be enough to ensure final victory in this kind of a war.

Sometimes we have grasped at myths. One of them has been the great success of the elections in September 1967. Whatever progress they have represented on the long and tricky road to self-government, we should not conceal from ourselves either the fact that they were marked by irregularities that go far beyond tolerable, Western-type corruption, or the fact that the dominant branch of the Saigon regime is not the assembly but an executive whose representative character is small, or the fact that both the assembly and the executive display South Vietnam's actual fragmentation far more than its potential unity.

Another myth is that we may now turn many of our responsibilities back to the South Vietnamese. It is a myth in the sense that if we turn them over to the present Saigon regime, we are in all likelihood going to accelerate the decomposition of our protégés and find that all the reasons that led us in 1965 to rush in operate even more strongly half a million men, God knows how many ruins and casualties, and three years later. On the other hand, if we turn those responsibilities over to an enlarged and improved regime in the south, that regime may negotiate with the Viet Cong terms of settlement that, at worst, could be far removed from those we still seem to hope to achieve in Paris and, at best, could have been obtained less bloodily some years ago.

It would be a myth to believe that because of the military "stalemate" our foes might accept a kind of piecemeal solution (of local accommodations and cease-fire zones), as if the significance of a stalemate in this sort of asymmetrical war were the same as in Korea, as if there were truly organized political forces on both sides of the "stalemate," as if communists were interested in a partition of South Vietnam, and as if one could avoid the crucial issue of ultimate control. It would anyhow be another myth to believe that we can achieve by negotiations with Hanoi what we have failed to win on the battlefield—the guarantee of a united, noncommunist, independent South Vietnam in which communists would be disarmed and reduced to the position of a minority political party as in Greece.

And it was—or should I say "is"?—a myth to believe that what we were engaged in was nation building. This was both an illusion fed by a social science imbued with engineering pretensions and an ideological justification for the less savory aspects of our role.

In the first place, no state can do more than create or restore the conditions in which another nation's citizens can take the political, economic, and social measures that will provide the nation with a sense of community, adequate institutions, and essential services. Political development is not simply a matter of techniques. The institutions that we as Americans know well and may want to propagate are not only limited by the peculiarities of our national experience, but they are also mere forms; the substance must be provided by the foreign nation's will and purposes. Nation building means creating values, distributing goods, and sharing power; if the "builders" are aliens (colonial masters or disinterested social experimenters), they will sooner or later be the targets and victims of their subjects.

In the second place, whereas a war is often the crucible of national consciousness, internal peace is the requisite for nation building. The disruptions of civil war may create the conditions for future nation building: by sending to the cities large numbers of peasants in search either of a refuge or of a better income, by weakening the hold of the traditional family, of village notables, of regional, religious, or ethnic separatisms, by enriching certain "modern" classes and impoverishing other groups, etc. But out of such upheavals can come either final chaos or nation building; and the chances of the latter depend on the success of pacification or on the advent of a negotiated peace. The destruction of an old building, the scattering of bricks and stones, the delivery to the construction site of cement, mortar, and sand are not to be confused with the construction of a new edifice: on some sites nothing ever gets built. We have too often confused the side effects of war with the labors of peace.

Finally, we have grasped at another, familiar kind of reassurance which could hardly be suspected of being an illusion or a myth, since it is (or so it seems to us) the shorthand translation of hard facts: statistics. As long as the quest for certainty in the realms of essential uncertainty remains within the bounds of social science, one can marvel without indignation. But when the same fallacies become props of policy, irony is not enough. We have copulated with figures and discovered at the end that it was incest, for the figures were all too often not the offspring of external achievements but the creations of our own fantasies. We have forgotten, first, that many of the statistics that comforted us were false, partial, or suspect in their origins; second, that even the believable figures had to be interpreted and were meaningless out of context: thus, figures about the percentage of the population controlled by us, or about the miles of roads returned to safety, or the number of incidents, could either mean progress toward pacification and victory or indicate a temporary shift in enemy strategy—such as his regrouping for the Tet offensive. One always comes back to our original sins—ignorance of the context and excessive self-confidence.

In Vietnam all the reasons that we gave for fighting the war now ring hollow. Some of them were never really relevant. We exaggerated both the role of China in the conflict and the degree to which a victory for Hanoi would mean an expansion of China's power and prestige: "it is hard to see how any likely outcome in Vietnam will . . . speed up China's long and difficult effort to become a great power. . . . China's power in Asia is dependent much more on factors other than what happens in Vietnam."[6] We have also exaggerated the domino effect of national liberation movements: they break out only where there are objective and subjective conditions of serious discontent, administrative and social neglect, ethnic or religious grievances, class inequities; and they do not reach the proportions of a civil war unless the degree of decomposition or inadequacy of the polity is very high. The chances for a communist domination of such movements depend very largely on the communists' aptitude for capturing the nationalist symbols. Thus the two main deterrents are—positively—domestic attention to and reform of legitimate grievances and—negatively—careful American abstention from too close an identification with threatened regimes, which could deprive them of their claim to represent their nations.

Many of the reasons we have given, while impressive, either have become irrelevant or cannot be used anymore as arguments for the war. The notion that our failure to save South Vietnam from a communist takeover would, by itself, have a domino effect in Southeast Asia, weaken other governments and make them eager to appease their communist neighbors is not false. But the force of the argument has never been sufficient to allow us to prevail in Vietnam, and indeed the argument required that we prevail at a reasonable cost: the higher the costs of our involvement, the more disquiet in Asian countries, not only because of the spectacle of the ruins accumulated by our protection, but also because of the likelihood that so massive (and frustrating) an effort would never be tried again. When a German politician praised the American undertaking because of his conviction that "what the Americans do for South Vietnam they would do for us," the only likely reactions are a mixture of shudder *and* disbelief. The lesson learned by other Asians from our policy may well be that, rather than leaning too closely on us, they ought to placate our foes instead of relinquishing to them the causes of nationalism, anti-imperialism, and antiwhite racism.

The argument that our effort in Vietnam was necessary to weaken China's position and improve Russia's within world communism also had some strength. Once again, however, the policy we followed failed to serve the goal. China's weakening, while obvious, can hardly be

[6] Donald Zagoria, "Who's Afraid of the Domino Theory?" *The New York Times Magazine*, April 21, 1968.

attributed to us: a combination of domestic turmoil and diplomatic clumsiness explains it. But insofar as we are concerned with China's view of the way in which national liberation movements can effectively tie down the world's greatest power, neutralize its nuclear arsenal, and carry forward the struggle against imperialism, the spectacle of our entrapment in Vietnam—"the fly that captured the flypaper"— can hardly be said to have disproved Marshal Lin Piao. As Professor Reischauer has written, if our goal was to demonstrate that such movements do not work, we have lost. As for the Soviets, whose enthusiasm for such movements has indeed been limited, our behavior has obliged them to display their solidarity with and support of North Vietnam, and it is only with the reversal of America's policy —not through its pursuit—that a chance for their playing a moderating role re-emerges.

The argument about the need to establish a balance of power in Asia remains valid. But we must observe, first, that the situation in Southeast Asia has evolved favorably for reasons largely independent of our stand in Vietnam and, connected with that fact, that (besides China) only in Vietnam have communism and nationalism been fused. Thus the upheaval in Indonesia had to do with a nationalist revulsion against the Chinese and a China-inspired communist party—and with the desperate instinct of survival of the Indonesian military, whom it is hard to imagine willing to let themselves be slaughtered but for America's stand in the jungles of Vietnam.

Further, America's policy can hardly be said to have contributed to a balance of power in Asia because we have not understood sufficiently what power means in the present international system. I have said earlier what I thought of our "buying time" argument: if the main threat to "free Asia" is internal disruption (supported, to be sure, from outside but triggered and sustained by domestic factors), our military enterprise only diverted attention and resources (as in Thailand) from the "nation-building" tasks in Asian countries. In Europe a balance could apparently be established largely by military means both because the threat seemed primarily military and because the politics, economies, and societies could absorb those military means and provide, behind the wall of deterrence and defense, the real basis for stability. In Asia neither the nature of the threat nor the nature of the societies justifies a transposition. There the imbalance between America's might and the local friendly powers' is such that a massive American military presence could only lead to a disastrous mixture of domination and disruption. Even if there were a serious threat of Chinese (or communist Vietnamese) invasion of neighboring countries, the answer could not simply be the stationing of large quantities of American troops: for the political, economic, and social implications would be such as to open the way for internal wars while we were trying to plug holes in the borders.

JOHN KING FAIRBANK: I think something further must be said for the record about Vietnam as a form of containment of China. In order to sell the American public, our administration accepted the interpretation of Vietnam as a people's war of national liberation. However, it seems to me that we too easily took that seriously. This interpretation was trumpeted abroad by us to show what our opponents were trying to do. The results are that we put ourselves on the line against a people's war of liberation; and if we are defeated in Vietnam or held at stalemate, then American containment of China seems to have lost, since we accepted this war as a confrontation between our policy and Chinese policy.

If we do not continue in Vietnam, no doubt we will accept the absorption of Vietnam into what might be called a Chinese sphere. At any rate, if a Chinese sphere does supervene in Vietnam, we are back to the islands and peninsulas of the Western Pacific, which is quite a feasible link-up of our diplomatic frontier with our strategic power frontier. This is the kind of link-up of frontiers we did *not* have when the "open door" was our policy and we could not oppose with any naval strength or otherwise Japan's encroachments on China. It is, however, the kind of link-up of frontiers we maintained during the Korean war in protecting Japan, Taiwan, and the Philippines by naval and air power. Getting out of Vietnam, then, will take us out of the extended frontier where power cannot be applied, where we have oversold ourselves.

This certainly can lead to a viable position for the future. It raises the question of whether we try to continue what we call a containment policy. I am sure we should change the term or drop it and get on to a new policy.

RICHARD M. PFEFFER: As one of the few other China people in the room, let me pursue this for a moment. I take it you were not denying that what we have in Vietnam substantially is a "people's war of national liberation." Rather you were suggesting that the problem lies in our misconception of this war as a form of Chinese aggression, which thereby puts it within the ambit of the United States' containment policy.

JOHN KING FAIRBANK: We define the war of liberation in our terms as Chinese aggression and expansion. The Chinese see it in their terms. However, their terms are not ours.

RICHARD M. PFEFFER: Presumably there should be some reality—beyond semantics and cultural differences—in the notion of Chinese aggression. Most people who argue the case for Chinese aggression speak in terms of abstract models of revolutionary war, since the level of Chinese influence in Vietnam is rather limited, and the level of Chinese involvement—compared to that of almost any other major power supporting either side in Vietnam—is certainly limited. Here again we have misconceived reality.

§§ ALBERT WOHLSTETTER: Phrases like "balance of power," "sphere of influence," "containment" need a great deal of rigor, operational definition, and added concrete information if they are to be much use in dealing with the complex political and military relations among and within the states of Asia. Whatever the realities of Chinese aggressiveness in general, and however one might realistically describe the past and future role of the Chinese in "liberation wars" near their periphery, it is plain that we misconceived a good many other realities in Vietnam. In Vietnam, the United States entered a conflict in which the chances were poor to start with for affecting events in the direction of basic United States interests and aims for the political and economic self-development of the "third world." The skillful communist leadership benefited from its success in the long struggle against the French. They had built up a formidable apparatus of cadres in the south. The heritage of French colonialism left the noncommunist alternatives for leadership weak and badly divided.

The nature of the threat, the feasible and worthy objectives of our support, and the main alternatives for achieving such objectives were misconceived. The issues were wrongly defined at each of the major successive stages of decision. They were defined wrongly, moreover, not only by official policy, but also frequently by factions within the government and by the critics of the government—and not least by the critics. The question was not whether to "escalate" or to "de-escalate." The concept of "escalation," prominent especially in the last few years, merely caps the general confusion. It indicates that we can order and measure the alternatives for choice on a linear scale. Shall we reduce or increase the intensity of the fighting? Or (since the latter is affected by the decisions of the North Vietnamese) should we scale our own effort up or down? How many men should we keep in Vietnam? How much should we spend? How many, and which, target constraints should we remove? These were the wrong questions.

If we were to try and help in Vietnam, the basic questions concerned not "how much" but "what for." Such questions were clearly posed at least by 1961—perhaps most clearly by British advisors in Vietnam.[7] Should we concentrate on the slow, persistent attempt to help construct a viable government capable of economic and political self-development, able to protect an increasing proportion of the population from subversion and terror, and so to reduce the local support for guerrillas and infiltrated northern forces? Or, on the other hand, should we focus our major efforts on trying to hunt down and annihilate guerrillas and the main-force units of the DRV? While the level of forces needed is not entirely in the control of one side, the first alternative would have required smaller military forces than the second. It would subordinate conventional military operations and, among other things, would aim to prevent the establishment of secure base areas by the Viet Cong and DRV main-force units; but it would not expend its efforts to "search and destroy." It would have taken years and might not have been successful at all. The second alternative required the application of brute force massively and at a much greater rate than was politically feasible for the United States and in any case would have destroyed much of the basis for viable government in South Vietnam. On my observation, one of the

[7] While I have some differences with them, since the beginning of 1962 I have owed much of my own view of the alternatives to talks with British advisors in Vietnam, in particular to Robert Thompson, Dennis Duncanson, and John Barlow.

things that predisposed us to the latter course was impatience and the distaste for any long-term involvement. This explanation runs quite counter to current views that attribute to the United States government the desire to get involved everywhere and specifically to get bases or a "sphere of influence" in South Vietnam.

In any event, the United States government tended never to face such basic choices. Instead, it "escalated"—more slowly and less extensively than requested. But it did not change the objectives. In this way it got the worst of both worlds, what might be called "a mini–brute force policy": a slow application of brute force in the hope of quickly achieving objectives that could be achieved, if at all, only by a massive and rapid use of force—and the wrong objectives at that. The bombing of North Vietnam, for example, was wrong even in its own terms: it was poorly adapted to reducing the number of North Vietnamese forces in South Vietnam. And the bombing and the artillery in South Vietnam were not for the most part in "close support"; they exacted much too high a toll in bystanders and friendly forces. (This does not, of course, justify the VC's deliberate putting of bystanders in peril.)

Let me elaborate a little on mini–brute force. While a brute force policy was mistaken, it is conceivable that in its own erroneous terms it could have been successful if it were actually massive enough. And this was not, as is usually said, a matter of the absolute limits of United States resources. After all, the United States raised armed forces including, in gross, 16,354,000 military personnel in World War II, with over 12,000,000 on duty in 1945, when our population was less than 140,000,000. We have the resources to raise over 20,000,000 men now—more than one for every North Vietnamese man, woman, and child. By brute force we could simply pave North and South Vietnam in concrete. Something less than that undoubtedly would accomplish the "search and destroy" job—however blindly. Of course, even a much less total mobilization of massive force to meet so limited a challenge was not politically feasible. This in itself, quite apart from the more important consideration of what the problems of a small country under attack by communist insurgent forces are, might have suggested transformation to other objectives. In fact, a change of objectives was never genuinely made. Time and again when requests were made for more resources or the removal of further constraints, the government response was to grant something less than the amount asked in resources or in the removal of constraints —but not to change the objective sought. As a result, we had the wrong objective pursued by a brute force tactic with far less than the amount of force that the objective required: in short, a mini–brute force policy.

The recent government decision to turn down a request for 206,000 more American ground forces in South Vietnam, courageous though it was, leaves unsettled a basic issue—one that will remain so long as the negotiations drag on in Paris. It does not alter what our forces in Vietnam are doing and for what purpose. They are still chasing Viet Cong, still focusing on annihilating elusive DRV main-force units, still largely ignoring the need to establish a politically secure base area relatively free of VC cadres, the need to protect the population, and to have a government that operates under the rule of law.

§§ ITHIEL DE SOLA POOL: First of all, I want to go on record as rejecting the entire formulation of the issue we are here discussing. It is entitled "Vietnam: Misconceptions in Action." This is like being asked whether one has stopped beating one's wife. It seems to be simply assumed here that the American role in Vietnam has been based on misconceptions. Of course there have been many misconceptions. No complex policy is ever right in all details. However, the basic conception that American national interest was at stake in Vietnam, that the people of South Vietnam oppose the Viet Cong, and that we should not allow a forced communist takeover was sound and remains sound.

Now I want to return to some of the other points raised by Professor Hoffmann. What Stanley Hoffmann has offered us is for the most part a declaration of political faith. Each of us will agree with some parts and disagree with others. But the main factual content of the argument is a single prediction stated as a fact. The prediction is of the failure of the American effort in Vietnam. He has frequently used the word "failure" to describe the American situation there, supplemented by uses of such synonyms as "fiasco," "disaster," and "tragedy."

Perhaps I misinterpret Professor Hoffmann's point. Perhaps by "failure" he means something other than military defeat. Perhaps he means only that we have not achieved our goals easily and quickly, as we hoped and expected. Perhaps he means that we are paying an inordinate price for our goals. In that sense we certainly have failed —but more in the United States than in Vietnam.

The agonizing political lesson that racks this country is that there has been a failure of our own political system. The intensity of dissent, the lack of public understanding of our national policy, and the divisions that rack American society today have thrown into some question the stability of government in the United States, the capacity of our political system to govern effectively, the basic commitment of the American people to the payment of the costs of our national goals. These are failings of which we usually accuse the Vietnamese, but the criticism is more fairly addressed against ourselves.

But let us not exaggerate the gloomy performance of our political system, disappointing as it may be. There is no evidence that either the government or the majority of the public are ready to withdraw abruptly in disarray from Vietnam. The passionate critics would like to believe that the curtailment of bombing and the beginning of the Paris talks represent a reversal of Administration policy and a decision to accept defeat. Since they did not believe the President earlier when he said he wanted negotiations and a political settlement, they are forced now to perceive him as reversing his course. I cannot read the mind of the President. But as a supporter of the Administration's basic policy I feel the negotiations are a culmination we have long desired. I feel no sense of any major shift in policy. To negotiate at this point despite the continuation of the war is a logical course in pursuit of our goal of a political settlement that will assure a non-communist South Vietnam. That is a very limited goal, one that does not call for more than the suspension of fighting with roughly the present balance of power and authority in the south. As far as I can see, the communists do not have basic dominance of the noncommunist regime in the south. I cannot see that we have failed yet in pursuit of our goal of a political settlement reflecting the real present balance of power in the population of South Vietnam.

Clearly the situation in Vietnam is a disaster and a tragedy for its many victims, and it has been of advantage to neither side. Clearly, also, major tactical and strategic mistakes have been made, and there is a question, as Hoffmann points out, whether our difficulties in Vietnam mostly represent wrong policies, as he is inclined to feel, or valid concepts clumsily applied. In either case, criticism and self-criticism are clearly called for. But to recognize the problems and misery that accompany this war is not the same thing as purporting to know what its outcome will be while it is still raging.

The war is not over, despite the talks in Paris. There is no reason to assume that either side is yet ready to give up its major goals. Casualties are higher than ever. Critical battles loom on the horizon. At this stage it would still take a soothsayer, not a social scientist, to know what the outcome will be.

In the nature of war, each side sees the likely outcome differently. No rational government would fight which did not believe that by so doing it might obtain a significantly better outcome than it would get peacefully. Clearly there are differences of prediction within the two sides just as there are between them. Within the Lao Dong party in Hanoi the more technocratic wing, using the slogan of "construction and reconstruction," looks with dismay at the devastation of their economy, the desperate drain on their manpower, the overwhelming force of American fire power, the presence of half a million American troops, the inability of the NVA and VC to win any battle militarily, the continuation and even consolidation of the so-called "puppet regime" in the south, and last but not least, at the chaos of the Cultural Revolution in the ally to the north. In this light, this faction favors seeking a better settlement than they can foresee gaining on the field of battle. But there are also those in Hanoi who still believe that the balance of forces is moving their way, that the American people will not tolerate war much longer, and that with continued resolute combat all Vietnam will be theirs. Clearly there is enough optimism left in Hanoi for them to fight on fiercely for a while.

Divergences in prediction on our side are no less great. At one extreme there is General Westmoreland, who has just once more told us that the foe in Vietnam "seems to be approaching a point of desperation" and that enemy forces are "deteriorating in strength and quality," having lost a hundred thousand dead this year already. The Viet Cong, General Westmoreland tells us, are now recruiting only three thousand men a month in the south, though he puts infiltration from the north at fifteen thousand a month. At the opposite extreme is Stanley Hoffmann's view that the war is already lost. A certain reserve about both these extreme statements seems to be in order. Hoffmann's argument is proof by assertion; Westmoreland at least presents some data which, if true, would lead fairly heavily to his conclusion.

Past experience, however, would justify a certain appropriate skepticism regarding that evidence. It would be the height of *hubris* however, to borrow one of Dr. Hoffmann's epithets, to dismiss *a priori* all the evidence of what the other side is suffering. It may be of some interest to note that while all of us here, including myself, regard the Tet offensive as a major defeat for our side, the opposite view, that it was a defeat for the Viet Cong, not only is propounded by a few government propagandists but is the widely held view of the Vietnamese man in the rice paddies. In considering the ultimate outcome of the war in Vietnam, a healthy agnosticism is still very much in order.

Having asserted that the war in Vietnam is a failure, Dr. Hoffmann next tells us that "the root of the tragedy is the demonstrated absence in the south of the capacity for sustained self-government." The Viet Cong is asserted to be the only national movement that cuts across religious and social lines. In fact, the Viet Cong is an overwhelmingly rural and Buddhist organization. Its recruitment base is primarily among the 35 per cent of the population in that social stratum. Among them the VC may well claim the sympathy of a majority, but VC success among other social strata, such as the urban population, has been negligible.

Nevertheless, one must concede the gross inadequacies of self-government in the south. South Vietnam shares a lack of political development with Bolivia, Nigeria, Indonesia, Iraq, and nearly one hundred other countries in the underdeveloped world. However, the incapacity for self-government is less in Vietnam than in most of them, for Vietnam has a long tradition of sophisticated politics. It has largely been the politics of personal intrigue, but in the last three years we have seen a remarkable development of representative political institutions. However dismaying the continued military struggle, Vietnam's rapidity of political development in the recent past is hard to parallel elsewhere in the underdeveloped world, and that despite the continuous ravages and emergencies of civil war.

For two years following the Diem dictatorship, there was utter instability. For the last two years, however, Vietnam has had a stable government which has shown the ability to change its top leadership without destroying the basic national coalition. During this recent period a military dictatorship evolved into a comprehensive civil-military regime giving voice and representation to virtually all elements not on the enemy side and giving participation in the government to a majority subset among them. This evolution began with the election two years ago of a constituent assembly to draft the constitution. That assembly was able to make their document stick despite the opposition of the ruling generals to a number of key points. The elections held under the new constitution had extremely significant results.

Passionate critics of Vietnam hold the *idée fixe* that these elections were stolen, for they are unwilling to recognize that the government of South Vietnam may legitimately represent the general tenor of the people. Electoral practices of local bossism or fraud, which in areas like India or Chicago they deplore but recognize as the by-product of the painful evolution of democracy in any domain ruled by the culture of poverty, became for the critics an excuse to dismiss the elections as a nullity. All evidence to the effect that fraud did not deny the people their voice has been brushed aside by them.

The major issue of South Vietnam's presidential election campaign was negotiated peace—an issue openly and loudly debated despite the ongoing war. The majority vote showed a willingness to persevere, though the peace candidate came up with a very respectable 18 per cent of the vote, an estimate in close concurrence with independent opinion measurements among the two thirds of the population in the government's domain.

In the senatorial election military authorities gave secret orders to support three tickets and to oppose one other at all costs. The three tickets the military rulers supported all lost, and the one they opposed won. In the elections to the house, there was an even more representative result. It is a body truly reflecting the checkerboard pattern of Vietnam's divided population.

Local elections were also held a year ago, restoring to the villages in the government's domain the power to choose their own chiefs, a power Diem had taken from them in 1956. When they voted, the villagers once more demonstrated the high measure of validity of the elections by defeating an estimated one third of the incumbents.

The first cabinet under the new constitution was a weak one. It has now been replaced by a cabinet that well represents the central tendency of South Vietnamese civil politics as the vote last fall revealed it.

Participant politics is becoming increasingly possible. Censorship has been abolished. Transistor radios are everywhere and have become the country's prime news medium. In the post-Tet period various new manifestations of civic mobilization have begun to appear. Student-organized relief activities for refugees have been impressive and large-scale. Self-defense groups have sprung up in various hamlets and urban neighborhoods. Even corruption, that plague of transitional politics, has begun to come under some repression. The kingpins in the graft syndicate that dominated Vietnam and indeed represented a kind of shadow organization to the government were the four corps commanders. Their position has been smashed and some of them removed.

There is much that remains to be done before Vietnam can be considered to have completed the transition to a responsible, representative, let alone democratic, political regime. The most important remaining reforms are to provide a bridge between the government in Saigon at the top and the autonomous village at the bottom of the political system. Elections at the village and national levels have laid the foundations for representative government at each of these extremes. However, at the province and district layers between, the government continues to be run by army officers who have been assigned the jobs of province or district chiefs. An elected village chief faces his district chief as a servant to a master. He receives orders and may ask the district chief for money, cement, fertilizer, and armed reinforcements. But the power relationship is one-way. The next needed step in the political development of representative government in Vietnam is the establishment of district councils *with power.* They can provide the milieu of bargaining and negotiation that marks the two-way power struggle between a legislature and executive anywhere. This would be a great step forward in giving Saigon effective political relations with the countryside.

It is no longer true, as it indeed was in 1964, that the only capable political structure in Vietnam is the Viet Cong. It is no longer obvious that except for American forces the Viet Cong would take over Vietnam. I do not believe that anyone can now be sure what would happen if all United States and North Vietnamese forces were withdrawn. The increasing references to a reduced American role and to the gradual transfer of activities to ARVN and to GVN hands is not, as snide critics assert, simply a face-saving formula by a noncandid government to camouflage its defeat. The formula means, rather, just what it says, and is being stressed now because a Vietnamese structure is emerging which has the capacity to take over more responsibility. Measures of military discipline such as desertion rates or combat performance, measures of public support for the GVN such as intelligence flow from people to officials—all tell the same story of political progress.

None of these favorable political indicators deny or contradict the very unfavorable military indicators of continuing harassment by the enemy. The increased flow of improved enemy arms and of infiltrators, the unremitting, harassing attacks on population centers, the increased casualty rate—all have their reflections in declining confidence among the public in the government's ability to protect them. The improvement of governmental capacity in South Vietnam is far from the whole story of the war and may or may not be the decisive factor in the outcome.

EQBAL AHMAD: Professor Pool has talked about the political successes in Vietnam. Professor Hoffmann has insisted that we continue somehow to delude ourselves with this kind of information. I would like to compare notes on elections to see what those elections in Vietnam actually meant.

My feeling would be, given the nature of the Vietnamese conflict, that probably each of the elections—and I believe this last was the fourteenth election in Vietnam since 1950—has actually helped to hold together the National Liberation Front. Let me explain why.

A guerrilla war, by any standard, is predicated upon the fact that the civilian population, or at least a large part of it, is overtly neutral and covertly supporting the guerrillas; for if the people become overtly for the guerrillas in large parts of the area, the guerrilla war will become a full-fledged civil war of conventional type and the civilian population will be subjected to open war. Therefore, what the guerrillas try to do is not to expose the civilians to governmental reprisals of any sort.

We were faced with this problem in Algeria in 1958 for the first time, when elections were held for the Fifth Republic. The political commissars of the Algerian National Liberation Front argued very cogently that the National Liberation Front must boycott the elections but must not enforce the boycott. In other words, it was believed that we should use this occasion to go to our population and say to them, "We have boycotted the elections but despite the fact that we are Arabs and honorable men, your lives are more important than our words. Therefore, if you feel in any way constrained to go and vote, go and vote; we shall understand." In most of Algeria 95 per cent of the population voted for France in 1958.

When I was in Algeria this past summer, Algerians were very excited about Vietnam—more excited, in fact, about Vietnam than about Arab guerrillas in Israel. When they started collecting money, they contributed 4 million francs to the Vietnamese National Liberation Front and only 2 million francs to the Palestine organization. When you ask them why, their answer is that the Vietnamese people were doing better.

Now, when I talked to these same people about America's record in Vietnam, they said that the Americans were doing very bad things there—they were burning villages, and, further, they were holding elections. Each time I asked them what was the matter with that, they repeated the statement of the Algerian National Liberation Front: "If you have to go and vote, then go and vote." They remembered that when as individuals they did actually go and vote, they felt degraded by the situation. The act of voting, at least in Algeria in 1958, became a matter of self-incrimination.

The result was that the political support for the National Liberation Front became more active. A guilty Algerian who had voted did more in terms of supplying information to the FLN.

Now, it seems to me, in line with all of this, that what you are considering really to be a great success in political terms, may very well be one of the great failures. I feel, in connection with these Algerian elections, that a repressive power that holds elections under such situations is out of its mind.

IthIEL DE SOLA POOL: It seems to me that we have here a beautiful example of a central problem in relation to this whole discussion:

the relationship between fact and broad generalization. You have raised a lot of very interesting questions of fact, and this is a level at which I think we can operate. Let's talk specifically about the village elections in Vietnam.

The villager is dependent upon the local hamlet and village chief for a number of things, including, for example, getting his identification papers, which often takes a long period of time and usually costs him a bribe, or getting his deferment from the armed services. According to large numbers of statements made by villagers, the most significant thing about the local election was that it put them into a bargaining position with these local officials. The enthusiasm of the villagers for the elections was not a question of national identification with Saigon; it was a matter of very simple and clear advantage. The power that the villagers gained was shown in the fact that about a third of the incumbents were defeated.

In a short discussion of this kind nothing can be conclusively proved. However, having looked at this problem in Vietnam, I have no doubt that the reactions to the elections were very different from those you have described in Algeria. What bothers me is the tendency to answer difficult questions about Vietnam simply by broad generalizations. Those who say that the people must support the Viet Cong because a guerrilla movement has to have popular support to survive, or who say the Vietnamese must want the Americans out because nationalist Asians are against the Western presence, have bland confidence in these *a priori* generalizations, which happen to be quite contrary to the facts. Backed by these presumptuous generalizations about what the facts must be, the generalizers become impervious to reality.

GEORGE KAHIN: Inasmuch as Professor Pool raised the importance of knowing the facts for the effective functioning of social scientists, it should be made clear that it is very difficult to get some of the relevant facts. Some of us, at least for the last six months, have been trying to get from our government the district-by-district election returns with regard to the constituent assembly elections and those of last fall. They still are not being made available to us.

Nevertheless, it is quite clear that one problem the United States has encountered in trying to build up political strength in South Vietnam is that a government having a significant representative quality would probably be a government which would press for policies contrary to those we were trying to forward ourselves. One of the dilemmas we have had is that opening up really free elections in the south would probably yield a leadership which would not suit our interests; more specifically, it would be a leadership which would be very likely to work for a political accommodation with the NLF.

The elections held in the south have been so organized to screen out most of those still there who have strong nationalist credentials. In all these national elections there have been provisions for throwing out, not merely those who were charged with being procommunist or neutralist or proneutralist, but also those who had been arrested for political reasons by the French unless they were first cleared by special courts appointed by Marshal Ky.

COLONEL HAYNES: During the national elections I happened to be G-3 in I Corps, the northern five provinces in South Vietnam. The NLF, for whatever reasons I am not certain, made an all-out effort there to disrupt the elections. They blew up bridges, mined roads, blew up civilian businesses, attempted to keep people away. Nevertheless, we had about an 85 per cent turnout in the senatorial and presidential elections and about a 78 per cent turnout in the house elections.

With regard to pacification, I think that pacification in our area is beginning to work. I have been away since January 1968, but we have a combined action program whereby we put in a Marine squad with a platoon of Popular Forces. I think this probably has been a most successful effort. It has certainly proved itself in considerable part during the offensives against Danang and surrounding areas, for, as you know, the Viet Cong did not get in. The information we were given as a result of the combined action units around there enabled us to thwart their efforts. I do think there are some hopeful signs—I do not think it is all a failure.

A Democracy Intervenes

§§ SIR ROBERT THOMPSON: I must assume that it is the grand strategy of the United States to promote peace, freedom, progress and prosperity throughout the world and, for that purpose, to maintain both its power and prestige, not least in relation to those of its possible enemies. I would define United States power to include military, technological, and economic advances, the unity of its people, and the strengthening of its alliances, while prestige covers its reputation in every sense, including moral, and its influence for good in the world.

In terms of grand strategy the initial intervention must be justifiable and acceptable to the great majority in both countries, and the justification must be maintainable through every stage of the involvement. The intervention, which implies the application of power and the commitment of prestige, must also be effective and successful if there is to be no harmful effect on grand strategy. Further, the manner in which the success is achieved is as important as the success itself. Power can be applied, but not brute force. "Massive retaliation" is not the successor to the gunboat. It is no good "winning" in such a way that both the power and prestige of the United States lose their credibility. In the long run and in terms of grand strategy that, too, would be defeat. The form of the intervention, or response, must therefore be tailored both to achieve success and to maintain the justification. Failure, or a long-drawn-out agony eventually successful, can also lead to the argument within the United States not to get involved again and within other countries not to accept any form of United States intervention or aid. Both are clearly dangerous conclusions, but after Vietnam they will have a strong following.

One fact of life emerges. The less the justification, the quicker the successful action must be. There is no doubt that if victory in Vietnam had been achieved by 1963, there would have been resounding applause all round, and even if achieved in 1966, after the commitment of the United States forces and the bombing of the north, little harm would have been done and most criticism would have been stilled. The longer the period and the larger the scale of the involvement are likely to be, the better must be the cause if damage to grand strategy is to be avoided. This all leads to the awkward conclusion that it is safer to back a quick winner who may be wrong than a slow loser who may be right.

As intervention proceeds, factors may arise which require either a reduction in the aim or even its abandonment. For this reason there should always be some flexibility in the policy so that more than one option remains open. Where, however, the policy is maintained and an increasing cost is accepted, the aim should always remain positive and constructive at the point of intervention. It is hardly fair to the country and people involved if it is not. To suggest now that the American intervention in Vietnam can be justified on the grounds that, even if it fails, it has at least given time for the fences beyond to be mended, is not exactly the purpose for which the South Vietnamese have made such sacrifices.

Another great problem affecting democratic governments is that a policy may change when a government changes through the process of elections. For this reason no major involvement can be undertaken unless the commitment has a large measure of popular and bipartisan support so that it is binding on successor governments. This was the case in Malaya during the Emergency and over confrontation, and has been the case in Vietnam. But if there is now any hint or indication of a change of policy, then it is bound to have a most damaging effect on confidence, which is the most precious of all the assets. Confidence, in fact, will be Hanoi's priority target during the rest of this year, both in Vietnam and at the negotiating table.

To a lesser extent Western democracies are also weakened because decisions and action are frequently timed to suit the convenience of domestic politics rather than the needs of the situation. It is my own view that if the decision was going to be taken to involve American combat forces in South Vietnam, then it would have been far better to have committed them early in 1964 rather than in 1965, when they were only just in time to prevent total collapse. It will be one of the historical questions whether President Kennedy would or would not have done this when President Johnson could not.

THEODORE DRAPER: Sir Robert raises a broad general issue of the relationship between justification and success when he says: "One fact of life emerges. The less the justification, the quicker the successful action must be. There is no doubt that if victory in Vietnam had been achieved by 1963, there would have been resounding applause all round."

By "justification" I suppose we mean political justification, and by "success" military success. If so, then I am not sure about Sir Robert's proposition. We have had two cases in recent American history of quick military successes. One of these was the case of Guatemala in 1954, and another the case of the Dominican Republic in 1965.

If we look at both of these apparent successes, the problem is not what it appears to be. In the case of Guatemala the operation was a ridiculously small one, involving a few men and a few planes. The Arbenz regime was easily overthrown because it lacked control of the Guatemalan army. We got away with it there with an absurdly small outlay, but it turned out that there was an intimate connection between the Guatemala coup of 1954 and Castro's victory in 1959. The lesson Castro drew from the Guatemalan coup was that you have to overthrow and destroy the existing army, root and branch. Guatemala's experience made Castro's position very persuasive to most Cubans. It may be, therefore, that what seems like a success in one country may lead to an even greater failure in another country and that the total cost of the Guatemala coup is not yet in.

In the Dominican case the intervention was an unmitigated political disaster. It was a political disaster because it demonstrated that the United States did not know the difference between reform and revolution, between what was at most a little social democracy and communism. This is again something we are going to have to pay for in country after country, and the returns are not yet in.

Where our politics cannot be justified, a military success, even of the quickest kind, won't retrieve the issue for us. It will merely purchase time in a very superficial way. For the cost of political bankruptcy tends to go far beyond the country where we exhibit it and far beyond the immediate issue. On the other hand, where there is a deep, clearly understood political justification, we can actually take a great deal of military failure and overcome it. Where political justification is lacking, no kind of military success will in the long run carry us through.

JAMES C. THOMSON, JR.: Two points. First, Sir Robert Thompson has said: "In terms of grand strategy the initial intervention must be justifiable and acceptable to the great majority in both countries, and the justification must be maintainable through every stage of the involvement." It seems to me that this degree of "acceptance" for the act of intervention is almost impossible of attainment, not to mention measurement. It was certainly difficult to achieve in our initial or later stages of involvement in Vietnam.

Second, it is impossible to deal with the Vietnam intervention without taking into account our government's preoccupation with public relations. Throughout the conflict, words have been of paramount importance. I refer here to the problem of oversell and the impact of rhetorical escalation. As has been suggested, in an important sense Vietnam has become of crucial significance to us because we have said that it is of crucial significance.

The key here is domestic politics: the need to sell the American people, press, and Congress on support for an unpopular and costly war in which the objectives themselves have been in flux. To sell means to persuade, and to persuade means rhetoric. As the difficulties and costs have mounted, so has the definition of the stakes. This is not to say that rhetorical escalation is an orderly process; executive prose is the product of many writers, and some concepts— North Vietnamese infiltration, America's "national honor," Red China as the chief enemy—have entered the rhetoric only gradually and even sporadically. But there is an upward spiral nonetheless. And once you have said that the "American experiment" itself stands or falls on the Vietnam outcome, you have thereby created a national stake far beyond any earlier stakes.

The Strategy of Intervention

§§ SIR ROBERT THOMPSON: All intervention by a major power in the affairs of a smaller power is political in intent, whether it is the commitment of military forces on a grand scale, whether it is the provision of economic assistance, or whether it is merely the offer of free education overseas. The difference is only one of degree, i.e., the extent of the involvement.

All intervention is designed to influence performance, alignments, and thereby events in a manner favorable to the major power and its policies. For this purpose there is a vast orchestra of instruments available, from the flutes of culture through the strings of economic aid to the drums of military power. All can be played either in turn or in harmony. The problem is the harmony.

The extent of the involvement at any stage will be influenced by the past relationships of the two countries concerned as well as by the circumstances which give rise to the intervention. United States involvement in the affairs of Latin American countries is likely to be easier than in, say, African countries for many obvious reasons; whereas British involvement in the affairs of former colonial territories, where relationships remain good, could be easier still. British troops, for example, were immediately committed to support Malaysia in its confrontation with Indonesia without any unfavorable reaction.

Another point affecting the extent of involvement and the problem of harmony is that all intervention tends to be progressive, not only in the physical sense of a continual one step more, which through lack of balance increases the problem of harmony, but also in the political sense. In this respect the major power gradually makes its commitment more absolute, thereby reducing its options and, in its relationship with the smaller power, passing from a position where it is reluctant to appear as interfering at all, through one of intervention with undertones of colonialism, to one where it is prepared to play god with the future of the country. It is obvious that President Eisenhower in 1954, when he offered "to assist the Government of Vietnam in developing and maintaining a strong, viable state capable of resisting attempted subversion or aggression through military means," did not envisage the military and legal escalation of the war, the progressive United States political intervention in Vietnamese affairs, nor the almost complete American responsibility for the outcome. Is the United States now prepared to impose an unfavorable peace which may decide the fate of the country on the government of South Vietnam?

Somerset Maugham once defined the inevitable as "only what a fool hasn't the wit to avoid." If this harsh definition is accepted, then how can an apparently inevitable process be avoided and how can the instruments of intervention be used to achieve success? This needs to be considered in terms of grand strategy, policy, and strategy.

The question whether or not to intervene in a particular case which fits the grand strategy is a matter of policy. The first consideration is the extent of the national interest involved, the second the nature of the threat or the enemy, the third the weaknesses and assets of the country concerned, and the fourth the availability of suitable resources. It is probably true to say that where the threat is very limited or abstract, e.g., famine, poverty, illiteracy, etc., and where the assets of the country in terms of its form of government, the character of its people, its social and economic structure, etc., are stronger than its weaknesses, e.g., a poor administration, arid soil, overpopulation, etc., then the national interest does not have to be so great to become involved. But the greater the threat and the more pronounced the weaknesses (or "contradictions") within the threatened country, then the more will be the resources that may have to be expended and the greater will have to be the national interest before becoming involved.

Many questions have to be answered correctly, and the answers then have to be weighed in relation to each other before a decision can be reached. I remember on my first annual leave from Vietnam in the spring of 1962 being asked two questions immediately by the then Foreign Secretary about the South Vietnamese: "Will they fight?" and "Are they worth fighting for?" I answered "yes" to both, which I certainly think was correct at the time. But there was a third question which Americans should have been asking all the time: "How far are they worth fighting for?"

The decision to intervene cannot be reached unless the aim has first been fixed. My own attempt to define the aim in the case of South Vietnam has been on the following lines: to establish a South Vietnam which is free, united, independent, politically stable, and economically expanding. This is not too far removed from the aim originally expressed by President Eisenhower, except that he added "capable of resisting attempted subversion and aggression by military means." This was an error because it slanted the aim and influenced the measures taken to achieve it. The achievement of my aim would certainly have defeated subversion and would in turn have deterred aggression by military means. Because such action would have been too overt and would have been universally condemned. The wrong definition of the original threat (the Korea complex) and the build-up of too large and conventional an army to meet it were the beginning of the tragedy.

Depending on the answers to the questions, it may not appear possible to achieve the ideal aim. The aim must be feasible at a reasonable cost, and it may be necessary, therefore, to set a limited aim in the hope that some initial success and changing circumstances will enable more to be achieved later. Indeed, my own aim should be qualified by the addition of the words "at a cost acceptable to the United States."

Having decided to intervene and having laid down the national aim, the major power must then decide what means will be allocated to achieve it. This is the final policy decision. The deployment and application of the means, both military and civil, is strategy.

Before deciding the strategy, a full assessment has to be made both of the threat and of the assets, including all factors which are relevant to both. If it is assumed that the threat is communist subversion with outside support, which could lead to insurgency and increasing infiltration, then all its strengths—e.g., its propagation of a nationalist cause, its social reform program, its organization, etc.—and all its weaknesses—e.g., minority support, lack of weapons, etc.—must be analyzed and clearly understood. All the assets and weaknesses (the "contradictions" which will be exploited by the enemy) of the threatened government must be similarly analyzed. This is not a task which can be carried out solely by an intelligence agency or military intelligence. It requires a professional team covering all fields of government. When the assessment has been made, then the strategy, conforming with the national aim, can be formulated in a single plan applying all available means to achieve the aim. It is at this point that there should be a review as to whether the means are adequate, and if not, whether they should be increased or the aim reduced. In practice, at an early stage in an insurgency the means are likely to be more than adequate.

The assessment itself should clarify what the strategy should be. Broadly the strategy should be designed to reduce the potential of the enemy's threat and to exploit his weaknesses while improving the government's assets and eliminating its weaknesses. The strategy, therefore, is both constructive and destructive, both offensive and defensive, both positive and negative. We hear a lot today about defeating the main enemy forces, pacification, and nation building. The problem is to get these in the right order and well balanced at all stages. The constructive offensive aim must come first, and that is nation building. The destruction of the enemy forces comes last, and their containment during the nation building is defensive. Pacification, or the restoration of government authority throughout the country, is the link between the two.

If the strategy goes wrong and a proper balance is not maintained, then the cost will automatically rise. A situation will develop where, instead of policy dictating strategy, it is the other way around. Strategy will first begin to dictate the means required and second the measures required, and the policy-makers will be dragged along with it. As the demands go up, the question which should be asked is not whether they should be met, but whether the strategy is correct.

The key to intervention is the strategy, that is, the deployment of the means to achieve the aim. The means, as suggested, are many: economic, financial, educational, cultural, political (in the narrower sense of support or pressure), and military. They must all be fitted together in one plan in order of priority and be correctly balanced. No progress will be made unless the advance is balanced, coordinated, and consolidated.

To ensure this there are two initial requirements. The first is a good working relationship between the major power and the threatened country. It is in this area that the greatest political difficulty will arise, both for the threatened country and for the major power. The former will be most sensitive about protecting its newest and most precious asset: its independent sovereignty. On the other hand, the major power will not wish to appear, either in the threatened country or before world opinion, as interfering internally within the threatened country or imposing any form of control which might be construed as colonialism. It does, however, have to be recognized that any power which is prepared to offer its blood, treasure, and prestige in assisting a threatened country must have some say in what happens. The country being assisted cannot expect, merely out of deference to its sovereignty, to be allowed to squander these gifts recklessly. It follows that the working relationship must be established on a strong basis. This requires a formal agreement of some sort.

Normally this would be a treaty, not one of protection in the old style, which would be quite unacceptable to both parties and in fact impractical to work, but one made between two sovereign states—thereby emphasizing the sovereignty of each—and laying down the arrangement by which the two parties would consult in order to reach agreement on joint action. (I fully recognize the great difficulty under the United States Constitution of making such a treaty. Nevertheless, it should be possible to achieve some such formal agreement instead of leaving it to the very loose, although admirable, concept that the United States "is helping the people of Vietnam to help themselves.")

Even now in Vietnam joint action is still a critical problem. While recent arrangements have achieved a better coordination of the American effort, it is still impossible to find an individual Vietnamese below the president who can issue an order that carries weight throughout the government of Vietnam.

One desired result of the formal agreement would be the establishment of a joint war council with suitable representation for both parties, such as ministers of the threatened country and local heads of agencies providing aid. All major decisions affecting both parties would then be put to this council for decision and approval. The council would be served by a small joint secretariat which would issue such decisions as directives and instructions to government ministries, supporting agencies, and military commands to ensure that they are distributed and obeyed right down the line on both sides. It would be the responsibility of the council to review policies, to supervise their implementation, and to make such modifications as necessary.

Preferably the prime minister (or president) of the threatened country and the ambassador of the United States would not be members of the council, so that in the event of disagreement between the two sides on the council the matter could be submitted to the respective governments at this higher level. The prime minister and ambassador can then reach agreement, or if this fails, they can suspend consideration of the particular subject until a more suitable opportunity. This at least will avoid tension and squabbles at the council table, where there should be no question of one side being in a position to outvote the other.

Obviously it is desirable that there be good personal relationships between counterparts at every level. These are more readily established if their respective responsibilities and obligations are formally defined both in the agreement and in the council's directives, one of the first of which should provide for the necessary coordination to implement decisions below council level at province and district. Personal relationships, however good, should be used only to grease the wheels of the machinery, not to take over its functions. If two counterparts at any level, including the prime minister and the ambassador, discuss a certain line of policy and reach agreement on it, then this agreement should be processed through the appropriate coordinating machinery in order to ensure that it is issued as a directive and that all relevant details are covered. If this is not done and action is taken on such a verbal agreement by both parties through their own channels, there is bound to be misunderstanding and there will certainly be a lot of loose ends. Loose ends always flap, and will flap hardest at the end of the line where the agreement has to be implemented on the ground.

One great advantage of such a formal agreement is that the major power becomes identified with those policies of the threatened country which are designed to achieve the aim. It does not become so apparently involved in other policies of the local government, with some of which it would not wish to be associated. The major power, in its political involvement, wants to get across that it is supporting, not individual members of the local government, but the people of the country and policies that are of benefit to the people. There is always the difficult problem of local individual politicians to whom the major power does not want to become too committed. While it will be necessary to work with them in order to achieve the aim, it is not always desirable to be committed to all for which they stand. They must be used rather than supported.

A further advantage of formal machinery is that it will help the major power to solve the second vital initial requirement. This is that all its own agencies and officials must speak with one voice and act in unison in furtherance of the aim and in accordance with the plan. Perhaps the most depressing feature of the American effort in Vietnam for many years has been its lack of unity. It was not until the summer of 1967 that any real steps were taken to solve this problem. Even now it is not ideal.

Any lack of unity in the ranks of the major power will naturally spill over and cause disunity within the government of the threatened country. There will also be an attempt on the part of local ministries and departments to play one agency off against another in the demands for material aid and especially weapons.

Even within agencies there are a number of human tendencies

that must be kept in check. Where relationships between two counterparts are good, there will be a temptation to increase the aid, out of turn and not in accordance with the plan, because it will be thought that such additional aid will be more effectively used and that the "response" should be met. The switching about of aid in this manner will soon throw the plan and programs out of balance and cause confusion. It will also lead to a situation where individuals are merely fighting their own little war without regard to anyone else. This became very apparent in Vietnam from the beginning of the strategic hamlet program onward, with the result that every province was fighting its own war. This can be fatal when one is up against an enemy whose organization and control are superb and rigidly monolithic.

Directors of agencies must also beware of their specialists, who are likely to have a narrow view of the war as a whole and who have an interest solely in completing their own pet project. That is what they are there for, and they will press ahead with their project in order to complete it within their tour of duty, without regard to whether their action suits the particular phase of the campaign or makes any contribution to victory. This will have two effects.

First, there will be a tendency to overload the country with aid beyond what it can absorb at any given time. Much of that aid will be irrelevant, and some of it will mainly benefit the enemy (symbiosis).

Second, the capital and provincial cities will become overcrowded with an unnecessary foreign presence. Saigon apartments today are full of well-intentioned experts, who would make a greater contribution to victory if they returned to the United States. A minor facet of this unproductive activity is that these people, while they are in the country, tie up a fair proportion of the better-trained and -educated Vietnamese, who could be much more usefully employed. The cabinets of United States departments are stuffed with research reports which few have read and upon which no action is going to be taken. It may be fascinating to discover that the dreams of the Popular Forces are only .05 per cent sexual, but it is not likely to win the war. It merely suggests to me that they are underpaid and underfed, and everyone knows that anyway.

To check all these tendencies and to ensure a united effort, the ambassador must be a proconsul with absolute authority locally over all policy and agencies. The problem that needs to be solved is that of the command channels between agencies locally—including military headquarters—and their head offices in Washington. It is easy enough to say that all policy questions affecting any agency should be routed through the ambassador for his approval and that direct communications between local agencies and their headquarters should be confined to administrative and logistic measures within approved policy, but definite machinery needs to be established to ensure that effect is being given to this.

If the strategy of intervention is to be successful, the first two prerequisites are, therefore, organization and control. Control presupposes that the ambassador will be given full support at the highest level in Washington. The relationship of General Templer with Sir Winston Churchill and Mr. Oliver Lyttleton (the Minister responsible for Malaya) and the complete support given to him was the key to his success. The General was given a free hand, within his directive, and full backing. Churchill was reputed to have said to the General on his appointment: "General, to few men in this world is it given to have absolute power. Relish it!"

For the reasons I have indicated earlier, it has been difficult for the United States to impose and maintain control. When President Eisenhower committed the United States to assist the government of Vietnam, he hoped that the aid would be followed "by performance on the part of the government of Vietnam in undertaking needed reforms." In this context, while aid in many forms can be injected, there is one aspect which will constantly frustrate the donor. It does not necessarily follow that standards and ways of life can be simultaneously transferred to a people living in a totally different environment and in almost a different age. It takes a long time to influence cultural and political changes. Ideas will seep in naturally, as they have done for centuries, and standards may slowly be improved, if only by imitation. This is an evolutionary process which can be slightly accelerated by the form of aid but not by its volume. Neither the provision of material aid nor the threat to withhold it are suitable levers for this purpose. In conditions of insurgency it is madness to suppose that reforms can be achieved by a revolutionary process. The only revolution is the one which the insurgent is promoting.

In terms of "performance" the donor can only assist the local government to function more efficiently. Improved performance in this respect will create a more fertile and able soil for the seeds of political and social reform and of higher standards. The people must grow these for themselves. Some will flourish, some will wither, while others may take years to germinate. The real purpose of all aid, therefore, should be to help the local government improve its organization and services and to get its departments working more efficiently. For this reason both the form and the volume of aid require very careful consideration.

In every field, including the military, training is the first priority. Whereas on the military side standards are well-established and training, as a result, is comparatively thorough, there is a tendency on the civilian side to lower the standards, to skimp the training, and, in times of crisis, to indulge in crash programs. This is a fatal mistake. Unless an effective administration is maintained and constantly improved by the recruitment and training of the best young men in the country, all national policies and all ideas for political and social reform remain completely meaningless, because without performance by a professional administration none of them can be carried out.

This training requirement applies to both administrative officers in the ministries and provinces and to all technical departments, including the police force. The training of professional officers and qualified technical assistants at all levels in the administration to provide services and to perform duties which are of direct benefit to the people is far more productive (and probably cheaper) than constant crash programs for the training of political and revolutionary development cadres. If this training is promoted right from the start and continued without interruption, then a steady production line will be established by the time the situation becomes critical. If, instead, because demands are urgent and impatience wins the day, training is reduced and short crash programs are instituted, there will be a constant supply of inexperienced, incompetent, useless officials who will be incapable of implementing any policy and who will merely add to the prevailing confusion.

Many factors have contributed to the decimation of the administration in Vietnam, including terrorist assassinations, *coups d'état,* and the draft. The government machine is the first asset which has to be secured and its weaknesses eliminated. As an asset no conscious effort was made to improve it, and it is now less of an asset than it was in the 1950's (compare, for example, the handling of the refugee problem in 1954–55 with the present). I have not yet met any American in Saigon who has any clue as to what the establishment or structure of any Vietnamese ministry or department should be to enable it to carry out its functions. It does not require much "assistance" to work this out, together with terms of service and pay, simplified and more modern government procedures, and the consolidation and clarification of the law.

The introduction of an adequate and equitable taxation system, with emphasis on indirect taxation, is another vital measure, because lack of revenue is one of the major weaknesses. This is one area where the Viet Cong have out-administered the government of Vietnam. Undertaxation was an unfortunate colonial legacy.

The second priority for aid, particularly during an insurgency, is to improve the communication system of the country, including roads, bridges, canals, small airfields, and radio networks. This is important from the point of view of deployment of forces, but far more so to increase the marketing potential and development of the rural areas of the country. It does not need massive projects, though a coastal steamer service, which could have been promoted as a commercial proposition, was an obvious deficiency in Vietnam. I remember being asked in 1962 by M. Thuan (secretary of state at the presidency) what I thought of a proposal to build a major bridge over the Mekong. I said it was crazy. Such a project would tie up all the engineering resources of the country for years, and there were hundreds of little bridges that were more important than the Mekong, where the ferries worked perfectly satisfactorily.

The third priority is economic aid, and in most underdeveloped countries this means one thing only—to improve the agricultural production of the country. The aim is growth rather than development, in the hope of achieving a synergetic process with as many self-generating side effects as possible. A 5 per cent increase in agricultural production alone makes a far greater impact on the economy of a peasant country than a 500 per cent increase in the production of manufactured goods through subsidized promotion of secondary industry. It was "economic assistance" for which President Diem asked. Figures are often quoted to show that the great majority of the aid given to him was economic, yet in 1960 the amount of USOM aid devoted to the improvement of agriculture was about 1 per cent. Most of the economic aid was indirectly designed to support the military program—that fatal slant.

Without the training of personnel to improve efficiency and without more production to increase revenue, all attempts to improve social services—the fourth priority—will fail. This applies equally to the fifth priority, which includes all the minor projects of a rural aid program designed to benefit the peasants that are not covered by the previous priorities.

If the items of aid are tackled in this order, then it will be easier to control both the form and the volume of aid. I am sure it is true that the less the aid given—so that the threatened country is compelled to rely on its own resources and to improve its tax collection—the more satisfactory the results will be. (Above all, the temptation should be resisted by the country giving aid to carry out projects itself through outside contractors because the local government is unable to undertake them.)

The volume of aid must be kept to a level which the country can digest without overloading either the administration or the economy. However tempting it may be to rush ahead when great resources are available, the inevitable result will be that the government machine will grind to a halt. It is not, after all, the primary purpose of government ministries and departments to receive aid. Their function is to govern and administer the country, not to act as chain stores for retailing foreign aid. A point to bear in mind is that if the insurgency expands, the capacity of the local government to absorb aid will decline. This is where ruthless control must be exercised to limit projects and items of aid solely to those which will be immediately productive.

With regard to the form and the volume of aid, it is necessary to consider how far contributions should be made to capital and annually recurrent expenditures of the local government. The emphasis should be on the former. There should be a great reluctance to become involved in annually recurrent expenditures, particularly where it may lead to the introduction of a commodity import program to provide the necessary currency. Such a program plays havoc with the normal commercial life of a country and is likely to cause commercial demoralization. As a side effect, it may even vitiate aid provided through other channels because of competition between imported commodities and those produced by secondary industry. This problem with regard to textiles in South Vietnam was finally solved when the United States Air Force bombed and gutted textile factories during the Tet offensive!

On the military side I have mentioned that training, because standards are well established, is normally thorough, though more could have been done in training junior leadership. There is also little problem in providing capital in the form of equipment, weapons, transport, barracks, airfields, etc. But, as with economic aid, here it is even more important that the threatened country should not be overloaded with armed forces which it cannot possibly support and which throw the whole political, social, and economic stability of the country out of balance.

In Vietnam the temptation to use the enormous surplus military resources of the United States could not be resisted. I have always regarded, and still do, the creation of a large conventional army inside South Vietnam as the basic cause of the failure to defeat communist insurgency there. The very size of the army fomented political instability because political power inevitably rested, and still does, with control of the army. It also compelled the introduction of the commodity import program to pay for it. Its conventional organization encouraged local warlordism and the mounting of operations quite unsuited to guerrilla warfare. Because the army was the source of political power and could offer reasonable careers and prospects of promotion, it also attracted all the best young men in the country, so that other essential services were starved. This has led to the absurd situation in which nearly all the important civilian posts in the country are held by inexperienced army officers, while skilled civilians have been drafted into the army.

There were many other harmful side effects of the creation of a large conventional army, such as an automatic escalation of costs (a soldier is the most expensive individual), the rule of force rather than the rule of law (a soldier is a blunt instrument), and the usurping of civil functions (a soldier is covetous of power).

What is required instead, particularly in the early stages of combatting insurgency, is a small elite army, highly mobile and capable of being deployed and switched to operations anywhere in the country in accordance with priorities laid down in the plan. For the main security framework within the country a territorial force also is required. This can only be the police force. It is an incredible commentary on the present situation in Vietnam that the police force has not yet reached a strength which the country would require in normal times of peace and has hardly been trained except to carry weapons.

If and when additional armed manpower is required, it should be recruited into a paramilitary type of force stationed in the localities from which it is recruited. This force should be hooked to the framework of the police force at least for operational purposes. In Vietnam the proliferation of forces has drained the country of its productive manpower without greatly increasing its capacity to defend itself.

It is a matter of judgment, rather than formula, to decide the size of the army an underdeveloped country can support. It is bound to vary, but there is a limit—perhaps roughly one division to 4 or 5 million people. If, when that limit has been reached, a further threat of a military nature develops, then is the moment for the major power to decide whether to commit its own forces. The great danger of the Indonesian threat to Malaysia during confrontation was that Malaysia would be forced to expand its army (of less than two divisions) at the expense of its other programs. That was avoided by the commitment of British forces at the outset.

As part of the process of strengthening the government's assets, the question will arise as to just how far the major power can, in support of the aid program, bring political pressure to bear on the local government to undertake "the needed reforms" expected of it. Great caution has to be exercised in this sphere to avoid creating either an issue where it did not exist or resentment by the local government being pressured to reform at an unacceptable pace.

Land reform is a good example of the first. In the early years of the Diem administration some progress was made in the break-up of large rice-field estates and the redistribution of land. This, however, was not really a major issue in South Vietnam, where there is not an over-all shortage of land. The main problem with regard to land has been its administration, i.e., surveys, issues of titles, land acquisition, and the opening up of new land. There remained plenty of uninformed critics, however, who continued to scratch where it didn't itch, thereby creating an exploitable weakness.

When a government is under pressure in time of war or insurgency and its main concern is the defense of the country, there will always be a tendency to hold firmly to the reins of power, to impose restrictions, to rely on the faithful and to ignore the "nervous Nellies." There will be few opportunities to press for "the broadening of the administration." It was interesting to watch this same process in action in the United States during 1967. One could almost hear the ghost of President Diem saying to President Johnson, "Mr. President, why don't you broaden the base of your administration?"

In approaching political and social reforms the best line to take is undoubtedly a long-term rather than a short-term one. If pressure is brought to bear on an Asian minister to do something immediately, he is bound to look at the problem personally in terms of how it affects his own power position, his support and his relationship with his colleagues. If, however, his mind can be projected into the future and the question is put to him in terms of what he would like to achieve in his lifetime, then I have not yet met one who does not put forward both ideas and policies which are in every way desirable and acceptable. If this projection is encouraged, then it becomes easier to push him slowly along the steps toward its ultimate fulfillment. The process requires patience and timing. Nothing can be more calculated to halt progress than to prod hard at the wrong moment. There is in any case a built-in antipathy to the foreign advisor and to aid with strings attached, even if the only strings are those of acknowledgment and gratitude.

There may also be a tendency on the part of the major power or some of its representatives to expect more of those being aided than they themselves would be prepared to do in similar circumstances, partly because they have not thought the problem through in relation to the scene. A senior member of the American administration was once discussing with me the cliché about President Diem broadening the base of his administration. I turned to him and said: "It is all very well, sir, but if it was you, what would you do?" This completely floored him, and he turned in vain to an aide for the answer. There are now some contenders for the American presidency who quite blithely advocate that the present government of South Vietnam should accept a coalition government with the NLF, when, as far as I am aware, they have not yet announced their own readiness to appoint Mr. Stokely Carmichael as Secretary of Defense or Mr. H. Rap Brown as head of the F.B.I.

It may be noticed that in the aim which I suggested I did not use the word "democratic." The form of government which a small underdeveloped country will eventually adopt is one entirely for its own decision. Nothing could be more fatal to its political progress than to try to ram British or American institutions down its throat. These are there for it to study and imitate, if it wants to, in its own good time. But by assisting it to become "free, united, independent, politically stable, and economically expanding," the best possible foundation for the eventual adoption of a democratic system of government is being laid. Without this secure base and the rule of law, democracy on the Western model is for the birds.

Much prominence is now given in South Vietnam to the many side effects of the war—inflation, corruption, nepotism, black market, prostitution, and so on. For an Asian country, South Vietnam has always had its fair share of these, but no more than others. Their rapid growth can be attributed to the breakdown of government, the trend of the war, and the massive scale of intervention, all of which have encouraged an every-man-for-himself outlook. As one of the indications of how the war is going, the military are fondest of quoting the casualty figures. If, however, a general was asked how he would equate this seeming advantage with the demoralization of Vietnamese society, he would be inclined to brush it aside as irrelevant. It is not the South Vietnamese alone who are entirely to blame for the current state of affairs. They may be corrupt, but they have also been corrupted.

The objective of strengthening assets and eliminating weaknesses applies also to the conduct of the war itself. It is a basic principle of counterinsurgency that a government must secure its base areas first. "Base areas" include, not just main towns, ports, and military installations, but also the highly developed populated areas on which the country depends both for its manpower and its economy. At the outbreak of an insurgency these areas are the least threatened, for the main insurgent activity will occur in remoter areas, on the fringes of jungle and swamp. By securing these base areas first, at a time when the process should be comparatively easy, the government is not only providing itself with a safe base but is consolidating its control over the material assets of the country. This will tend to confine the insurgent to remoter areas where the assets are less. The failure to adopt this principle is well exemplified by the present situation in

Vietnam, where there are no secure base areas, where the insurgent threat is not confined, and where the Viet Cong have access to all the assets.

On the negative as opposed to the positive side, it should be the objective of the government to reduce the enemy's assets and to exploit his weaknesses. The greatest weakness of an insurgent is the very fact that he is in rebellion against the constituted authority. There is a very great advantage in being the government. It is not just that the insurgent is committing treason but that he is also committing nearly every crime in the penal code. He is also destructive, for it is one of his objectives to cause a breakdown of government and to destroy the government's assets. The government should be able to show that, enticing though some of the promises propagated by the insurgent may be, the prospect of their fulfillment, judged by performance elsewhere—e.g., in North Vietnam—is remote. Not everything in the promised land is rosy. One of the Canadian commissioners on the I.C.C. told me that he was traveling one day with the Polish commissioner by car from Hanoi to Haiphong, observing conditions under which the peasant was harvesting. He asked the Polish commissioner what would happen if the peasant was treated like that in Poland and got the reply: "There'd be a counterrevolution, and I'd be in it!"

Just as the insurgent is trying to cause a breakdown of government, so must the government make its main target the breakdown of the insurgent organization. It is a basic principle of counterinsurgency that the government must give priority to destroying the insurgent's political underground organization, not his guerrilla units. I do not think guerrilla units can be destroyed unless the political underground organization is broken first. Even if they could be, the war would be far from won. In fact, it could still be lost. But if the political underground organization is broken, then the guerrilla units must automatically wither.

The key to success in this field is an efficient intelligence organization, which has never existed in Vietnam. One of the reasons for this has again been the preponderance of military control. Military intelligence is interested only in the order of battle, in guerrilla and main-force units. It is not concerned with the laborious process of identifying the individuals in the political underground organization, commonly referred to as the "infrastructure." It has proved impossible to persuade the military that if you target on the infrastructure, this will lead to the order of battle, but if you target on the order of battle, you will not get the infrastructure. Another reason for the intelligence failure has been the proliferation of the intelligence services, both Vietnamese and American. In the Saigon area alone in 1966 there were seventeen intelligence organizations operating, most of which did not talk to each other. Only now, ten years late, is a serious attempt being made to solve this problem.

A failure of strategy, in applying the means to achieve the aim, will frequently lead to a policy of increasing the means. Costs, in every sense, will then soar until they reach a point where they are no longer acceptable. If the enemy can contrive a situation where his costs are indefinitely acceptable while the costs of the threatened government and the major power are not, then he has achieved a winning position. In this situation a further escalation of costs is obviously out of the question and the remaining options are only to reduce or abandon the aim.

If it is still practicable to switch the strategy in Vietnam and so reduce the costs, it would be interesting—as a first step in this process—to study what, in fact, could be maintained if costs were cut from the present $30 billion to $20 billion (and later less) and whether, if such a reduction were made, it would be necessary to reduce the aim. It is one of the functions of a successful strategy to ensure an economy of effort, to keep the cost down in terms of men, money, and materials, and to maintain justification and support for the intervention.

The history of war has shown that the most successful strategy is always indirect, and the same applies to the strategy of intervention. The less direct the intervening power is in its approach to every problem, the more likely is it to be successful. It has never paid to go head first down the line of toughest resistance and, when that failed, to pour more in.

§§ JOHN McDERMOTT: Before commenting on Sir Robert Thompson's statement, I want to make a few remarks about the framework for discussion. Since 1965, discussions of Vietnam have been dominated by a focus on the role of the military. There has been a tendency to cast too much of the blame for the present situation on the military. The Vietnamese problem is not that easy. Nor can you argue that the failures are administrative—that this AID chief or that CIA chief "goofed" from 1954 through 1959. In the early years the Diem government in fact had the benefit of fairly sophisticated and quite technically competent American advice. They had learned some lessons by observing the French, but the application of the lessons did not work out for two reasons.

In the first place, they tried to build in South Vietnam a Western puppet government. Secondly, they failed to understand what the North Vietnamese government had achieved in the period after the Geneva agreements. I am not just talking about economic development. I am talking about North Vietnam's achievements in popular participation in the political and social process, in avoiding the worst excesses we associate with communism, in laying the groundwork for a fairly decent society, and in political decentralization.

With this preliminary, let me come directly to what Sir Robert Thompson has just presented to us. It is a strong point of Sir Robert's presentation that he shows limited enthusiasm for the more comprehensive nation building schemes so popular in American policy now and in the past, in Vietnam and in a host of other places. I would take an even stronger position on this question than Sir Robert, who merely assigns such nation building a limited role as an object of policy. For a number of reasons I am persuaded that nation building is not a desirable object of policy and, obviously of greater importance, that it very likely cannot be done.

Perhaps it is hard to realize now, but as late as, say, 1961, AID and other reports originating in South Vietnam were able to point to rather extensive American-assisted progress in many areas of Vietnamese life. The affected areas included road and telecommunications, agricultural extension, training of middle level officials, health and educational services, and so forth. Having had access largely to published reports, it is very possible that I am deceived as to the degree of progress actually recorded, but I think not. Extensive conversations with persons who served in Vietnam in the late fifties, as well as moderate access to field reports, confirm this conclusion. At least until 1961 and *in terms of the scheme then and now used by officials committed to the nation building enterprise*, South Vietnam's development was very near the outstanding success story its enthusiasts claimed; there really was a "little *Wirtschaftswunder*."

If this is true we need to revise our views on the possibility and desirability of nation building, as that term is understood. Since I have written fairly extensively on this elsewhere, perhaps the following brief argument will suffice to make my objections clear.

There is no meaningful sense in which South Vietnam has an economy; it has many economies, and their relationships to one another are largely unknown. I am not an economist, but I am not just speaking poetically. South Vietnam, and by extension other underdeveloped nations, has many economies in the sense that economic changes in one region, village, commodity, or sector bear little known relationship to changes in other regions, villages, commodities, or sectors. The reasons for this state of affairs are not hard to find: among the main ones are the relatively arbitrary way in which prices are set, buying habits in which nonprice factors are strong, marked regional differences, and poor economic communications. These reasons, of course, are very much part of what is meant by an underdeveloped economy, quite as much a part of that meaning as is low productivity.

The existence of many subeconomies thus implies that capital inputs, whether in the form of capital investment per se, goods, improved technique, or the presence of advisors, are inputs into only some of these subeconomies; and this in turn implies that the result of the input is as likely to be grave economic distortion as it is to be quickened economic growth. Something like this appears to have happened in South Vietnam, with the import subsidy program playing a leading but by no means a solo role. The reports indicate, and my conversations confirm, that urban South Vietnam experienced considerable prosperity in the fifties, a prosperity which was not shared by the countryside—in fact, a prosperity which caused significant disruption in the countryside because the presence of cheap Western goods in the larger cities tended to destroy important markets for local products. Thus I share with Sir Robert a low opinion of the worth of the import subsidy program, but *the argument against that program appears to be generalizable to any sort of capital assistance, in short, to any kind of outside assistance.*

This is not to argue that large scale crises will follow all assistance programs. It does mean that economic distortion, such as we have witnessed in South Vietnam, is a system property of assistance programs, as is unpredictable social disruption in some of the subeconomies of the underdeveloped country. Both of these will combine to cause some measure of real injustice and suffering and a consequent growth of political resentment.

Nation building theorists are aware of this problem, though they express it in a different language. They also advance a cure, and in this case the cure is worse than the disease. The cure for the economically unpredictable effects of aid programs is to equip such programs with a large array of United States advisors who will monitor their effects and make adjustments when the need arises. But the capacity of foreigners, with limited language resources and using Western economic indicators, to monitor a myriad confusion of subeconomies is not very large. Moreover, the experience of the Vietnam program indicates that it is very difficult for foreign advisors to shake free of the economic and social perceptions of the elite of the host country, an elite very likely receiving important benefits from the program. Thus assistance programs will tend to look successful even when they are not, and the discovery of distortions, disruptions, injustices, miseries, and resentments will tend to be delayed, perhaps beyond the point at which repairs can be effected.

The other liability of the monitor cure is that it creates "commitments," in Richard Barnet's sense. The more advisors you have, the more important their work; and the more talented the personnel, the more effective will be the lobby you create within your own government to increase the commitment still further.

Sir Robert Thompson's recommendation on the importance of building up the capacity of the host government to govern is not a solution. It is a bad recommendation. There is no paradox here. Stripping the recommendation of all euphemism, what it asks is that we increase the capacity of the government to exert control over its people and the various economic and social processes they engage in. In the absence of assistance to the population as a whole in the techniques of controlling their government, the recommendation is tantamount to encouraging the growth of authoritarian governments in the underdeveloped world.

A friend of mine has commented that the military junta is the chief form of government in the free world. That this is true is very much related to the one-sided character of outside assistance. It should be taken as an axiom that assistance is never neutral as regards the political relations of the governed to their governors; by strengthening the latter, you weaken the former. You are then responsible for the mischief which flows from the imbalance.

It is the height of fashion now to accept the necessity of authoritarian governments in the "third world." But consider the following model for economic development which results. Rapid economic changes create an increase in social disruption and political resentment; the process accelerates by means of capital inputs whose effects cannot effectively be monitored, in a political environment in which the populace is decreasingly able to influence the behavior of its government, including behavior which aggravates existing social fissures. All in all, a dangerous mixture.

The dysfunction here is a dysfunction in the model itself. Wise administration, caution in the number, kind, and size of projects, will tend to diminish the dysfunction but not to eliminate it entirely. The lesson of Vietnam is that dysfunction may grow rapidly from small beginnings (1957?) to a critical stage (spring 1960) before making itself felt even by the elite of the host country. In the Vietnam case it was another twelve months before the American government became aware of it.

The policy of nation building is defended as much for its supposed humanitarian aspects as for its contributions to our national power. I remain unconvinced that it can bring about stability, growth in any meaningful sense, the net alleviation of misery, or any of the other good things its enthusiasts claim for it. Two policy biases flow from my position: technical assistance should be wrenched free of its nation building aspects; project assistance—probably limited to agriculture, primary education, medical and some social services, i.e., local impact programs whose effect is calculable and easily monitored —rather than developmental (planning) assistance should be the rule.

Diplomacy should replace intervention. The two are very different. Intervention assumes that the smaller nation's international stance can best be influenced by penetrating its domestic politics—its army, trade unions, finance ministry, police, political parties, more generally its development planning. Another name for intervention of this kind is "neoimperialism." Diplomacy places the main emphasis on influencing the smaller nation's international stance directly, using a wide range of sanctions, some pacific, some not, some public, some not. The point is not that diplomacy is nicer or more liberal than intervention, merely that it intrinsically involves lower stakes and that it lacks a built-in escalator.

Western conceptions of nation building are capital intensive. They accept that an underdeveloped nation is that precisely because it lacks capital. The remedy is to import it in the form of private investments, credits, aid, subsidized goods, advisors or training programs. That supposedly is the humane remedy, but Vietnam indicates that it isn't. The other remedy, Stalin's and that of the Industrial Revolution, is to sweat capital out of the populace by working them harder and allowing them to consume less—forced saving.

Neither of these pictures of how economic development works is applicable to the NLF zones of Vietnam prior to 1965. Yet the NLF achieved considerable economic growth in those years. I think it is now conventionally accepted that the level of educational services and medical care was higher, political administration and economic management more effective, in their zones than in those of the GVN.

Another way of looking at the same thing: today's Viet Cong utilize more in the way of resources against us than their Viet Minh forebears (in the south) did against the French. The differences in magnitude appear to bear no relationship to the differences in outside assistance. On either way of looking at it, the NLF zones have developed utilizable resources of considerable magnitude, and from any perspective this represents significant economic development.

NLF development has contributed to the growth of a social system that has many enviable properties. This statement holds up even when we ignore, for the moment, everything other than their military forces. The Liberation Armed Forces have shown high capacity to adapt Western technique to local conditions, to do so rapidly and under very difficult conditions. They have been able to train very large numbers in advanced techniques, to replace heavy losses in technical personnel without marked loss in quality. The VC have excellent fire discipline, maneuver well in battle, show impressive radio technique, and coordinate their arms very effectively.

When I was in South Vietnam, company-grade United States officers were unanimous in believing their VC opposite numbers to be their professional equals. Moreover, the quality of NLF officers did not appear to deteriorate in spite of the high casualties they suffered. The population of the NLF zones—under what appear to be almost unendurable conditions because of the intensity of our fire power—continued to show high morale, continued to carry out those functions necessary to support their army, and continued to maintain their own life services—food, shelter, community organization, etc.—at a high level. In spite of reports to the contrary which originate in our official circles, there is really no reason to believe that the populace of the NLF zones dislike their Viet Cong government any more than the northerners dislike Ho's government, for the latter gets no more in the way of loyalty, ardor, and effectiveness from his people than the NLF gets from theirs. In both cases, north and south, this does not force us to believe the populace is wild about its government—only that they find it tolerable, that they respond to its efforts, that their private purposes are not so violated or frustrated by it that they are open to disaffection, and that at least in some cases it excites their enthusiasm.

Both the NLF and the DRV argue that their scheme of development places politics first. They argue that people are more important than technique and abstract doctrine, that the party cannot coerce the people—the path to revisionism—that it can only lead them, and that the masses have latent creative energies which need only to be set free of traditional social and political forms in order to achieve startling gains in their own lives and in the power of the party, movement, and state. To Western ears these phrases have the sound of pure cant or calculated deception. Yet the success of the other side in achieving things that we have tried and failed to do argues that these phrases are not entirely cant, not entirely deceptive, that they have operational meaning, and that they function within a more effective political language than that used by the nation builders.

If there is a single critical difference between the development schema used by the other side and that used by ourselves, it is this: their Marxist orientation has led them to recognize that underutilized labor is the pivotal resource for rapid economic and social development. According to available Vietnamese village studies, something in excess of 40 per cent of South Vietnam's rural labor force is largely idle eight months per year; perhaps 20 per cent are idle all but a few weeks in the planting and harvesting periods. In the NLF analysis all that stands between this idle labor and its productive employment are outmoded social and political institutions in which the bulk of the rural population have small stake. Vast capital inputs are not initially necessary to produce large economic gains. All one need do is encourage individual and village self-interest to ignore or overturn the traditional institutions, and vast reserves of labor and morale are set free. After that the party's role is not to goad further effort on the part of the populace; the surge is still there. All one need do is try to steer it into socially desirable (for the party) directions.

Two very good things follow immediately in this model. First, the things which are important to the rural populace tend to get done first. The NLF zones and DRV development history indicate that startling advances are initially made in primary education, elementary medicine, in the basic diet, and in sanitation. In North Vietnam this initial surge was followed in 1955–56 by a crude communist party attempt to introduce draconian Russian and Chinese forms of organization into agriculture. Following the suppression of the Nghe An revolt in 1956, North Vietnamese agricultural policy was drastically modified and has since marked up great successes. In line with deliberate policy, increases in gross production have not had first priority, though there has been a strong and largely unsuccessful effort to boost production. The main effort has been directed to building a viable rural society, able to contend against drought and flood, able to provide growing medical, educational, social, and cultural services, and able to feed itself adequately while similarly feeding the cities.

Second, the rural population begins to play a significant political role. The engine in this schema of development is the rural labor force, not foreign capital and advisors or the efforts of a small elite of technically trained persons. Western nation building schemata disenfranchise a majority of the population from economic and social participation in the development process itself. It considers them as drag or inertia. Authoritarianism—the political disenfranchisement of the population—follows on this as night on day. To the degree that communist development schemes must rely on popular cooperation, to that same extent can the populace exercise political sanctions against the party. These may take many forms: lack of enthusiasm for party priorities, covert resistance such as laggardliness or carelessness with tools, even open criticism of this or that directive of local cadres. When, as in Vietnam, the party forbears from administrative coercion, a bargaining relationship of sorts is established between the party and the populace. That is, while North Vietnamese society is by no means democratic in the Western sense, *neither is it authoritarian,* either in the sense that South Vietnam has been authoritarian or in the sense that is traditionally and accurately associated with communist rule. (I have seen no reliable information on these questions which would confirm the same conclusion for the NLF zones. I suspect, however, that the same holds true there, to a lesser degree.)

The communists of North Vietnam have learned a lesson understood and applied by our own founding fathers. Nations with poorly developed economies cannot function humanely or effectively without severe limitations on the power of central governmental authorities. Thus in spite of the strong authoritarian traditions to which twentieth-century communism is heir, we witness principled efforts to limit the coercive power of the central party apparatus without at the same time any weakening of the drive to build socialist economic institutions. In Vietnam, at least, this has resulted in a society which is perhaps not ideal by many standards but is at least morally tolerable. The nation builders offer no rival claim.

SAMUEL P. HUNTINGTON: One issue in this discussion turns on the relative priority to be given to the administrative type of activity as against the more political type. I think that in addition to arguing the priorities of the matter, we should look at the consequences of each. It seems to me, Sir Robert, that if the stress is put on the administrative side, the effect, particularly when it involves a very substantial foreign participation and contribution, is precisely to strengthen tendencies toward centralization and to build power at the top or from the top down. This complicates the subsequent problem of trying to promote local organization and to increase participation of local groups.

It seems to me that the history of all of the pacification efforts in Vietnam from the fifties down to the present is precisely the history of this effort to start from the center and work out through administrative means. We are trying to do that right now with the revolutionary development teams. This can have very harmful consequence on local power structures and local groups. Indeed, it often has the effect of undermining these groups, when in the long run they are the very groups we should be trying to strengthen.

DANIEL ELLSBERG: It was very heartening to hear a very American "can do" attitude sounded by Sir Robert. His remarks could almost be paraphrased by the old Seabee slogan: "The difficult we do immediately, the impossible takes a little longer." But we must address ourselves to the question of whether time is really a solvent for all our problems.

All the measures Sir Robert has proposed would have been useful at the various times he proposed them, would have been worthwhile, would have strengthened the situation; they were, in fact, necessary. But was there any likelihood that any of these would be done in Vietnam? They were in fact not done, and the high odds that they would not be done should have become clear to us very early in the game in Vietnam. Regarding administrative strengthening, policing, intelligence improvements, and the other things he describes in looking at the strategic hamlet program, it is frequently said that the governing concepts were good but that they were carried out badly. But it was incumbent on us to ask in the beginning whether it was *likely* for them to be carried out by a government like Diem's advised by Americans.

I believe there are only two ways that one could imagine these kinds of steps having been taken, and both ways, really, are ruled out by Sir Robert.

One would have been a comprehensive kind of American control. Certainly the success in Malaya reflected not British "advisors" but British control. The British were in a position to run things in Malaya. Could the Americans from the beginning have exerted the same kind of control in South Vietnam? In any case, they were not inclined to intervene to that extent, for that purpose.

The other method would have been some kind of popular Vietnamese pressure. Mr. McDermott suggests that we should help the people control their government. In principle this is not an unthinkable sort of assistance. But Sir Robert deprecates this quite strongly.

I would argue that such political change in the relations between governed and governors has many positive implications for the success of the venture and the feasibility even of the administrative changes Sir Robert wants. Take administration as an example. Without detailed and informed pressure by the United States as the intervening power, is it imaginable that the Diem government would have achieved the kind of spontaneous strengthening of administration that Sir Robert wants? In fact, even with that pressure there was a weakening of administration from 1954 to 1964 largely because of political factors.

Similarly talent that could have been drawn back from France and other parts of the world was excluded from government either deliberately or because the persons involved would not associate themselves with a government of the nature of Diem's. The same is true of the governments after Diem. They have denied themselves this kind of administrative talent.

Moreover, even the best administration in the world would not have survived the fall of Diem, which was a direct result of defective political relationships between governed and governors. I think, therefore, that Sir Robert's sarcasm about United States talk and efforts to broaden Diem's regime is a little misplaced—especially right now and especially in view of the analogy Sir Robert draws to the Johnson Administration. One almost has a feeling that his sarcastic comments about how L.B.J. would have received a suggestion to broaden his government were written before March 31, 1968.

The fact is that our own government was toppled at that point. At least, it came as close to it as our system allows, and by very much the same kind of agitation that toppled Diem, and for many of the same reasons. The Congress having been bypassed in 1965 and inadequately consulted since then, the public having been ignored and misled, resentments were built up which created a situation where the President of this country was not able to get easily and safely to airports and auditoriums to campaign—just as, as early as 1961, I observed that Diem needed large military escorts to get to the airport.

Failure has always been overdetermined in Vietnam, but in the case of Diem it happened at least in part because he disregarded the advice we had given him to do something to improve popular support for his regime.

STANLEY HOFFMANN: I would like to emphasize a very important point of difference between Sir Robert Thompson and Mr. McDermott.

Sir Robert has offered a series of recommendations about what an aiding government should do in order to strengthen and develop the capacity of a recipient government like that of South Vietnam. He offers us a list of priorities, such as training, economic aid, developing communications, and so on. Mr. McDermott's point, if I interpret him correctly, is this: the kind of aid just mentioned can be useless or harmful if the assisted government does not have the kind of strategy for mobilizing the population and the strategy of economic and social growth which Mr. McDermott thinks the North Vietnamese government has been able to develop—but which was not within the realm of thought of either the South Vietnamese or their American advisors.

Here, then, is the important issue. Are the recipes which Sir Robert has derived from the successful experience in Malaya not only necessary but also sufficient in all circumstances? If so, then he is correct in his own judgment that the situation in Vietnam in 1961, while bad, was salvageable. On the other hand, perhaps McDermott is right in indicating that there are circumstances in which the political-social situation is such that the set of recipes Sir Robert has suggested will produce nothing at all. In other words, there may be certain kinds of economic and administrative aid, divorced from concepts about the social process and political participation, which are counterproductive.

GEORGE KAHIN: It seems to me that we encounter difficulties in this discussion at the very outset if we focus primarily on the 1960's as the take-off point. If we do that, it is very difficult to differentiate two kinds of intervention. One is intervention in a state that already exists and has its own political cohesion and its own sense of nationalism. The other is an intervention in one nation in order to carve out a separate political entity—and under circumstances where the mainstream of nationalism is already against such an operation and where most of the flow of that stream is already well channeled politically by a group of leaders with very strong nationalist credentials who also oppose the intervention.

Shortly after the end of World War II Vietnam, like Yugoslavia, had a national revolution which swept back and forth across the whole length of the country and was not confined to the north. While it was weaker in the south, it still had very appreciable strength there.

We were misled in the mid 1950's by the artificial reprieve after Geneva from general political competition.

Now, let's assume that in Yugoslavia at the end of the war there was *one* nationalism (rather than co-existing Serbian, Croatian, Slovenian, etc., nationalisms), and the United States had undertaken to support a group in part of this country against the main thrust of nationalism. How successful would we have been?

FRANCES FITZGERALD: It is correct to say that the fact that the Viet Minh defeated their colonial occupiers gave them enormous respect. But I am not sure that you can generalize the effects of nationalism. There have been many nationalists who have had a strong impact on their countries without successfully generating national movements or national governments. Sukarno, for example.

An important point we have missed about the North Vietnamese regime is that it is not simply nationalist. It has also been successful in solving the social problems which have occurred as a result of the breakdown of traditional society in Vietnam as a whole. On this point I would go even a bit further than Mr. McDermott when he said that the North Vietnamese turned out to be really quite acceptable insofar as our moral values were concerned—that they encourage a lot of political participation, etc. What is important is that they seem to have behaved in a manner that is morally acceptable to the Vietnamese.

WILLIAM R. POLK: I would like to recall some of the ways in which at least part of the State Department in 1961 and 1962 thought about the process of guerrilla warfare. At that time—and today as well— we did not have a single adequate political history of any guerrilla war. Practically every study dealt with the military or security aspects of guerrilla warfare. Inevitably the emphasis on security led to administrative prescriptions for counterinsurgency.

For example, in much of the early thinking in 1961 about the Vietnamese conflict the experiences in Greece, Algeria, the Philippines, and Malaya were our teachers. But the lesson we learned from each was that the political outcome of the confrontation depended directly upon the administrative and military prescription. In Greece it was in the form of American military assistance; in Algeria, French regroupment of the Muslim population; in Malaya, the creation of fortified villages; and in the Philippines, civic action. In Washington there was a general feeling that once these prescriptions were combined, they would produce a successful answer to the insurgency in Vietnam.

However, a more sophisticated look at any of the specific issues destroys the simplistic models. For example, I have always believed that in the Greek case it was not the application of large-scale external assistance or, indeed, even the closing of the Yugoslav frontier, which was lethal to the Greek guerrilla cause; rather it was the split in the Greek communist party. It was not until Greek communists began killing one another, as they did after Tito's defection from the Cominform had been duplicated in the split between the nationalist and Cominform wing in the Greek communist party, that the civil war collapsed. Hence, unless this sort of split could be duplicated in Vietnam, the lesson of Greece was probably not pertinent in the way in which it was being drawn.

The critical political factor in the case of Vietnam may be missed if we use 1962 as the take-off point in our discussion. The critical political factor, as Professor Kahin suggested, may go back to 1945 or 1946.

It seems to me that as a rough rule of thumb one can say that something like 80 per cent of the process of guerrilla warfare is political, 15 per cent administrative, and only 5 per cent military. Applying this scale to the Vietnamese conflict, one can say that the political issue was largely decided as early as 1946, the administrative issue by about 1957, and that we are talking today only about the residual 5 per cent.

ALBERT WOHLSTETTER: To shift the discussion somewhat, Sir Robert Thompson and Mr. McDermott joined another issue nicely. Mr. McDermott poses an extreme view, a view toward which influential bodies of opinion now seem to be tending. What Mr. McDermott is really saying—not consciously but close to it—is that growth itself is not good. Economic assistance, for example, is bad for people, since it encourages what he calls "distortions."

A common-sense answer to this objection is that not all things grow at the same rate. Some decline, some increase—at least relative to others. It is characteristic of all growth, aided or not, that it proceeds unevenly. France is a case in point. In its formidable economic development there were polar differences as one part of the economy got ahead of the others. Still, if you are going to make any choices in investment at all, you always invest in one thing rather than in another. There will be some disruption as some industries decline while others advance. An available body of literature suggests that any rapid economic change is likely to be disruptive and to cause some resentments. This, however, would happen with or without assistance. If you regard this as being evil, you should really oppose even a growth that is entirely self-generated.

But, Mr. McDermott, you are not being consistent about your own implied thesis. You talk about a number of kinds of aid which you regard as being legitimate, such as aid to education, medical aid, and so on. You mischaracterize many theories of economic development by supposing that they stress only capital equipment. Very few competent theorists of economic development stress capital equipment exclusively; rather they place a great deal of emphasis on development of human resources.

Even so, it is clear from the current literature on human capital that its development is also extremely disruptive. In the case of medical aid, we have many examples of the disruptive effects it has in terms of decreasing death rates and increasing population. So if you are really against any sort of growth and imbalance, against the growth of one thing relative to another, you also should be against any aid for development of human resources. In short, Mr. McDermott, you appear to oppose any attempt to support or influence change, including economic growth and economic self-development, in the "third world." Your stand thus seems to be an extreme example of an ominous isolationist trend in America.

THEODORE DRAPER: I would like to say something else about Mr. McDermott's position which raises two questions in my mind.

First, Mr. McDermott argued that it was impossible for Americans, despite their enormous resources, to "monitor" what was happening in Vietnam. He implied that foreigners with limited language resources using Western indicators cannot monitor a myriad confusion of small-scale subeconomies. All this may be true, but from the rest of his remarks it developed that with fewer resources—in fact, with very little

—he very confidently felt it was possible to monitor the achievements of North Vietnam and the Viet Cong.

Second, after he argued against all sorts of socioeconomic and political intervention on the ground that it was neoimperialist, he then talked about diplomacy replacing intervention. It seems to me that if one is committed to the concept of neoimperialism, the diplomatic process will be as neoimperialist as anything else. I don't quite understand why one should be sympathetic to neoimperialist diplomacy or seem to substitute it for neoimperialist intervention.

JOHN MCDERMOTT: The second part of your question might be disruptive to the present flow of discussion, and it would be best to discuss the matter at a later place. As for the use of the word "monitor": it means that you have people in a country who can somehow keep track of a program to see how it is operating. Perhaps I should give you an instance of what I had in mind. During the 1958 phase of the recurrent reforms of the import subsidy program in South Vietnam, there was great pressure to increase the proportion of producer goods brought in under the program and to diminish the proportion of consumer goods. One of the effects of the pressure was that some consumer goods which customarily found their way to the countryside—small radios and bicycles in particular—seemed to be cut off. This apparently caused some resentment. After all, bicycles are very useful things in South Vietnam. Therefore I use the word "monitor" in an administrative way.

If you cannot monitor the situation, if you do not have fairly easy and convenient ways of monitoring, it seems to me that the aid program, whatever the faith of the economist in its abstract growth, is not very useful. The administrative criterion should be something you can follow for the program's impact on various people. If things start to get out of hand, you then can make adjustments. My comments about the North Vietnamese government are political remarks based, not on the continuance of this or that program, but on taking an overview of several years. There is no confusion in that whatsoever. I have no idea how one goes about monitoring this or that project in North Vietnam.

THEODORE DRAPER: How can you tell us, then, that the level of educational services and medical care is higher in one area than another if you cannot in some sense monitor it, by which I mean keep track of it? You have made some assertions here that indicate a much greater knowledge than you may have.

JOHN MCDERMOTT: I do not really understand the force of that objection. With regard to medical services, the World Health Organization released a report on the incidence of tuberculosis in North Vietnam compared with other countries in the region. On the basis of their figures they say that tuberculosis is not a serious problem in the northern region of the country. I know from personal and other experiences that it is serious in the south. This seems to me a judgment one can make. Maybe we are wrong, but there is at least an evidentiary basis on which to make the judgment.

The real problem we should come back to is that I don't think it is very easy for foreigners to monitor particular programs in another country. There are different mechanisms in a modern economy that you do not have in Vietnam. This means that in Vietnam there are no easy ways to calculate the effect of various programs. You have to have people on the spot keeping watch on factors involved.

My judgments on North Vietnam represent, as I said before, aggregate judgments which lump together events of the decade. There is now an extensive literature on the impressive internal accomplishments of the present North Vietnamese regime, which is important because it bears on our own theoretical responses to different nation building schemes, different schemes of development.

I would not like to be put in the position of having to say that five years from now the North Vietnamese regime is going to be very tolerable as a regime; I don't have enough sense of it on a political dynamic basis. But one can speak of the past in this respect.

LEROY WEHRLE: I think the question that was asked—can we or can we not monitor strictly economic results?—is an easy one to answer. But it leads to another question which is more important: what do we seek to achieve on the political front by our economic programs?

I would suggest here that one can say flatly that we have not been able to monitor the political effects; more importantly, we have not adequately sought to determine what we wanted to achieve politically with our economic programs. With regard to Mr. McDermott's statement that we are not able to measure strictly economic results in Vietnam, well, this is a kindergarten business and not very difficult to do.

Much more important is the question of what we want to do with our economic efforts in Vietnam? Do we seek, for example, to disperse political power by decentralizing it among communal groups? Do we seek to strengthen the Vietnamese commercial class against the Chinese class? It is here that we have much greater difficulty, first, in defining what we want to do with the kind of power we throw around, and second, in monitoring and determining whether we have achieved what we are trying to do.

Epilogue:

iv The Lessons of Vietnam

The World of the 1970's

SIR ROBERT THOMPSON: Today we come to the point where to produce a new alibi, having lost the alibi of Diem, people are saying the failure in Vietnam is due to the fact that Vietnam is unique. Well, I frankly do not think that you are going to get away with that alibi, because if you do exactly the same thing in Thailand that you have done in Vietnam, you are going to lose Thailand also. And if Vietnam was unique, Thailand cannot be.

§§ SAMUEL P. HUNTINGTON: Recent experience and recurring United States introversion make "No more Vietnams" a likely guideline of American policy for the foreseeable future. On the other hand, however, the United States will presumably not relapse back into prewar isolationism and will retain a variety of interests in other countries. The expansion of the American nongovernmental presence—economic, social, and cultural—may well continue.

Major instability and conflict in other countries will inevitably have some effect on American interests. During a period of introversion the perceived effect may well be considerably less than it has been in the past. Nonetheless clearly some types of situations may occur in the future which could generate severe pressures—external and domestic—for United States military intervention. Perhaps the most obvious of these can be grouped into four general categories.

(1) *Authoritarian breakdowns.* Much of the world is governed

(to use the word loosely) by narrow-based authoritarian regimes of doubtful legitimacy and less adaptability. These include, first, primitive and personalistic dictatorships, as in Haiti, Nicaragua, and many African countries; second, traditional monarchies, as in Libya, South Arabia, Ethiopia, Iran, and Thailand; third, conservative authoritarian regimes, as in Spain, Portugal, and Taiwan. The political systems in all these cases are highly fragile. In any one of the three types a coup or simply the death of the ruler (naturally or through assassination) could trigger a complete breakdown of authority, the eruption into politics of a large number of hitherto suppressed social forces, and the degeneration of the society into a state of anarchy inviting intervention by communists, Americans, and others.

(2) *Communal wars.* The obvious possibilities here include blacks versus whites in South Africa, Rhodesia, and Portuguese Africa; Negroes versus Indians in Caribbean societies, such as Guiana and Trinidad; Chinese versus natives in Southeast Asia; tribal conflicts in Africa; and the almost infinite opportunities for racial, ethnic, linguistic, and religious wars in India.

(3) *Peasant revolutions.* Societies where the bulk of the agricultural population is not effectively related to politics obviously furnish fertile ground for revolutionaries attempting to carry out their own version of a Maoist upheaval. The recent lack of success of such movements in Peru, Guatemala, and Bolivia does not eliminate the possibility of future success. Among the areas where peasant revolutions seem most likely are the Philippines, Central America, Andean South America (exclusive of Bolivia), and northeast Brazil.

(4) *Anti-American assaults.* The continued existence of a significant American presence in many countries could give rise to violent attacks on that presence by anti-American nationalist movements, which in turn would generate pressure for American military intervention to protect American interests. Among the countries where this type of violence is possible are Thailand, the Philippines, Taiwan, Okinawa, Panama, the Dominican Republic.

All of these forms of instability are likely to be widely prevalent in the future. Whether any one of them would actually generate an apparent need for American military intervention would, of course, depend upon the location, size, strategic importance, and political commitment of the country concerned. Anti-American assaults are most likely to provoke an American military reaction. The likelihood of such assaults, however, can obviously be reduced by decreasing the extent and, equally important, the visibility of the American presence overseas. In many countries, also, authoritarian breakdowns, communal wars, and peasant revolutions could break out and pursue their own course without involving the United States. One of the more hopeful developments in world politics, indeed, has been the extent to which the United States has been able to remain relatively uninvolved in a communal civil war in the largest country in Africa. On the other hand, in some cases the United States might well feel that sufficiently vital interests were at stake to justify military intervention.

GEORGE KAHIN: I want to follow up the several passing references to Thailand. First of all, Thailand provides a classic case of Jim Thomson's "verbal oversell," involving an exaggeration of the present insurgent threat. In some cases there has been conscious exaggeration by American officials stationed there as well as by Thai officials. When you talk to them, they say this is the only way sufficiently to alert people in the United States—Congress in particular—to ensure that Thailand's minimum needs for economic support are met.

With regard to the over-all potentials of insurgency, I would suggest that discontent in Thailand is still a latent force, largely channeled by the establishment. The king is still a powerful symbol of nationalism, pretty largely at the service of the military-civil bureaucratic hierarchy that runs the country. Moreover, there is a relatively high degree of ethnic homogeneity, although this is eroding to some extent.

Let me turn one by one to the significant insurgent areas. The one we hear most about is the northeast. The northeast certainly has regional sentiment. Ten million of the thirty million people of the country live in this area, and they speak a variant of Thai different from that spoken in Bangkok and which is close to Lao. It is an area traditionally badly neglected by the central government. It is an area in which until recently Bangkok sent its bottom-of-the-barrel civil servants to work. A regionally-rooted insurgency of modest proportions —more modest today than a year ago—has developed there. It seems, in addition, that some individuals trained in North Vietnam have been returned to the area within the last year and have helped the insurgency.

However, this is a multifaceted insurgency. The area—something like our southwest in the 1880's—has a high degree of cattle rustling, and a lot of the insurgent activity there today simply involves cattle rustling. Apart from that, the area also contains returned mercenaries who fought in Laos in several wars of recent vintage, apparently on both sides, and who have come back with military training of sorts, with a taste for adventure, and sometimes with arms. There also are several local factions which have been considerably outraged by Bangkok's neglect. In some cases severe reprisals have been visited upon these local leaders.

The expenditure per capita in the area is still lower than in other regions of Thailand, despite the fact that we have done a good bit through our various efforts to change this. But I think this is an insurgency that is much more under control than it was a couple of years ago.

Nevertheless, one of the things that makes it difficult to control is the presence of American bases there—with all their disruptive by-products. The insurgency did not become very significant until after we put the bases in. One of the ironic examples of this disruption has been that while both Bangkok and United States officials have desired to build up local police forces, many policemen have left to serve as auxiliaries in the defense of American bases because the pay is so much higher.

Sir Robert Thompson is much better qualified to talk about insurgency on the borders of Malaya. However, let me say that if it has any potential, I think it is largely not in the hands of the communists, but will depend primarily on Bangkok's relations with the Malay population in Thailand's southernmost provinces. It is not now too much of a problem.

Another area is near the Cambodian border. Here, it seems to me, some of our chickens are coming home to roost. Members of South Vietnam's Cambodian minority have been given training in South Vietnam and then transported by air across Cambodia to southeastern Thailand, from which they have probed across Cambodia's western border. But since then the Cambodians have begun to retaliate, and the border has become a very live one.

The most minatory insurgency of all is the one in the north. It has strong ethnic overtones. There is, in addition, an important ecological factor here, in that groups who come over the border from Laos and elsewhere to practice agriculture find insufficient land. Therefore they either have to compete with some of the existing landowners or cut into forest preserves in defiance of Thai officials. The problems of this area are further complicated by the presence of the Chinese Nationalist (KMT) troops, who previously operated in Burma. For reasons of expediency Thai police have turned over responsibility to these Chinese in a sizable area on the Thai side of the border.

Speaking of Thailand generally, I would say that if the United States reduces its military presence in Thailand and if it does not intervene further, then the Thais ought to be able to look after themselves very well. One of the long-term problems is that too large an American presence shields the Thai elite from political and economic realities, insulating them from problems they would otherwise deal with directly and soon enough.

CHESTER COOPER: I would like to add a footnote to George Kahin's description of Thailand, with which I agree. I think his point about the overestimation of the threat in Thailand in a sense reflects not only our attitude toward Thailand but our experience in Vietnam. One wonders, if Vietnam were not there and etched into our collective memory, whether the reactions to the threat in Thailand would be somewhat different.

The only thing I would add is that the insurgency, which I think is contained and containable, nonetheless may take on different dimensions depending on what happens in Vietnam.

Intervention and the Future of American Foreign Policy

CRITERIA FOR THE FUTURE

§§ STANLEY HOFFMANN: The broader implications of our Vietnam experience can all be summarized in one formula: *from incorrect premises about a local situation and about our abilities, a bad policy is likely to follow.* Our policy in Vietnam has been exemplary in the sense of providing a complete catalogue of all the mistakes that can result from false premises. Let me proceed to three imperatives and two final lessons.

A first imperative is to examine with greater rigor and depth each of the situations of trouble in which our intervention is at issue. The world has shifted from a period in which international alignments were the domestic priority to one in which domestic issues are the international priority. In such a world the possibility for any one large power to control other nations is far smaller: neither Soviet or Chinese subversion nor American intervention can easily master the complexities of local social, economic, and political problems or overcome the resistance of local nationalisms. Yet in such a world, as chances for remote manipulation decrease, cases of endemic internal violence increase.

Consequently, first, we must shift from a vision of the world which at least implicitly gave priority to the notion of an external threat (spread across borders either by blatant means of outside intervention or invasion, or else by devious techniques of subversion) to an understanding of the *domestic priority,* i.e., of the fact that the opportunities open to our foes as well as to us depend on the internal realities of the various areas. This is why, for instance, there is no universal, standardized model of "national liberation." It was not the Maoist model that worked in Cuba, and the Cuban one failed in Bolivia. It was China's neglect of these domestic realities that has led to her various setbacks.

Yet in both China's and Russia's ideological pronouncements (for reasons that have to do with the focus and message of Marxism-Leninism) there is much more awareness of those domestic priorities than we have shown. Whatever reservations one may have on specific proposals he made throughout the years, one must pay tribute to George Kennan for his constant understanding of this point.

The "internalization" of conflict results from the excessively high costs of conventional war, from the fact that the stakes of world politics are, more and more, the shaping of domestic societies, and from the phenomena of social mobilization which make the waging of foreign policy increasingly dependent on internal support, images, and institutions. Consequently the policy-maker needs to find in the works of theoretically oriented social scientists not merely broad generalizations about the international system or about political development, but more particular and differentiated theories that attempt "to account for the policy-relevant variation among" cases.[1]

[1] Alexander L. George, "Bridging the Gap Between Scholarly Research and Policy-makers: The Problem of Theory and Action," Rand Document, May 8, 1968. The implications of Vietnam for social science and for its relation to policy deserve a separate study.

Second, we must learn to distinguish much more carefully between types of intervention. Each one and each combination has its own advantages and drawbacks, and precisely because no great power can ever abstain altogether from intervention, it is important to understand what these assets and liabilities are. In the continuum that goes from nonintervention (which, as Talleyrand remarked, is also a kind of intervention) via aid to military expeditions, we need marks and signs. Thus intervention can be distinguished according to (1) scope; (2) type (military, economic, etc.); (3) whether it is overt or covert; (4) whether it consists in deliveries (for instance, of advice, arms or goods) or in denials (for instance, a suspension of aid)—and one can see that it may be more advisable to support democratic legitimacy abroad by depriving unpopular or illegitimate tyrannies of our military aid than by giving such aid either to democratic insurgents or even to democratic governments whose resources could better be used in other ways; (5) whether the purpose of intervention is essentially negative (to avert a threat, to prevent a crisis) or essentially positive—and we have to remember, for instance, that the bigger the scope, the more problematic a purely negative intervention becomes, whereas the capacity to achieve controllable, positive results from the outside is always limited, the more so as one moves from the economic to the political sphere; (6) whether the measure is part of a strategy of competition with one's major rivals or part of a strategy of cooperation—an important distinction, for we may be compelled in certain cases to intervene in reply to intervention by our major rivals, whereas we would not have done so unchallenged; also we may seek a multilateral framework for large-scale cooperative intervention, even though competitive ones may have to remain unilateral; (7) whether the focus of intervention is the control of internal behavior in a foreign nation or its external conduct.

Our main experience is in the latter area: we are primarily used to contests in which "winning" means imposing our strategy on an adversary in open battle. As for affecting internal affairs, we have a great deal of experience in the realm of economic aid; we also have some experience with waging successful, swift, and superficial coups. We have much less experience with the kind of intervention in which we found ourselves ensnared on behalf of the Saigon regimes: an asymmetrical fight against a foe who obstinately refused to play our game while being inventive and flexible enough to adapt his tactics to our presence, against a foe who succeeded in keeping the initiative even while we thought that our forays—on the ground and in the air—meant that it was ours, and in a territory and over stakes that made "winning" the gradual by-product of military control, social change, administrative and political reform, institutional creation and organization.

We must learn in particular to distinguish between two kinds of intervention: on the one hand, marginal ones (which does not mean unimportant; they can be decisive) that allow a threatened society to deal with its problems in a way that strengthens its cohesion but does not jeopardize its autonomy and self-respect and, on the other, interventions that are so massive that they are counterproductive either because they weaken the assisted partner (by spreading corruption, disrupting his administration or his economy) or because that partner lacks the institutional ability and social cohesion without which our intervention will be in vain.

There is no substitute for area expertise, historical knowledge, and the kind of informed judgment that allows one to separate a hopeless case from a merely difficult one. There is, in this respect, at least one clear message from Vietnam: when a regime that is oppressive or ineffective or both is faced, not with an ordinary insurgency, but with a movement that is both superbly organized and capable of mounting an effective government and a social revolution in the areas it holds, the chances of reversing the trend are very poor. It would be as foolish to mistake every rebellion for a genuine social movement as it is to mistake every political leader for an authentic force. The key issues are those of the roots, the organization, the appeals. We must learn to distinguish movements that are broad, effective, and legitimate from pseudo movements. Once again the ability to discriminate is a prerequisite of policy. This ability requires in turn a social science more interested in asking the key questions of historical sociology than in collecting swamps of data.

A second imperative is to re-examine critically the limits of our power. This does not mean indulging either in an orgy of self-doubt or in a repudiation of an ungrateful outside world that resists our good intentions. It means assessing several factors more realistically.

First, we must more realistically assess the limits in the present international system of the kind of power that we have in greatest amounts: military and economic. Having written abundantly on this topic elsewhere,[2] I will merely sum up my point here.

The new conditions of the use of force, the rise and strength of the nation-state, the heterogeneity of the system—all reduce considerably the direct ability of any major power to shape the world according to its wishes. There is an excess of the power to deny over the power to achieve gains. In other words, our greatest impact comes through creating conditions in which the forces on which we count—the defenders of the status quo or the champions of moderate reform—can work. Our forms of help—military deterrence and various kinds of assistance—cannot succeed in denying all enemy gains, for they are not capable either of preventing him from exploiting at our expense (and through similar techniques of assistance, ranging from military to diplomatic) regional interstate disputes (as in the Middle East), nor are they capable of transforming an internal situation as hopeless as Vietnam. Moreover, when our deterrence and assistance succeed in consolidating noncommunist regimes, there is no guarantee that these regimes will use their own power in ways that will please us, as we found out in various parts of the world.

Second, we must more realistically assess the specific limitations that our history, our style, and our institutions impose on our effectiveness. It is imperative that we know ourselves better. To be sure, one could argue that our massive resort to technological power in Vietnam results precisely from our exploitation of what we know to be our greatest asset. But this has to be weighed, not only against our ignorance of local realities that vitiated this asset, but also against our neglect of some serious psychological weaknesses of our own: an overbearingly self-confident approach to complex problems; a tendency to reduce them to mere issues of management, without questioning the realism of the ends and therefore the adequacy of the means; an optimism that makes us believe that a superficial, often verbal, community of values with foreign elites entitles us to be their guides and enables us to solve their problems; an activism that conflicts with the needs for prudence and patience and often reduces our associates to the position of subordinates and makes them resentful of our protection and of their dependence; an underestimation of the

2 *Gulliver's Troubles, Part I.*

way in which other people's history and customs condition their reactions to present issues; a lack of understanding of social revolutions,
of the kinds of violent movements that develop when there are no
procedures for peaceful change and that often are not led by the kinds
of elites with whom Americans are comfortable. This lack of understanding results from our own inexperience with such revolution and
makes us reserve our sympathies to noncommunist, purely nationalist
elites.[3] Finally, there is our tendency, when challenged, to be far
more concerned with proving ourselves than with finding out whether
our objectives are worthwhile or reachable and whether our involvement serves them adequately.

What has been most striking in Vietnam is our way of turning that
intricate contest (in which, by our own admission, we are not fully
in control even of our side) into a test of our resolve, competence,
and moral and material superiority. This is an old and not disgraceful
feature. But precisely because of its importance in our make-up it
should make us careful about getting involved. At least we should be
careful to get only into confrontations that are so essential as to
justify this heavy investment of our pride, if not only in confrontations
we can win, so as to avoid the self-lacerations of defeat (this would
not be a very realistic imperative).

A third imperative, following from the first two, is precisely to
redefine more carefully our national interest in the international competition. Again, I will refer the reader to another piece of writing,[4]
and make only a few remarks here. First, for several reasons we must
learn to distinguish between two kinds of threats to "stability" (a
much-abused notion). On the one hand, there will arise in scores of
countries risks of internal disruption that may be helped from abroad
yet correspond to domestic realities. We must learn to live with such
perils and to accept violent social and political change—even if private
American interests happen to be the targets, even if communists should
occasionally be the local beneficiaries and communist powers the
likely allies of the local winners. For there will never be any manageable international system if our statesmen pretend to play the role of
cosmic Metternichs. Unless the consequence of those upheavals would
be to put into power regimes hostile to us in important countries,

[3] Cf. United States reticence toward the French resistance in World War II.
[4] *Gulliver's Troubles,* ch. x.

such changes would not seriously endanger our position in the international competition.

As for a revolutionary communist takeover in countries that are of great importance in the world balance of power (by which I mean, not the nuclear balance, which seems safely in the hands of the two superpowers, but the conventional military balance and even more the far less tangible diplomatic one), while it would undoubtedly be a blow to American interests and a source of international instability, it is hard to see how the United States could prevent it (would we have tried to overthrow a communist regime in Indonesia?). We can only provide such countries with limited assistance to help them consolidate their internal cohesion, and avoid providing communist or procommunist forces there with a cause through our excessive involvement.

This does not mean that we must refrain from any help to a foreign government even if the insurgents it fights are, not merely helped, but effectively controlled by Moscow or Peking so that behind the appearance of local revolution there is the reality of great-power aggression. But this is not a very likely scenario. Nor does this mean that we should suspend economic aid just because it risks pushing us down the slippery slope that ends in military intervention. It means only that we should expect economic aid to breed, by itself, neither social and political stability nor external compliance, and we should grant such aid as a limited cooperative and positive form of intervention, justifiable both in narrow terms and broadly as a humanitarian contribution from the rich to the poor, preferably through mutilateral channels. Nor does this mean, finally, that there may never be internal disruptions of such magnitude and potentially so dangerous for world order that external intervention becomes just and necessary; but by definition such intervention will have to be collective in order to be legitimate and effective.

On the other hand, we should be concerned with the external implications of internal changes; we should be especially interested in preventing domestic disruptions from engulfing the major powers and domestic revolutionary regimes from exporting their recipes by force. Our national interest in the moderate management of conflict ought therefore sometimes (as in intra-African conflicts) to lead us to promote formulas for international or regional localization and neutralization, and in other places (as in Southeast Asia, where the threat comes from communist regimes) to encourage us to promote regional efforts at self-defense against risks either of invasion or of military interference with communications, under an American guarantee or with as unobtrusive a military assistance on our part as possible. Similarly, in Vietnam our effort now ought to focus on the distinction between the settlement of the internal issues (which should be left as much as possible to the various factions of South Vietnamese) and the solution of the external implications of South Vietnam's self-determination (such as the withdrawal of foreign troops, neutralization of the country, the conditions of eventual unification of Vietnam, the guarantee of the borders in the area, and the immersion into this process of as broad a section of the international community as possible).

Second, we must learn to establish a hierarchy of interests, of which the separation described in the previous paragraphs is but one example. We must be guided by the following considerations. (1) Not every part of the world is of the same importance to us. An area's importance depends largely on two sets of factors: the intrinsic importance of the country or region for us because of resources, population, political influence, and (as in the case of Israel or South Korea) abundance and intimacy of ties with us, and also its importance to our main adversaries. (2) Even in countries or areas that are important to us, we may have a hierarchy of concerns. Whereas one could argue that in all such instances we have an interest in preserving them from outside aggression, the scope of our interests beyond this must vary from case to case. In particular, a prudent foreign policy must beware of turning into a major stake the internal control of a highly unstable polity that we are badly equipped to preserve and reform. A prudent foreign policy must avoid total identification of the United States with any foreign government, both for the latter's sake and for our own; for we know that our capacity to control does not grow along with our involvement. The closer the identification, the smaller our freedom of maneuver and the greater the risk of our becoming the blackmailed victims of our ally, yet also the higher the likelihood of his losing his national legitimacy. We must learn to remember that even when the domestic milieu becomes the battlefield of international politics, it is foreign policy that we wage. To remind ourselves of the foreignness of foreigners is to realize, not only that we have—quite properly—less control over them than over the men and goods of our national polity, but also that what may be in their national interest (such as certain kinds of "political development") is not necessarily either in our interest or a proper concern of our foreign policy. This is not "neoisolationism"; it is the art of distinguishing the essential from the irrelevant. It is blind activism or overinvolvement, not the ordering of one's interests, which breeds an isolationist reaction.

In Vietnam, although a Viet Cong victory was important to Peking as a test of its doctrine, such a victory was never tantamount to Peking control. Therefore the area itself should not have been deemed essential to us to begin with. Moreover, the nature of the threat there was such as to justify a deliberate effort on our part to *minimize* the importance of domestic control and to concentrate our efforts on the external aspects.

Here lies one important lesson: in present-day confrontations, when the superpowers for obvious reasons engage only a small part of their military resources, tests of will are resolved less on the basis of the ratios of military might than on that of the "balance of interests as manifested in the relative capacity of the opponents to convince each other that they will support their positions with war if necessary."[5]

Let us apply this to Vietnam. Our escalation in the south and in the north was an attempt to convince Hanoi and the NLF of our determination to support our position massively. But we failed to convince them that what was at stake—the control of South Vietnam—was of such overriding importance to us that we would pay for it the price of sacrificing more important American interests, such as our interest in avoiding heightened tension with Russia and war with China, our interest in avoiding a depletion of our military forces in Europe, in avoiding a domestic crisis over escalation—all interests that would have been threatened had we decided that denying the enemy control of Saigon was worth either even greater efforts at trying to "win" or a perpetuation of an indecisive war.

We failed to convince them because, as we discovered the depth

[5] Robert E. Osgood and Robert C. Tucker, *Force, Order and Justice* (Baltimore, 1967), p. 152.

of our earlier illusions, we failed to convince ourselves. After the long and bloody detour of an escalation that was an escape from unsavory realities, Hanoi and the NLF prevailed when we understood that the only way out of the lasso was an end to the war. On his side, the enemy succeeded in convincing us of his determination. We came to realize that within the limits of escalation which were tolerable to us, he could continue to fight for stakes that were infinitely more important to his existence and *raison d'être* than our stakes were to ours; and we came to realize that within the limits set in the south by the nature of guerrilla warfare and in the north by his own sense of prudence, he was indeed waging an unlimited war; whereas we were fighting a war both too limited and too brutal, both too classical and too absorbing to provide real victory. So we gave up the fiction, backed by an impressive display of force, that Vietnam was the Wilderness of the international civil war. And the enemy imposed on us the reality of his resolve and of the difference between our power to destroy and our power to create.

There is one final lesson from Vietnam that ought to be remembered when the issue of intervention arises again. In international affairs the normative requirements of political order and the normative requirements of ethics do not always coincide: not all moderate international systems, not all world empires have been based on or have dispensed justice. But it is both the moral duty and the political interests of statesmen to avoid policies that compound political and moral error, political inefficiency and ethical ugliness. In Vietnam our political and our moral roads, paved with good intentions, have led to hell.

That same inadequacy of our means to reach unreachable objectives and that same tendency of the means to make the goals even more illusory, which have marked the political course of the war, also justify moral condemnation. For the ethics of foreign-policy behavior is an ethics of consequences. No policy is ethical, however generous its ends, if success is ruled out. And no policy is ethical if the means corrupt or destroy the ends, if the means are materially out of proportion with the ends, if they entail costs of value greater than the costs of not resorting to them—three precepts violated by our conduct in Vietnam.

The ethics of foreign policy must be an ethics of self-restraint: our moral duty coincides with our political interest. From neither point of view can one support any policy of universal intervention. Here again, prudence on the one hand and the ethical judgment of the ends and the relation of means to ends, on the other, converge.

By definition, political interest and moral duty in political affairs can be spelled out only case by case, and general guidelines are of little help. But the extreme case of Vietnam gives one a good, if tragic, idea of the kinds of things that cannot be brought off and should not be undertaken, of the bad effect of letting general principles and familiar techniques of action be sloppily applied without sufficient consideration of the special circumstances of the case and of the special disabilities of the actors.

The saddest aspect of the Vietnam tragedy is that it combines moral aberration and intellectual scandal; and yet maybe we should be impressed by the rather rare fact that in a world where these two sets of values—those of moral action and those of political effectiveness—are often far apart, they have been reunited in so exemplary an instance.

§§ ITHIEL DE SOLA POOL: Effective intervention—and I predict that there will be a number of effective interventions in foreign crises in America's future—requires exactly the combination of moral stance and political understanding that Professor Hoffmann has so well identified. The immediate problem for American policy in Vietnam is to reduce a nation's suffering: to check killing, terror, and oppression that arise from many sources. Given the double and triple binds of the historical heritage, there is no easy answer even to that immediate problem. Certainly there is no easy answer to the long-term problem of how far, where, and when America should commit itself in the future to involvement in securing international peace and stability. It is the duty of scholars to look objectively and soberly at the various contradictory aspects of reality, not to produce rhetoric in which broad generalizations conform to people's abhorrence of dissonance by portraying the bad as all bad and the good as all good. Vietnam can look that way only from twelve thousand miles away.

The recognition of the complexity of reality brings me to a point which Stanley Hoffmann makes superbly and forcefully. It is a powerful plea for the importance of knowledge as a basis for action. The high point of his remarks is an attack upon the platitudinous application of broad slogans of policy without knowing the actual facts of the situation. As he says, "From incorrect premises about a local situation . . . bad policy is likely to follow. . . . There is no substitute for area expertise, historical knowledge." Unfortunately, at the time our basic Vietnam policies were set, "our understanding of South Vietnamese society was poor, the expertise at our disposal limited. In such circumstances, we tended to distort our analysis by reducing South Vietnamese uniqueness to elements that seemed familiar and reassuring—to features that we had met and managed elsewhere." The true Vietnam experts that this country had in 1965 could be counted on one's fingers. Moreover, as James Thomson points out, these experts were not called in by the makers of Vietnam policy, and the more critical the decision, the less so.

Hoffmann's powerful plea for local knowledge instead of platitudes is unfortunately faulted by an irrational distaste on his part for numbers. Many of the things we need to know are matters of amount. How many of the Vietnamese people sympathize with the Viet Cong or with the government? Where is major corruption to be found? What is the rate of inflation? What are the rents that are truly paid? Many of Hoffmann's statements are quantitative. He describes, for example, villagers "torn between identification with the Viet Cong which they respect but fear and identification with a regime for which they have no respect." Some peasants certainly feel that way, but how many? Are they 20 per cent? 40 per cent? 60 per cent? Are they found everywhere or mostly in some regions? The answers to such questions cannot be dismissed as "swamps of data." Fortunately the United States government is not a totally know-nothing organization. Late, but better than never, it has started putting itself in the position to answer questions like that.

There has been too much ignorant wisecracking in the press about the figures being collected on the progress of pacification. The usual remark (Hoffmann has a more vivid one) talks about running the war with computers. As every high school graduate knows, any measurement has a margin of error. I happen to have a pretty good notion of the margin of uncertainty in these particular figures and of how much effort is being made to reduce it. I also know how much better our knowledge is now than it was before we had these admittedly approximate figures. But that is only part of the point. The important point is that the collection of good data, far from mechanizing the war effort, is humanizing it.

Before the Hamlet Evaluation System was instituted, the typical American district advisor had very little contact with the hamlets in his area. He advised the district chief and had no pressing requirement to get deeply involved with what was on the minds of the villagers. Today he must fill out a monthly report which he can do readily only by getting to the hamlets and talking there. The results have been extraordinary, not in producing magic numbers, but in giving the advisor a sense of his problem.

This is simply one example of the vital importance of applied social science for making the actions of our government in foreign areas more rational and humane than they have been. Right now the anti-intellectuals—and Senator Fulbright, astonishingly enough, with them—are trying to deny policy-makers the capability to learn what they need to know if they are to avoid the disease of overgeneralized reaction that Stanley Hoffmann so well identifies. Without social-science area knowledge to correct their instinctive clichés, our military officers are likely to march us into futile battles and our foreign-policy makers into repeated crises, like the Red Coats who marched according to their rule book against the embattled farmers of New England.

That has been the lesson of every recent intervention crisis. We marched into the Bay of Pigs because those area experts who did know were not consulted. In the Dominican intervention we succeeded, and successes are seldom questioned. Nonetheless, the fact of the matter in retrospect is that we did not know at the time who was on what side. Both our civilian and our military authorities needed good political analysis more than they needed anything else.

Our need for better social-science knowledge can perhaps be identified as the first lesson of Vietnam. In a world in which we will continue to be involved in a series of overseas crises located in diverse and strange cultures, the prime requirement is available social-science area experts who know the language and the country. They are needed, not only in the field, but also in the highest policy-making councils. Until the Secretary of State, the Secretary of Defense, and the President are adequately and directly served by the top experts on each country in crisis, and until we massively increase our social-science knowledge of crisis areas, we will make drastic mistakes over and over again. That is the first of three major lessons of Vietnam.

The second concerns the conduct of war by a democracy. Mankind, regrettably, has not yet reached the point of totally rejecting war. But a democracy in the present era cannot deliberately choose war as an instrument of national policy. The people in a democracy will not fight willingly for long unless they believe that combat is forced upon them by an aggressive enemy. Pearl Harbor and the North Korean invasion of the South were signal events to which the American public could and did respond. There has been no such event in Vietnam. The lesson looks clear for revolutionists or aggressors seeking to impose their will on a foreign country; the lesson is to act covertly and gradually. It would be naïve to think that the experience of Vietnam precludes an American military response to future overt dramatic aggressions against our allies. Our response, however, may well be timid if the provocation is not obvious.

To the American government the lesson is that it must find effective ways of responding to limited disruptions by means short of war. We have learned, for example, that divisions of troops are not very effective against undergrounds, and we will have to learn how to use police and intelligence operations.

Our worst mistake in Vietnam clearly was to initiate the bombing of the north. Before that started, it was my view that the United States as a democracy could not stand the moral protest that would arise if we rained death from the skies upon an area where there was no war. After the bombing started, I decided I had been in error. For a while there seemed to be no outcry of protest, but time brought it on. Now I would return to my original view with an important modification, namely, time. Public reactions do not come immediately. Many actions that public opinion would otherwise make impossible are possible if they are short-term. I believe we can fairly say that unless it is severely provoked or unless the war succeeds fast, a democracy cannot choose war as an instrument of policy. Any other sort of war will destroy the cohesion of the democratic community that wages it.

A third lesson in Vietnam is more specifically American. It is that the politics of this country will continue to be polarized between an isolationist impulse to avoid involvement in other people's problems and an internationalist impulse to promote our own values in the world. We are likely to oscillate dangerously between these extremes. Professor Huntington's remarks identify this oscillation as a lawful cycle, like the business cycle of old. I wonder, however, whether we have not reached the end of such a regular cycle. Time alone will tell whether major exogenous events will push the pendulum dizzily one way or the other.

Right now it is fashionable to say that the American public will accept no more Vietnams. Perhaps that is a partial truth for the moment, but it would take only another catastrophe that occurred because we sat on our hands and avoided intervention to push the pendulum back the other way. Whatever the last catastrophe was shapes the direction of the public's indignation at the incumbent administration. Just as the fall of Czechoslovakia oriented us toward the Marshall Plan and NATO, and as the fall of China shaped our response to Korea, and as Cuba conditioned us to act in the Dominican Republic, so a passive acceptance after Vietnam of some communist takeover elsewhere—or even there—would be the prelude to a revived activism in American policy.

In the long run, it seems to me sure that the isolationism now so rampant in the McCarthy campaign and in the anti-Vietnam protest is a transient thing. It is transient for two reasons. The first reason is that American money and armed power have been a major stabilizing force in the world. If we cease using them, it is fairly predictable that the result will be a catastrophe somewhere, and with that will come the revival of the internationalist impulse. The second reason is surer though more remote: it is nuclear proliferation. Treaty or no treaty, there are many in this room who will live to see several underdeveloped countries with the means to launch nuclear war. The United States, I predict, will not stay passive in the face of such a threat. When we come to realize that we can live in safety only in a world in which the political systems of all states are democratic and pacifically oriented, the immediate lessons of Vietnam—whether of success or of failure or a combination of the two—will recede into a dimly remembered image.

In the nuclear age the world has become a small place. In various ways we will all become more alike, and more like America as we know it today. People everywhere want some aspects of American culture, such as automobiles, TV sets, refrigerators, and Coca-Cola. Vietnam illustrates this trend, too. Other aspects of our value system, such as participatory politics, civil liberties, social mobility, pragmatism, and a pacific orientation, are also spreading, but less readily and universally. Were it not for the nuclear threat, the world might well remain heterogeneous in these respects. However, in the era of technological change on the edge of which we now stand, American policy-makers will not be able to view with indifference aggressive dictatorships with nuclear arms, no matter how small or remote they may be. Vietnam, therefore, is not likely to be the last case in which this nation finds itself trying to cope with dangerous armed ideologies in countries far from our area of normal concern and at the potential cost of much American sacrifice. The lesson we must learn is how to cope with such situations by better means than contests of fire power.

RICHARD M. PFEFFER: Professor Pool's professed faith in social science moves me to return to a point Professor Hoffmann touched on a number of times. It is not simply that civilians must bear a large portion of the blame for this war; more particularly, it is social scientists who must bear a large portion of the onus.

I find a striking lack of recognition of the real limitations and deficiencies of social science in Professor Pool's remarks and, more generally, even in a book so critical of American social scientists as the one edited by Irving Horowitz on Project Camelot. Almost everyone contributing to that book, with few exceptions, still maintains a kind of *hubris* about the capacity of social scientists to both understand and manipulate.

Yet we now can see that it was the influx into government of a group of intelligent social scientists, of which many of us like to think we are members, plus the shift from a policy of massive retaliation to incrementalism that set the tone for the kind of easy escalation we have followed in Vietnam. Incrementalism is particularly important in this context, where most of us seem to agree that there is a lack of clearly defined concepts of national interest and clearly defined concepts of national capacity. Without such clear concepts—however difficult they may be to come to—there are few ways in an activist society to stop incremental escalation.

STANLEY HOFFMANN: I would like to go back to some of the points made earlier by Arthur Schlesinger and Henry Kissinger, with whom I entirely agree.

What strikes me most in reflecting on the Vietnam experience (and, temporarily, I will gladly withdraw the word "failure" if it annoys Professor Pool) is that it is, at least to me, a symptom of a generalized intellectual failure—and here I will use the word. We have two kinds of explanations around this table—conceptual ones and organizational ones—the organizational ones being largely represented in the positions of Yarmolinsky and Barnet. I would not minimize the role of bureaucratic momentum or inertia, but one can exaggerate this element and thereby conceal from one's own eyes the intellectual failure itself.

When all of the institutions, agencies, and organizations end up making the same kind of mistake, then it must be for reasons going a bit beyond bureaucratic organization. It is perfectly true that success for each agency became the fulfillment of its own norms, but what is interesting is to try to understand why those norms were set up in the first place. Here one has to go back to those elements of intellectual history or of the American political style which Professor Schlesinger previously mentioned.

I must also say that I agree with much of what Mr. Ahmad said earlier. It seems, for instance, that there has, first of all, been a failure to understand the change in the nature of the international system. In our approach to international affairs we have had very much an expectation of symmetry, an expectation that the adversary would play according to our rules. And we have voiced surprise and discontent when he did not.

Today there are new conditions of international relations. We are now involved in an international system where the stakes are different from what they used to be, where the players are different—more numerous and diverse—and the forms of relevant, i.e., usable, power are not what they used to be. Yet we still analyze the world with conceptions of power derived from very different circumstances and on the basis of grand ideals not really applicable to a world in which the special national circumstances of so large a number of nations really set the limit of what any one of them can accomplish.

There has also been something else—a failure to analyze the conditions of successful insurgency. One thing has disturbed me in what

Mr. Draper said. Even if the war in Vietnam was part of a bipolar world conflict, and even if somehow the Viet Cong had been "controlled" (whatever that means) by Peking, we still could not have won there unless we understood the local circumstances, the nature of the political problems in South Vietnam. As a result, the discussion of the specific weaknesses of South Vietnamese society and politics would not have been irrelevant in any case. This, in turn, would have helped us understand the limits within which a military intervention could be successful.

I also think that we have not understood clearly enough that military intervention, when it takes place, is good only in order to deny the enemy certain kinds of advantages. It has absolutely no or very little relevance to nation building, stability, and so on.

We have not always been aware of the consequences of our own doctrines. We have adopted a doctrine of flexible response because of our dislike of a doctrine of the "rationality of irrationality," and the result, in the case of Vietnam, has been the irrationality of rationality.

We should try to understand, first, what it is that we do badly and, second, what are the consequences of what we want to do, of our doctrines and of our expectations. This strikes me, on the whole, as a more fruitful area of discussion than reforming what I have by now concluded is a thoroughly unreformable bureaucratic apparatus.

What is also most urgent is understanding a little better the political processes in foreign countries, and here I would agree with Mr. Pfeffer that modesty is a prime necessity of social science at the present time.

I have one last point in reply to Professor Pool. He objected to the word "failure." The only question I would ask him is, how much more evidence do you need? In particular, many of the things which you mentioned, such as the election of village officers, are strictly quite irrelevant. What would be relevant would be evidence that pacification is now undertaken by the villagers themselves with forces of their own, that these people are successful in protecting their own areas against the Viet Cong. I see no evidence of this. As for believing that we still can accomplish this today, I would say, well, unfortunately, there is a war going on which makes this very difficult, and what makes it even more difficult is that the kind of war we are running is quite counterproductive.

DANIEL ELLSBERG: Obviously a major lesson of Vietnam is that we must know ourselves better. My experience in Vietnam has led me to believe that we do not know enough about at least one aspect of ourselves, that is, the learning properties of our bureaucracy and government. Let me dismiss as a straw man one caricature of my earlier remarks. Obviously the issue is not that we cannot learn or that we never learn or that we never learn fast or effectively enough. The issue is that we need to learn a great deal more, to reflect more, and to draw many more implications from frequently uncertain facts which even in the most urgent situations sometimes lead only to amazingly and disastrously slow and unreliable interpretations.

That this is a simple point does not reduce its significance. Mr. Wohlstetter, in the fifties, was very important in drawing implications for our strategic plans and posture from what seemed a very simple perception—that electronic messages take time to be communicated and can be interrupted by some physical phenomena. Now, it would not seem that this was a great physical discovery. However, at that time our strategic plans were formulated as if this were not the case, as if messages traveled instantaneously and were thoroughly reliable.

Similarly the perception that organizations, in certain situations more than others, have bureaucratic and not merely human properties, which involve peculiarly bureaucratic insensitivities, blindnesses, or distorted incentives that delay learning or slow up learning or make learning uncertain—this perception is not as much in our consciousness for purposes of analysis and planning and policy-making as I think it should be.

It is especially important to try better to estimate the odds and the speeds of learning when one is involved in giving advice. Many of us in this room have been in the position time after time of giving advice whose appropriateness is premised upon the United States government or that of another country changing itself fast and in important ways. I can easily name specific examples of advice in which the speed with which governmental change would occur was critical to the appropriateness of that advice. Yet in few cases did the advisors concern themselves with that issue, and if they did, they rarely gave the right answer. Their advice, consequently, often led to very bad results. To give advice in the hope that all of one's own preferred tactics or instruments can and will in fact be adopted is often terribly unrealistic and can be dangerous and even irresponsible if we know that this is not the way it is going to be. It is very important in designing and giving advice, in other words, to ask oneself how advice is likely to be carried out.

I want to boil this generalization down to a very narrow but important prediction with regard to Vietnam and elsewhere. I think that at least one great failure probably still lies ahead of us in Vietnam. Saigon, to my mind, is unlikely to survive this year and, indeed, perhaps even unlikely to survive the summer. I make that prediction here because it illustrates my point.

Many people in the bureaucracy can see that this eventuality would be disastrous for us, whether you think in terms of negotiations or anything else. Saigon, of course, is pre-eminently *the* "oil spot" more and more, almost the only one; with a few other cities and towns it is the home of the supporters of the GVN, people who have been driven to Saigon by what Huntington regards as our "modernizing instruments" in Vietnam, bombs and artillery. It is easy to see that from any point of view it is not in our interest to destroy Saigon. But I think it probably will be destroyed—and by us—because it is in the interest of the Viet Cong to move us to do so. And the Viet Cong understand us better, perhaps, than we understand ourselves; and they understand how difficult it is for us to change our habits and how unlikely such change is. I think we will not learn fast enough.

I would say that it is important to prevent our destroying Saigon and that it can, in principle, be avoided. The President can give an order, and it could be effective. But it is essential in arriving at appropriate policies—in this case, as in others—to ask: will he in fact give that order, and to what degree will it be effective?

My own judgment in this instance, right or wrong, is that the President can keep our bombers from bombing populated areas in cases of isolated Viet Cong incursions into Saigon. But in a desperate situation, where bombers appear to be the only way to save American lives and the American presence, the President probably would not, in the face of the advice he will get from the military, resist the call for measures that would destroy Saigon, perhaps all at once, perhaps district by district.

Once having made that judgment of the real odds, one doesn't then curl up and die. For example, in this case I draw these implications. First, it is worth enormous resources to prevent the Viet Cong from getting into Saigon at all in large numbers; this means a redeployment of our forces, which we have not yet carried out to the necessary extent, and probably won't. Second, once we realize in a particular case that we are very unlikely to learn fast enough, we must conclude that time is strongly against us, and our attitudes in *negotiation* should reflect this conclusion; the longer we allow the fighting to go on, the more difficulty we will have because the VC have gotten our number: they have an effective tactic to use against us, and sooner or later they are likely to use it; in fact, they have found a way to exploit our reflexes—in Sir Robert's terms, a jujitsu technique; thus our bargaining position is likely to get worse over time, not better. Finally, it is essential, I think, to study the governmental and military learning process itself to learn much more about its limits and how one can speed it up.

ITHIEL DE SOLA POOL: This discussion reminds me in some way of arguments about laissez-faire in the history of economic thought. Like the proponents of laissez-faire arguing against planning, some of those here who criticize the American role in the world make the underlying assumption that the nature of the state and its bureaucracy is such that rationality cannot be expected of it, that no matter what the government does, it is going to be wrong, and therefore the best thing to do is to abandon its international functions.

As in the economic field, there is a great deal of sense to this argument. But most of us have recognized that in fact large-scale governmental economic policy is going to be with us, and while we may want to reduce it in some ways, we do have to face the problem of maximizing public rationality whenever governmental economic action proves necessary. The same thing applies to the role of the United States government as a stabilizing force in international affairs. Since policy will often be less than perfectly wise, we would like to avoid unnecessary involvement, but unless we accept the necessity of some governmental involvement abroad, we will have a chaotic and dangerous world. We must learn to be as wise as possible in these involvements.

I question the notion of a basic incapacity of government to learn.

There are examples of governmental learning in the economic field. Our government has learned how to maintain a stable economy. Albert Wohlstetter gave a very good example of learning in the political field when he pointed to the improvements during the past eight years in our management and control of strategic nuclear weapons. We have also learned to function overseas relatively effectively in such fields as public health and in certain aspects of agricultural change.

In relation to major issues, such as the nuclear one and the economic one, however, it is unfortunately true that we tend to learn only when we become desperate. It takes a great depression or a war or something of that kind to make us learn. Hopefully, if we can get out of the present mood of self-flagellation about our performance in Vietnam and begin to get more concrete and specific in the lessons we learn, then Vietnam may prove to be another event that leads us to that kind of creative desperation.

What is it that we must learn from the Vietnam experience? We must be specific about the problem of how to influence political outcomes in an environment where conventional military means are ineffective or are excluded to us. Here I would like to reinforce the point Mr. Ellsberg previously made in relation to bombing. In general, we have to find ways of coping with international problems that minimize the use of force. That, of course, means that we have to be skilled in the use of other instruments of influence available to us. The instruments we must use better are largely money, propaganda, political organization, and intelligence.

The notion that we will be able simply to watch the world go by without feeling massively threatened by some of the things that happen seems rather shortsighted. We need to learn to cope with genuine threats and neither acquiesce to them nor respond with inappropriate military devices.

STANLEY HOFFMANN: First of all, let me say that if any effort to draw critical lessons from Vietnam is going to be denounced as self-flagellation, then I do not see much hope for American policy. I was interested in Professor Pool's argument. It made me wonder whether the distinction between domestic politics and international affairs has been clearly understood. A government has a certain amount of control over the elements of the national economy, but it has much less control over what happens abroad. It seems to me that this is one area (among others) in which national borders still make quite a lot of difference. I am struck by how little attention we have paid to this particular phenomenon: our devaluation of borders, of the national fact. What has struck me most in our Vietnam experience is the constant and permanent overestimation of chances of success. We have always adopted the most optimistic reading of the realities. I am afraid that we may be doing just the same in the future if we switch from massive military intervention, which we are beginning to recognize as counterproductive, to massive intervention for political development, which is good old American activism all over again.

In that area, as in international relations in general, the more we understand political processes, the more—not less—uncertain we should get about possibilities of control. The fact is that we still know very little about what we can manipulate. This is especially true when one is dealing with foreign governments.

As I indicated earlier, it seems to me that as Americans (whether we be political scientists or statesmen) dealing with problems of social cohesion and political organization abroad, we approach them with one hand tied behind our back (because we are not colonial masters) and with the other hand full of the wrong tools: tools that have worked only for us.

This brings me back to a point of Sir Robert Thompson's initial statement in which he derides the various attempts at broadening the base of the South Vietnamese government. He points out that all that was needed was a stable and effective government. It did not necessarily have to be a very democratic one. Yet what the Vietnamese story proves is that there is a relation between the stability and effectiveness of a government and its popular base or lack thereof.

If we look around the world, we will find that there are quite a number of places in which social cohesion and political organizations just do not exist. Their existence would be the precondition of success, which American intervention has not heretofore been able to provide.

Now, if this is so, if our capacity to control is limited, we should ask ourselves what it is we ought to feel threatened by. I, for one, may feel threatened by nuclear proliferation in some cases but not necessarily in all. However, I do not think that the American national interest is threatened by all the millions of domestic disorders which are going to take place all over the world.

We have been talking about the alienness of China and Southeast Asia as an excuse for not intervening in the future. But in thinking of American policy toward France in World War II and since, I cannot feel very much more optimistic about the possibilities of intervention in more "familiar" areas either. One certainly ought not to lapse into isolationism, but we should redefine very seriously the kind of things we ought to feel threatened by and the kind of things we really can do to cope with these threats.

LUIGI EINAUDI: My comments derive, first, from Dan Ellsberg's points on American bombing and the lessons others may have learned from it and, second, from Ted Draper's comment on the Dominican Republic. As it happens, my conclusion fits rather nicely with what Stanley Hoffmann was just saying.

Over the past several years the Latin American military have tended to be recalcitrant about matters of civic action, often resisting its introduction in their countries. In the United States this has been presented as the behavior of right-wing incorrigibles. Yet I have found again and again, even before the 1965 escalation, in both internal Latin American working papers and in private conversations, that Vietnam is being taken to demonstrate that the United States does not know what it is doing. This in turn implied to them that any policy (such as civic action) proposed by the United States as part of a counterinsurgency strategy needed to be viewed with considerable doubt and reservation.

Without belaboring the point, I think one lesson of Vietnam that is going to condition the international environment for some time is, very simply, that the credibility of United States advice has been very substantially compromised, regardless of the outcome and also regardless of whether we choose to accept Vietnam as some kind of failure.

With regard to the Dominican affair and its implications for future United States intervention, let me say that the guerrilla groups see United States intervention as a means to recover some claim to the national legitimacy they lost as a result of Castro's association with the Soviet Union. They hope to regain national legitimacy by attempting to lead popular resistance to a foreign invader. Fortunately this is partly an act of desperation. Contrary to some popularly held theories which speak of growing guerrilla strength in Latin America, I would say, as I have been saying on the record for several years now, that there is no chance of a repetition of a Cuban-type guerrilla success in Latin America.

Unfortunately, however, this does not dispose of the question of United States intervention. Many Latin Americans believe that the Dominican matter demonstrates that the United States is capable of misreading more or less normal events in the traditional play of Latin American politics, even ones with minimal communist participation, as requiring extensive American intervention.

If one looks at changes of government in Latin America, one is struck by the recent relative absence of revolution and coups. I would suggest that what we are seeing is, to a certain extent, an effort by Latin American political elites, even very diverse ones, to protect themselves against the eventuality of American intervention by carefully avoiding creating the kind of conditions which might conceivably be misinterpreted by the United States. We are seeing, in other words, a moratorium—somewhat similar to that which existed during World War II—on extreme forms of partisan political activity and violence.

It is fairly easy to predict, therefore, that when the international climate changes, there is going to be in Latin America an extensive round of governmental changes similar to what took place in the period 1944–45. When that happens, what will be relevant will not be questions of counterinsurgency or guerrilla warfare but whether we will have used the time gained by this moratorium to decide, as Stanley Hoffmann suggests, which of these changes we are going to feel threaten us and what our responsibilities and responses on the international scene will be when confronted with a whole range of actions which will have relatively little to do with insurgency, however defined.

THE PURPOSES AND METHODS OF INTERVENTION

§§ SAMUEL P. HUNTINGTON: In the context of expectable major instability and conflict in other countries around the world, is there any way in which the United States could reduce the likelihood of having to choose between an introverted reluctance to act militarily, on the one hand, and the seeming political or diplomatic need to take such action, on the other?

Whatever happens in Vietnam, tendencies toward introversion will be a reality conditioning American behavior in foreign affairs for the immediate future. A primary problem facing the American political system—and certainly a top issue confronting the President who takes office in January 1969—will be to reconcile this new restraining attitude with the responsibilities which the United States accumulated during a quarter century of international involvement. In the past, periods of introversion meant isolationism in foreign policy: we could retreat behind the oceans. Today this is clearly not the case: Walter Lippmann's proposals that the world be divided into spheres of influence and that we limit our concerns to the Western Hemisphere and adjacent waters are very quaint and quite unrealistic. The nature of distance and the constraints imposed by distance have changed fundamentally and made old-style geographical isolation simply out of the question.[6] The problem now is how to adapt to introversion without succumbing to isolation.

One possible and rather likely way out of this dilemma is to reassess, not the geographical scope of American involvements—which will remain world-wide—but rather the purposes of our involvements and the methods we have used to achieve these purposes. Presumably two overriding purposes are the deterrence of overt aggressions and the prevention of domestic insurrections which would upset the international equilibrium in such a way as to threaten vital American interests. Over the past twenty years the United States has developed a fairly effective system for deterring conventional aggression. The continued achievement of this goal will require the United States to maintain substantial military forces, to deploy some of those forces overseas, and to continue to pioneer in weapons innovation. Quite clearly, no comparable system exists for preventing the authoritarian breakdowns, communal wars, and peasant revolutions which might create threats to the peace equal to those produced by overt aggression.

The principal instruments which the United States has used to in-

[6] Cf. Albert Wohlstetter, "The Illusion of Distance," *Foreign Affairs*, XLVI: 2, Jan. 1968.

EPILOGUE: THE LESSONS OF VIETNAM / 219

fluence domestic developments in other countries have been economic
and technical assistance, military aid, covert operations, and military
intervention. In the past these have not been very effective in promoting political stability; in the future, introversion is likely to make
them less available to foreign-policy makers. Economic and military
assistance programs will undoubtedly continue, but probably at greatly
reduced levels. The reluctance of any administration to intervene
militarily will be very great. The day of the massive foreign-policy
program may well be past. In these circumstances the United States
may be compelled to seek other, more appropriate political methods
in attempting to minimize violence and instability in foreign countries.
What we need, in a sense, is an equivalent for domestic violence of
the strategy of military deterrence for overt aggression. Such an
equivalent may conceivably be found in a policy of preventive political involvement.

In recent years many people have argued that earlier and more
extensive American political involvement in the domestic affairs of
other countries may provide an alternative to military intervention.
With respect to the Dominican Republic, for instance, John Bartlow
Martin has said that "political noninvolvement in such a country is
very likely to lead to military intervention—and did." Abraham
Lowenthal similarly concludes that "interference of the traditional
character has been counterproductive, but noninterference has been
ineffective and unsatisfactory; the result has been intermittent, *ad
hoc,* military intervention. The Dominican intervention of 1965
dramatizes the need to reflect on this troubling history, and to suggest
new ways to approach the dynamics of political, social, and economic
development in the Caribbean area."[7]

Similar arguments have been made about Vietnam. The United
States, it is said, consistently side-stepped the opportunities to play a
more direct role in shaping political evolution and political development: in 1957–58, when the insurrection was getting under way; in
1961, when President Kennedy greatly increased American military
assistance to Vietnam without first securing Diem's agreement to the
economic and political reforms recommended by General Taylor;
and again in 1963, when the United States stood aside while the

[7] John Bartlow Martin, *Overtaken by Events* (New York, 1966), p. 709;
Lowenthal, "Lessons of the Dominican Crisis," p. 9.

military overthrew Diem but did little to help establish a more viable political system to replace Diem. Commenting on this failure, Robert Shaplen wisely observed that in our relations with Diem "we seemed unwilling to confront the harsh and unpalatable fact that in today's world . . . subtle but firm political involvement in the affairs of other countries with whom we are engaged in a common enterprise is often the only way to get results and avoid military as well as political disasters."[8] As in South Vietnam, political efforts tend to be postponed until the society is in a state of almost complete disintegration, and at that point they inevitably have to compete with the seemingly even more urgent military demands for priorities and resources. The lead time in political development, however, is unquestionably a long one, and smaller and more timely efforts at political development can be far more effective in preventing an insurrection than larger and later ones will be in pacifying one.

Instability within a society, which may give rise to American intervention, in most cases reflects tensions and breakdowns of the modernization process. Presumably its likelihood can be reduced to the extent that the political system of the country can cope effectively with modernization. To do this a political system must, first, have the capacity to promote social and economic reform, that is, to initiate and to implement the policies required to adapt a society from traditional ruralism to modern urbanism. In general, social reform involves a more equitable distribution of the material and symbolic resources of the society. In most of the more complex societies of Asia, the Middle East, and Latin America, and even in parts of Africa, however, strongly entrenched traditional social forces, interests, and institutions still pose obstacles to reform. Reform requires the change or removal of these traditional forces. It thus requires a redistribution of power within the political system: the breakdown of the power of local, religious, ethnic, and class groups and the centralization of power in national political institutions and groups committed to modernization.

In addition to the ability to concentrate power and promote reform, a political system also must be able to integrate successfully into the system the social forces produced by modernization which achieve a new political consciousness as a result of modernization. Probably the

[8] Robert Shaplen, The Lost Revolution (New York, 1965), p. 151.

single most significant political aspect of modernization is the expansion of political participation. In most traditional societies political activity at the national level is the monopoly of a small ruling class or oligarchy. Modernization produces new "middle class" groups —intellectuals, businessmen, civil servants, army officers—who demand admission into the political system and the opportunity to share in office and power. In due course, political consciousness and participation extends to the lower-middle-class of the towns and cities, to the urban working class, and to the peasants. The expansion of participation to these groups and their integration into the political system may or may not be achieved through democratic means. The modern totalitarian system differs from the traditional authoritarian dictatorship precisely because it requires a much higher level of political participation. The fact that political consciousness and political participation are much greater in Castro's Cuba than they were in Batista's Cuba, however, does not make the former any less of a dictatorship than the latter. A developed political system, democratic or dictatorial, possesses political institutions—parties, interest groups, and assemblies—which can absorb the new participation and integrate the new social groups into the political system. The expansion of participation in an underdeveloped political system, on the other hand, which lacks strong and adaptable political institutions, simply increases the alienation of some groups from the system and leads to overt or covert civil strife.

Social reform and political institutionalization are thus two goals, the successful promotion of which in a modernizing country would reduce significantly the likelihood of United States military intervention.

Beginning in the last years of the Eisenhower Administration, there was an increasing tendency to make American economic assistance to modernizing countries contingent upon those countries embarking upon appropriate programs of social reform. In 1961, of course, the link between economic assistance and social reform was crystallized on a grand scale in the Alliance for Progress. The assumption here was quite clearly that by promoting social reform the United States would reduce the likelihood of Castroite revolutions in Latin American countries and thus avoid the dilemma of either accepting another communist state in the Western Hemisphere or intervening militarily to prevent it. After 1961 the role of social-economic reform as a means of preventing instability and violence was stressed again and again in negotiations between the United States and aid-receiving governments. It received particular stress, of course, in the relationship between the United States and the GVN.

There are, however, at least two major problems in emphasizing social-economic reform as an alternative to instability. The first concerns the presumed effects of such reforms. It is assumed that reform is a substitute for social revolutions. In some cases, however, reform may well be a catalyst of revolution. This was de Tocqueville's argument on the French Revolution; there are reasons to suggest its applicability to contemporary modernizing countries. Reforms aimed at urban and especially middle-class groups seem particularly likely to produce violence and disorder in their wake. Land reforms, in contrast, have usually had the effect of turning peasants from a potentially revolutionary force into a conservative bulwark of the existing order.[9]

In Vietnam, however, even this may not have been true. For a decade Americans urged land reform as a means of countering the Viet Cong appeal to the peasants. Yet one recent study has found the Viet Cong in the 1960's to be weakest in those provinces in which no land distribution had taken place in the 1950's and much stronger in those provinces where some land reform had been implemented. In addition, the greater the inequality of current land ownership in a province, the weaker the Viet Cong was in the province.[10] The assumptions and methods of this study can be debated. They have, indeed, been subjected to outraged criticism and passionate denunciation by AID true believers in the doctrine of "salvation through land reform." Whatever quibbles may be made, however, the conclusions suggested by this seemingly perverse statistical analysis can be bolstered by much evidence from other countries and other times. The promotion of social-economic reform may in some circumstances reduce the likelihood of civil violence; in other circumstances it may increase that likelihood.

A second problem concerns the effects of American efforts to pro-

[9] This argument and supporting evidence can be found in chapter 6 of my *Political Order in Changing Societies* (Yale University Press, 1968).

[10] Edward J. Mitchell, "Inequality and Insurgency: A Statistical Study of South Vietnam," *World Politics*, XX, April 1968, pp. 421–38.

mote social reforms. So long as American efforts remain relatively small and are limited to the carrot and the stick of economic assistance and its denial, the impact of these efforts on social change will be relatively small. Where the United States massively intervenes in a society, however, its effects on the promotion of social reform, economic change, and modernization are likely to be overwhelming and revolutionary. American liberals frequently think of United States involvement in the politics of another country as inherently biased on the side of the status quo. This is, however, only a half-truth. In fact, there would appear to be a direct correlation between the scope and direction of American involvement. *The more extensive the American involvement in the politics of another country, the more progressive or reform-oriented is its impact on that country.* In those countries which it has governed militarily or colonially the impact of the United States has generally tended to undermine and destroy the traditional order, promote social and economic equality, expand human welfare, and stimulate economic development. In the years since World War II, for instance, rapid and thoroughgoing land reforms have (with one exception) been carried out under two auspices: communist revolution (China, Vietnam, Yugoslavia) and American military occupation (Japan, Korea, and, at a second remove, Taiwan). The only other country which has carried out a land reform as sweeping as these is Bolivia, and that was done by a revolutionary government financed by the United States.

The revolutionary and modernizing impact which a massive American presence has on a foreign country is in part the result of conscious desire to promote reform and in part simply the by-product of the exposure of a traditional culture to the ways of an egalitarian, affluent, liberal, modern society. On the other hand, where the American presence is relatively limited—and in particular, of course, where the American governmental presence is limited—the net effect of the American impact tends to be much more conservative, witness most of the states of Central America. In a sense this relationship between the scale and the direction of the American impact parallels that which students of colonialism have noticed between direct and indirect colonial rule. Countries subjected to a massive and prolonged colonial rule, it is argued, were in a much better position to modernize and develop than those, such as the Middle East countries and China, which were subjected to indirect, marginal, and hence irresponsible colonial influence.

This seemingly positive relationship between intervention and re-form obviously creates problems for the American liberal. On the one hand, he is against intervention; on the other, he is in favor of reform. Outside of government, he can add up the balance one way or another. In the government, however, and anxious to promote social-economic reform (and this includes, I would argue, the bulk of State, AID, and CIA personnel, despite myths to the contrary), he inevitably also finds himself promoting more and more American intervention. Vietnam is the perfect case in point. There, as in so many other non-Western societies, the forces of traditionalism, elit-ism, apathy, corruption, family, and self-interest were so strong as to make extremely difficult achievement of reforms through the in-digenous political system. As a result the life of the American advisor was typically one of intensifying frustration. Adhering to the canons of advisorship, the new American arrival inevitably starts by at-tempting to become chummy with his Vietnamese counterpart and then gradually to induce him to take the actions which to the Ameri-can seem obviously needed to promote social welfare. The Vietnamese smiles approvingly and does nothing. The American becomes more insistent; the Vietnamese becomes more resistant. In the end the Vietnamese eventually orders some action to be taken, but then also ensures that it will have just the opposite effects from those which the American intended. By that time the American advisor, who arrived with such idealistic hopes and progressive ideas of promoting social good *with* the Vietnamese, has come to the conclusion that if any good is to be accomplished, it must be done by Americans *to* the Vietnamese. If he still has any time left in his twelve- or eighteen-month tour of duty, he will demand five more American assistants and plunge in to do the job himself. The desire for reform thus pro-motes the continual expansion of the American presence; and the expansion of the American presence promotes both intended and unintended social and economic change.

This issue of reform *vs.* nonintervention is perhaps most dramati-cally posed by the problem of corruption. Many of those Americans who have voiced doubts about the American role in Vietnam and have argued for a decrease in the American presence there are also precisely those who have argued that we must do whatever is necessary to eliminate corruption there. Achieving the latter goal, however, would inevitably mean much greater American intervention and involvement. The United States could, for instance, simply refuse to recognize or to cooperate with GVN officials known to be more corrupt than the average. If this policy was to be effective, however, it would soon mean the exercise of a veto power by United States officials over virtually all appointments in the ARVN and the GVN. The results might well be successful, but they would be achieved at a price. Which is worse: toleration of Vietnamese corruption or expansion of American colonialism?

Many AID and CORDS provincial advisors in Vietnam have tacked up on their office walls one of those many verses from the poet laureate of the British empire which now seem peculiarly relevant to American dilemmas:

> Now it is not good for the Christian's health
> to hustle the Aryan brown,
> For the Christian riles, and the Aryan smiles
> and he weareth the Christian down;
> And the end of the fight is a tombstone white
> with the name of the late deceased,
> And the epitaph drear: "A Fool lies here
> who tried to hustle the East."

The instinct of Americans, however, is to draw quite the opposite lesson than Kipling intended. If the East cannot be hustled, it must be replaced. If the Vietnamese won't reform and change their own society, we must reform it for them. And few phenomena are more unsettling in their consequences than masses of energetic and high-minded Americans intent on doing good.

If promotion of social reform seems unlikely to reduce the pressures for American military intervention, what about the promotion of political institutions capable of channeling discontent into peaceful paths? To some extent, of course, more effective political institutions are required for social reform. The assumptions about political development which underlie the American commitment to social reform, indeed, directly conflict with those which have been associated with American economic assistance programs. The latter have in part reflected the belief that economic development will create the social and economic conditions favorable to the emergence of broad-based, stable political institutions. The American commitment to social reform, on the other hand, presupposes the existence in the recipient country of a political system sufficiently well developed and authoritative as to be capable of inaugurating such reforms. As the experience of the Alliance for Progress amply demonstrates, this assumption is of questionable validity in much of Latin America. It is probably even less valid in Southeast Asia. If the United States is to make social reform a condition for economic assistance, it may also have some responsibility to help governments to develop the political institutions required to make such reforms a reality.

The development of broader-based political institutions is thus in some cases a prerequisite to reform. In other cases, of which Vietnam is probably one, the development of such institutions may well slow down the pace of reform. The concentration of power will give way to the dispersion of power, and the result will be less reform but more stability. In particular, it will mean less obvious signs of reform, which are the things that please Americans, and more toleration of Vietnamese practices and ways, many of which are abhorrent to Americans. Clearly, however, political stability in many modernizing countries will depend upon the creation of an institutional framework to provide for the peaceful participation of larger and larger groups of people in the political process. If a political system is unable to develop the organizations to serve this end, if its leaders, like Diem in South Vietnam in the late 1950's, instead attempt to close off the institutional channels for popular participation, the inevitably revolutionary leaders arise to mobilize popular participation against the political system rather than through the political system. To maintain political stability, consequently, the construction of organizations and institutions for peaceful participation in government must go hand in hand with the expansion of political awareness among the masses of the population. In particular, stability requires the development of political parties and party systems.

By and large, stable countries have strong political parties; unstable countries have weak parties. More importantly, countries which do have strong political parties can look forward to future stability with considerably greater confidence than countries with weak parties or with no parties. The future political stability of Thailand is more problematical than that of Malaysia, in part because Thailand lacks organized political parties to assimilate into the political system groups which inevitably will acquire political consciousness as the process of modernization continues. It is a bitter truth but a real one that probably the most stable government in Southeast Asia today is the government of North Vietnam. The relative political stability which has characterized that country in contrast to South Vietnam derives largely from the fact that in the north the organization of the communist party reaches out into the rural areas and provides a channel for communication of rural grievances to the center and for control of the countryside by the government.

Changes in the political stability of a country are related to changes in the strength of its party system. The emergence of South Korea from civil strife and instability after 1962 coincided with the creation by General Park and his associates of a strong political party which was able to provide effective rule and public order and at the same time promote economic growth and such needed reforms as the normalization of its relations with Japan. The contrast between India's political stability during the 1950's and the instability of Pakistan was due to the strength of the Congress party in India with its well-developed grass-roots organization, as contrasted with the weakness of the Muslim League in Pakistan, which at that time was little more than a clique of maneuvering politicians with no roots in the country which they were supposed to govern. The emergence in the 1960's of political stability in Pakistan coincided with the development of a new grass-roots political system through the Basic Democracies program and the reinvigoration of the Muslim League organization. At the same time, the decline in the strength of the Congress party threatened India with increasing political turmoil and instability.

The nature of the party system in the society largely determines whether new groups will enter politics peacefully or through revolution. After the urban intellectuals appear on the scene, the next crucial turning point in the expansion of political participation in a modernizing society is the inauguration of the rural masses into national politics. The timing, the method, and the auspices of the "green uprising" decisively shape the subsequent political evolution of the society. It may occur relatively rapidly, or it may occur slowly and proceed through several stages. In a colonial society the "green uprising" may occur under the auspices of the nationalist intellectuals who, as in India and Tunisia, mobilize peasant groups into politics within the framework of the nationalist party to support them in their struggles with the imperial power. In a competitive party system the peasant mobilization often takes the form of one segment of the urban elite developing an appeal to or making an alliance with the crucial rural voters and mobilizing them into politics so as to overwhelm at the polls the more narrowly urban based parties. If no group within the political system takes the lead in organizing peasant political participation, some group of urban intellectuals will mobilize and organize them into politics against the political system. This results in revolution. This almost happened in the Philippines. It did happen in Vietnam. It may be happening in Thailand.

The argument that the United States ought to encourage the development of more highly structured and broad-based party systems in modernizing countries always runs into at least three objections. First, many Americans question the legitimacy of governmental programs directly related to political institutionalization and party development. They recoil from any thought of "intervention," and particularly intervention in the politics of other countries. Yet the fact of the matter is that American intervention in the affairs of other countries occurs continuously in scores of ways. The United States intervenes to promote health, agriculture, land reform, industrialization, education, and military security. Why should it not also intervene to promote political development? The United States intervenes to help build civil services, police forces, universities, armies, and navies. Why should it not also intervene to help build political parties? Modernization means increasing political participation. That participation has to be organized. The principal institutional means for organizing that participation is the political party. Why should it be thought immoral or inappropriate to help strengthen these essential institutions of modern society?

Second, it is at times also argued that intervention to promote political development is bound to be ineffective or self-defeating. American support for a particular party or group, it is said, will be the kiss of death to this group. In some cases this may be true, but it should be noted that people in most countries think that the United States intervenes now to support particular groups, even when it does not do so. In many ways the United States suffers all the stigmata and disadvantages of political intervention and reaps few of the benefits. In addition, in many countries important groups have strongly urged the United States to play a more active political role, but the United States has hung back and refused to do so. It is also argued that American intervention in the politics of other countries runs counter to the general desire of the people of those countries to manage their own affairs and will consequently give rise to violently anti-American nationalism. Quite obviously, however, the control of politics, even more than that of the economy, will remain in local hands. The elites of each society will choose their own forms of political organization. All that foreigners can do is to advise them on the prerequisites and requirements of political organization, even as they do for economic development, and give them technical and material assistance in the development of political organizations.

Third, it as at times argued that the United States is so much a victim of liberal myopia that it is hopelessly incapable of understanding the political needs of foreign systems and of adapting its own goals and methods to meet those needs. Americans, it is said, will inevitably attempt to reproduce in the most unsuitable foreign soil all the characteristics of their own highly distinctive two-party, liberal, pluralistic, constitutional democracy. Obviously Americans, like anyone else, like to see the virtues of their own system and to flatter themselves by seeing it reproduced elsewhere. On the other hand, however, it is also quite clear that Americans have been able to rise above such parochialism in the past, and there is no reason why this should not be even more of a pattern in the future. Indeed, many of those critics who accuse the United States of attempting to export its own institutions, at the same time also accuse the United States of supporting reactionary and repressive personalistic dictatorships around the world. Such critics would be more persuasive if they were less inconsistent. In fact, of course, the United States has, wisely or not, supported and attempted to promote the development of the most varied types of political systems around the world. Surely few political systems differ more fundamentally from the American system than that which has existed in Iran. Yet the United States has engaged in the most active efforts to strengthen and develop this essentially authoritarian monarchy. Whether this is a wise policy or not and whether it will succeed or not are other questions, but we certainly were not inhibited in our efforts to promote monarchical development by the failure of the Iranian political system to conform to the American model. In similar fashion the United States has played an active role in promoting one-party systems in Tunisia and Bolivia, a military-led dominant party system in Korea, monarchical-bureaucratic regimes in Thailand and Nepal, and also, of course, a variety of competitive democratic systems in which the dominant groups have been socialist, Catholic, and liberal, as well as highly conservative.

Political involvements designed more effectively to promote the development of political institutions will certainly require levels of discretion and sophistication which have not always been present in our international behavior in the past. Such involvements may be designed to ward off the instabilities which could lead to military intervention, but conceivably they could in themselves become a cause and excuse for military intervention. The way to avoid this is to keep commitments to particular individuals and groups conditional and/or covert and deniable. In the past we have often felt the need to justify such commitments by saying that the future of the country rested with Mr. X or the military or some other group. In fact, however, our leverage varies inversely with our commitments. In Vietnam we became the victim of our own declarations: we talked ourselves to the point where, as Joseph Johnson neatly put it, our commitment became the commitment. In the future a more detached attitude toward foreign governments and leaders may well increase rather than decrease our influence. All commitments should be conditional, and many should be covert. In the past the logic of democratic politics tended to dramatize the commitment and play down the conditions. The shift to introversion and the resulting absence of public support which requires recourse to political means in foreign policy, however, may also give our leaders greater freedom to avoid the stark commitments which they have felt compelled to make in the past. The need to substitute more discreet political action for more massive economic and military action may also create the possibility of doing so.

The United States clearly can affect the political development of other countries only in marginal ways. Yet we also clearly have some interest in doing so, if only because such action might marginally reduce the probability of more Vietnams. There are perhaps at least five things which we might do in this area.

(1) We could consciously recognize, even if we did not publicize it, that a major goal of American policy is the promotion of stable political institutions in modernizing countries and particularly the development of strong political parties. Our support for and cooperation with political leaders or military juntas could depend upon their actively attempting to develop grass-roots political organization. If we do get irrevocably committed to any one leader, no matter how charismatic he may be, we could, like the Russians in Cuba, try to nudge that leader into the difficult task of building political institutions.

(2) We could devote much more effort to the study of the conditions and patterns of political evolution and to the elaboration of new concepts and categories useful for the analysis of societies undergoing rapid social change.

(3) We could evaluate economic and technical assistance programs in terms not only of how they contribute to economic development but also of how they affect political development. We could try to identify those types of economic assistance which may contribute to both forms of development. We could develop criteria and guidelines for balancing prospective economic gains against political losses and political gains against economic losses.

(4) We could inaugurate new activities directed specifically toward political development. These might include assistance to political parties, programs to develop and train political leaders, assistance to more broadly based and public-oriented interest groups, and more widespread support for community development programs.

Finally, we could create some office in our own government which would have a primary responsibility for political development. Until recently, the Agency for International Development has been, in effect, an agency for economic development. Somewhere, either inside AID or outside AID, we need an office for political development; the new Title IX office might serve as a staff nucleus, but it is clearly much too far down in the hierarchy to carry much weight. We need diplomats and economic planners, but we also need to recruit and train personnel skilled in the techniques of analyzing political change and promoting political organization. What we could use, perhaps, is a new-style CIA, more skilled in building governments than in subverting them.

All this may seem highly adventurous. But it is, I would suggest, a highly conservative prescription for promoting political stability and avoiding military intervention. Such a program of preventive political involvement would be less visible to both the American public and foreign publics. In an age of introversion and of hostility to massive expenditures overseas, this has much to be said for it. Stimulating political organization, in particular, would get the United States out of the job of attempting to promote social and economic changes on its own. Instead of trying to pressure a reluctant government to introduce land reform as a substitute for peasant revolution, we would focus on the promotion of peasant organizations which could then, if they wished to, put pressure on the government. Political involvements of this nature could well be more discreet, less expensive, and more productive of political stability than current reliance on economic development, social reform, and, ultimately, military intervention.

§§ EQBAL AHMAD: Professor Huntington's presentations are a mixed bag of welfare imperialism and relentless optimism. They reflect that strange compound of assumptions and attitudes which characterizes American policy in the "third world" and which invokes among those of us from the "third world" feelings of bewilderment and fear. The policy-makers in Washington will be pleased by his earlier assertion that Vietnam may not after all be regarded as a failure when there is a "reckoning of the benefits of the intervention." The worried doubters, however, are assured that the uniqueness of Vietnam makes unlikely a duplication of the Vietnamese situation. The acknowledgment of the risks of historical analogies should please the modernistic social scientists who object to this form of analysis. Yet the more traditional among us should have no great cause for complaint after the prescience of a prophetic cycle theorist has been praised. The invocation of the Klingberg cycle must gratify the isolationists and the pacifists with the knowledge that America has reached the end of its twenty-seven-year period of "extroversion." But the cold war liberals ought to be soothed by the intimation that while America may have to eschew military involvements of Vietnamese proportions, it cannot disengage from its responsibilities to the underdeveloped. The hawks, of course, can look forward to the next cycle of extroversion, sometime after 1984. Finally, those most vociferous of all Americans—the sociologists and political scientists—must rejoice over the promise of their promotion to an unquestionably lucrative and highly challenging role as engineers and architects of political ideologies, parties, and participation—modern day philosopher-kings engaged and anointed by a super CIA. Only the New Left radicals may find it difficult going, unless, of course, they derive a vicarious satisfaction from the speculation that in the event of a fourth major military involvement (the earlier three being World War II, Korea, and Vietnam) the "constitutional structure of the Republic could well be shaken."

Professor Huntington's remarks, in an abstract sense, are an excellent product of the American pluralistic, bargaining political culture. There is something for everyone within a defined boundary, and there is room for orderly settlement of differences provided there is a consensus on broad goals. Yet precisely for the reasons of its cultural symmetry, it fails as an analysis for underdeveloped countries which are still torn by cleavages on goals, and where antagonistic interests and values dominate social, political, and economic realities.

The phased modernization of West European countries, the United States, and even Japan enjoyed the luxuries of time, superior psychological, economic, and cultural resources, plus the opportunity of channeling to the colonies and the expanding frontier the tensions and ambitions produced by technology and social change. Yet they had their share of excesses, civil wars, revolutions, disorders, and ideological aberration. Today, the "third world" countries must undergo a triple transformation—social, economic, and political—simultaneously, in telescoped time and under the multiple pressures of colonial heritage and growing population. In the circumstances, our relative calm should surprise observers. We may hope to avoid the extremes of excesses—regression into colonial, racist, fascist, or Stalinist aberrations. Yet we shall inevitably experience conflicts and disorders in the process of reformulating our values and reconstructing our societies. If a superpower enters our world committed obsessively to orderly change and with an interest in maintaining stable clients, it will necessarily distort our development, sharpen our conflicts, and will also render itself vulnerable to the perpetual temptation of intervening militarily in behalf of its losing protégés.

Our formal independence has given us, at best, an unenviable position as pawns in the game of high politics. That is why we react in fear when one superpower serves notice on a country, as America has done in Vietnam, that it will cajole, coerce, and finally conquer a people that would not conform to its inverted image of freedom and democracy; and another great power insists, in the name of justice, on subverting a people driven by want and search for dignity, so that the attainment of justice becomes an excuse for the strangling of human freedom. Vietnam is important to us only because it has dramatized our agony and exacerbated our fears. And it leads me to conclude that unless there is a drastic change in Western attitudes toward a transforming world, the underdeveloped countries which stand in agony today at the threshold of the twentieth century could become the greatest suckers in history. But then who knows what price we may exact from the world for the destruction of our dignity, not to mention our lives and property, and our right to formulate our destiny without gross foreign interference?

The jealous nationalism of the underdeveloped countries is not simply a question of mood. It is a matter of survival. To the extent that even communist states like Cuba, North Vietnam, and North Korea, not to mention China, assert their independence from the dictates of the protecting power despite their acute dependence (on Russia) and their encirclement (by the United States), it is a measure of their responsiveness to this national need. It is curious, indeed, that in a discussion focused in great part on political development in underdeveloped countries, Professor Huntington has made no reference to this primary fact in our political life. I suspect that this omission, though unintentional, is not accidental. It reflects the antinationalist thrust of the United States, which, as suggested earlier, is related to certain aspects of the American political culture.

When a nationalist movement acquires a radical content, when it threatens to nationalize property and socialize national resources, when it becomes diplomatically assertive and neutralist, it initially elicits an unfavorable response from the United States. Its programs threaten potential or actual American investments; its diplomatic posture involves the loss of a potential or actual ally in the cold war; its revolutionary doctrine appears dangerously congruent with the communist enemy's. If a country threatened by such a nationalism happens to be a client state, then a United States–mounted *coup d'état* or sharp, swift military intervention seeks to restore the status quo. Interventions of this type include Guatemala, the Dominican Republic, and

Iran. In nonclient underdeveloped states such a radical nationalist movement is tolerated by the United States if it comes to power unexpectedly, or turns radical gradually and without serious challenge under a legitimate and popular leader—although relations with such regimes remain intermittently reserved if not restrained. Egypt is an example of the first type, Tanzania of the second.

American tolerance toward these countries appeared to be increasing in the Kennedy Administration; neutralists were not regarded invariably as allies of communism. There was even a tendency actively to encourage their radical posture, especially in the zones of French influence (Tunisia became an AID showpiece during this period and has since shown unabashed loyalty to the United States). The unusual popularity in the "third world" of the Kennedy Administration was due, not so much to actual change in United States policy, but largely to the feeling among us that America was beginning to understand the nature of our nationalism, that the puppeteer view of the world was giving way to a more sophisticated understanding of our drive toward sovereignty. But only among the East European clients of the U.S.S.R. has American policy consistently welcomed and, where possible, encouraged reactive nationalism.

Professor Huntington gives us a very keen analysis of how, in the American alliance with conservative nationalism, the interaction between United States economic aid and desire for reform promotes the expansion of American presence and finally ends in intervention. Military assistance produces much the same, if more dangerous, symbiosis between the United States and the recipient indigenous elites. The more a foreign power involves itself in native problems, the greater becomes its economic and psychic investments. As the relationship gets more institutionalized, it becomes harder to extricate itself from the commitment. The tendency then is to blame individuals and not the system, which inherently lacks the capacity to maintain and enhance its legitimacy. Hence one gets rid of a dictator only to inherit a worse one. United States–supported Latin American coups provide innumerable examples of this vicious cycle.

The case of Vietnam is also illustrative. There is now a general tendency in America to blame Diem, who had once been billed as a democratic alternative to Ho Chi Minh. Yet it is not fair to blame him for failing to introduce meaningful reforms and thus driving the

Vietnamese to desperation. It was morbid optimism to expect an absentee aristocrat to substitute for a heroic leader who had devoted a lifetime to the liberation of his country, and to bypass a leadership and cadres whose organic ties with the peasants were cemented by the bitter struggle for independence. Given his situation, Diem had no choice; his only possible weapons were a power apparatus to regiment the population, all-out support of minorities and the privileged, and widespread terror. These were not the aberrations of a program, but the program itself. And his assassination left the United States at the mercy of the musical-chair generals, who had earlier collaborated with France and who further degenerated into sanctioning the systematic destruction of a country they claimed to govern.

Professor Huntington ignores the important problem of legitimacy when he makes his recommendation in behalf of political development. I do not question his central positive theme, that the achievement of consolidation of power by a regime followed by advances in the area of social reforms and political institutionalization will reduce the chances of United States military intervention. Yet his belief that the United States should actively engage in fostering political development is fraught with risks and is likely, at best, to be self-defeating.

No foreign power has the ability to equip a native government with legitimacy (the essential quality of rulership) nor with the will and capacity to open channels for peaceful change—unless it is the case of a military occupation which for some historical or psychological reasons is accepted by the population.[11] In fact, the reverse is truer: identification with a foreign power erodes the legitimacy of a regime. And the correlation between growing legitimacy and willingness to open new domestic channels for participation is known to be positive. Even if I were to accept the questionable premise that the United States has not been involved in aiding and influencing political and administrative development in Vietnam, I should at least question the efficacy of such involvement. Given the absence of legitimacy and the reactionary character of the Diem regime, I doubt that a

11 Professor Huntington has cited the case of Japan. One may also ask why the United States did not achieve comparable success in Cuba and the Philippines? While it is not central to the argument here, it may be noted that Bolivia is not the only noncommunist or nonoccupied country to achieve thoroughgoing land reform. Algeria, Tunisia, Tanzania, Egypt, and Syria are among the others.

timely and firm American involvement in political development would have led to the creation of legitimate and popular institutions in Vietnam, thus preventing, as Professor Huntington appears to believe, the insurrection from spreading.

Professor Huntington seems to take an essentially technical view of political development. But the primary factor in promoting political institutions is not improved professionalism, as is largely true of the army, navy, hospitals, etc. Rather it involves a vision of society, the choice of values and goals. These are not exportable goods or skills that can form part of foreign aid programs. It is incorrect, therefore, to put political parties in the same category as hospitals and armies. Political institutions unsupported by operative values become mere formalities or else turn into bureaucratic instruments of control rather than of participation. Professor Huntington does not discuss the question of prerequisites for an institution-building effort. He somehow assumes the pliability of recipient regimes to American pressures for and advice on how to build institutions. The error typical of American policy is repeated. The dramatic failure of the American mission in Vietnam should at least have laid to rest this kind of technocratic evangelism and culture-centered optimism.

Legitimate rulers who have a value commitment to maintaining a measure of accountability to the populace and to creatively confronting the crises of participation, development, and distribution are unlikely to need foreign help in creating and running political institutions. The recent history of underdeveloped countries provides ample evidence that their leaders do not lack organizing skills, nor are they in need of advice on institution building. If they do not promote political participation, it is because they do not wish to do so. The Algerians, many of whom are in power today, created one of the most powerful and, under assault, indestructible political institutions of this century. Yet the FLN, unlike the Neo-Destour party of Tunisia or the Istiqlal of Morocco, did not really survive independence, and not for lack of foreign advice or pressure. Potentially it is still a revivable institution, for many of the old cadres and an eager populace are longing to be active participants again. What is lacking is the incentive on the part of Algeria's military leaders, who perhaps perceive in the development of popular institutions a threat to the power of the army.

Similarly Pakistan's Muslim League degenerated into factions and

Ghana's Convention party turned into a bureaucratic behemoth, not for lack of organizing skill nor because of ignorance on the part of politicians about the meaning and importance of political institutions. They weakened as popular institutions because the leaders perceived them as threats, or at least as useless for wielding power after independence had been achieved. These leaders lacked the radical commitment to social and economic transformation, on the basis of which they could continually communicate with the majority a consistent and functioning ideology which could provide guidelines against which political behavior could be tested and upon which political institutions could be based. They lacked an operative commitment to accountability which could ensure their adherence to institutionalized norms and practices.

These commitments are seldom acquired through pressures from allies. They result from social conflict or social movements, in response to continual, often violent pressures from below, or as a consequence of revolutionary upheaval. Unless an elite is already committed deeply and operatively to a set of political values, it is not likely to become so under foreign pressure. In fact, protective foreign involvement may only harden its unwillingness to distribute its privileges and power.[12]

Professor Huntington, in his discussion of political involvement, presents an excellent analysis of how the interaction between economic aid and United States pressures for social reforms produces the expansion of American presence as well as its frustration; the combination leads eventually to intervention. But he does not explain satisfactorily why similar involvement in political development will not produce the same result. In fact, the very forces which lead to a positive relationship between economic reform and intervention are likely to have a stronger correlation between political involvement and intervention. Political participation is even more difficult to sell to an entrenched ruling class than economic reforms, because it involves

---

[12] For this reason I believe in the "domino theory," in reverse. If the United States "wins" in Vietnam, it may have the effect of assuring the Thai rulers (whose propensity to promise elections has become proverbial) and the Filipino elite (who have the reputation of being the most corrupt in Asia) that the United States will save them from their people. The defeat of United States objectives in Vietnam, on the other hand, may have a salutary effect on their willingness to reform.

the sharing of power as well as resources. It is bound to produce greater resentment and truculence on the part of native allies, more frustration, greater psychic and material involvement, and more intervention on the part of the United States. Politics and power, more than economics, command the passions of men—especially well-fed men.

Professor Huntington's suggestion that the escalation of political involvement into military intervention can be avoided by keeping political commitments "conditional and/or covert" suffers from bad history no less than poor principles. Commitments, even conditional ones, have a vicious logic of proliferation. History is replete with examples of conditional commitments giving birth to unconditional ones. Vietnam itself is a case in point; need one recall that American boys were never committed to fighting the battle of Asian boys? As for covertness, how does one keep political activities of this magnitude covert in a democracy—or in a dictatorship, for that matter? And how does the professed commitment to the principles of participation and democracy square with the systematic denial to people of information on the nature of institutions to which they belong and to which they contribute?

Then there are the operational questions, far too many to merit detailed examination, but they all lead to the same thing—increasing military aid and "advisors" to incumbent regimes, and possible military intervention. Who will the United States aid in building political parties and organization? Professor Huntington does not exactly answer. But his assumptions are clearly drawn from the American culture of management. He mentions groups "within the political system" as against a "group of urban intellectuals" whose organization of the peasantry "results in revolution." He implies that United States political involvement will be on behalf of the groups within the system and, since they exist practically everywhere, in competition with the revolutionary intellectuals. I wonder whose definition of groups within and outside the system is to be taken—America's? the native government's? the military's? I wonder, too, how this concept differs from United States–aided counterinsurgency being practiced in Thailand, the Philippines, or the more tragic Guatemala? And what would happen if the revolutionaries somehow do succeed in mobilizing the peasants and do seriously challenge the American-sponsored party or system?

If my earlier analysis of American political culture has any validity, it points out the danger of continued United States interventionism, especially in the client states. By way of summary, it seems (1) that the United States is not yet able to tolerate, much less encourage, radical nationalism in client states; the tendency to accept and encourage nationalism as a vehicle for social transformation has been proportionately greater in the countries where the United States does not command direct influence; (2) that the United States expects of the underdeveloped countries a style and norms of politics which are unlikely to be fulfilled at this stage of their development; (3) that in countries where its involvement is significant, failure to conform to American expectations produces a vicious cycle of expanding American role in domestic affairs, erosion of the legitimacy of United States–supported elites, radicalization and enlargement of civil conflict, and military intervention in behalf of the status quo; while seeking order and stability, in fact the United States contributes to more disorder; (4) that the deeper its involvement in a country, the less flexible it becomes in dealing with diverse political groupings and the more it develops a vested interest in defending friendly governments against revolutionary forces; (5) that a colonial style, perhaps acquired in Latin America and reinforced by evangelism as well as incipient racism, persists and produces a relationship of dependence and protectiveness between native elites and the United States.

From these conclusions it should follow that if the dialectic of intervention is to be broken, scholars and policy-makers have to give attention to the manner in which the United States must disengage from direct involvement in underdeveloped countries. Such a disengagement need not be the result of isolationist sentiments. It must envisage a new role for the United States and new styles of relationships which will take into account the interest of America as well as of the underdeveloped. Yet such a change in policy must necessarily be preceded by not only an examination of America's assumptions but also a redefinition of its goals.

Professor Huntington implicitly endorses the assumptions and goals of United States policy. He does not identify either, although a few may be inferred from his discussion. There is a preoccupation with success; we are given a "useful reminder that consequences are all that count." The criteria of success, however, are left unclear.

Restoration of order, successful arbitration between conflicting native factions, organizing "honest elections" which the "right man" wins, and promoting reforms are cited as achievements of the Dominican intervention. He also argues that the "judgment that United States policy in the Vietnamese crisis was ultimately unsuccessful tends to be based upon an incomplete, perhaps misleading reckoning of the benefits of the intervention." Hence he defers a discussion of whether or not it was a salutary case of intervention.

One is led to ask, "benefits" for whom? For the United States? For the Thai and Filipino clients of the United States? For the men in Saigon who once collaborated with France and are now collaborating with America? Or for the people of Vietnam and Southeast Asia? If one judges from the point of view of the Pentagon or the White House, many benefits are already perceptible and more can be discerned for the future. For example, military officials are reportedly happy over the unusual opportunity to test and develop new weapons both for conventional and irregular warfare; a new generation of officers and men have gained combat experience in unfamiliar terrain; lessons learned in Vietnam have led to improved techniques of counterinsurgency and pacification in the other client states of Southeast Asia and Latin America. Domestically the war may have served as a safety valve for absorbing thousands of young blacks, the most aggressive of whom opt to extend their service in the military. And insofar as the intentions of the United States are still unclear, it is possible that, unwilling to negotiate withdrawal (the status quo being the *casus belli* is nonnegotiable), it will eventually acquire a piece of strategic real estate near China, inhabited by the beaten and sunk remainder of a once brave and proud people—a sort of modern Indian reservation in the heart of Asia. The ruling elites of Thailand, the Philippines (and elsewhere), and other war profiteers may also have reasons to extol the benefits of the intervention, especially if the United States can demonstrate its willingness to commit a genocide in order to save its clients.

To the Vietnamese people, however, the American invasion has brought few benefits. Professor Huntington's earlier contention regarding the "relatively limited and undestructive" character of this war notwithstanding, their losses have been staggering, and many of them are statistically immeasurable. No one seems to have counted the dead in this computerized war, but if one were to accept even the lowest estimated ratio of civilian losses to claimed enemy casualties, more than a million Vietnamese may already be presumed to have died. A quarter of the southern population has been displaced; the social and cultural fabric of the society has been badly torn. Even the ecological balance has been affected by defoliation and bombing, although only in the future shall we know the extent and permanence of this damage. And the end is not yet in sight.

The earlier argument that the right lesson of Vietnam may be an "unlesson" is based on a factually correct yet irrelevant observation. I can only agree with Professor Huntington on the uniqueness of the Vietnamese situation. But, as others have said, the uniqueness rests with Vietnam, not with American policy. It refers to the historical and political configurations which permitted the Vietnamese people to organize a successful resistance against American intervention. It does not refer to the assumptions, attitudes, and the pattern of relationships with indigenous elites which have frequently caused the United States to intervene militarily on behalf of a threatened status quo. The postwar interventions generally succeeded in obtaining their immediate goal of defeating a radical coalition and maintaining a friendly and manageable, preferably reformed status quo. The Philippines, Guatemala, Nicaragua, Iran, and the Dominican Republic are frequently cited as examples of success. In Lebanon it was a standoff; in Cuba, a fiasco; in Laos, a suspended failure. Only in Vietnam has the dialectic of intervention resolved into a seeming disaster; mistakes led to blunders, and blunders have been escalating into a crescendo of crimes. An effective style of protecting clients, which admitted American involvement in internal conflicts either by proxy (through advisors, training "special forces," and military aid) or by swift and discreet police action of short duration, has been stymied by the Vietnamese quagmire. Professor Huntington believes that the duplication of such a situation is unlikely, although he himself points out that Thailand and the Philippines, among others, are potential scenes for future United States military involvement in internal war.

Should we regard Vietnam as largely an accident for a policy which has a good record of "success"? Or does it put into question the basic attitudes and goals which define this policy for the "third world"? Is Vietnam an "unlesson," better forgotten? Or is it a lesson calling for a fundamental change in a policy which, even if it were relevant in the earlier decades, may now have lost its relevance, which even when "successful" by American definition may have been essentially self-defeating? The answers depend on one's perspectives and priorities. And they are shaped by our environment, our social, intellectual, and moral location. The dialogue between many of my American colleagues, some of them critics of the present administration, and myself has been breaking down because I am progressively unable to share their phantoms and their fantasies.

In underdeveloped countries the quiescence which followed independence is giving way to new disappointments and new demands which are unlikely to be satisfied by a politics of boundary management and selective co-optation—a fact which the United States, much like our ruling elites, is yet unable or unwilling to perceive. There is an increasingly perceptible gap between our need for social transformation and America's insistence on stability, between our impatience for change and America's obsession with order, our move toward revolution and America's belief in the plausibility of achieving reforms under the robber barons of the "third world," our longing for absolute national sovereignty and America's preference for pliable allies, our desire to see our national soil freed of foreign occupation and America's alleged need for military bases (at least in the rimlands surrounding China and the U.S.S.R.). As the gap widens between our sorrow and America's contentment, so will, perhaps, these dichotomies of our perspectives and our priorities. Unless there is a fundamental redefinition of American interests and goals, our confrontations with the United States will be increasingly antagonistic. In the client states of Asia and Latin America it may even be tragic. In this sense Vietnam may not be so unique. It may be a warning of things to come.

SAMUEL P. HUNTINGTON: Concerning the prerequisites for effective intervention, I think I discern an emerging consensus here that economic and military intervention can succeed only if certain political prerequisites exist in some sort of established political system or state. Now, if this is the case, then quite clearly economic or military intervention on a massive scale in underdeveloped countries cannot succeed because it is precisely an established, viable political system which is missing.

Consequently, if one follows out the logic, we should direct attention to the nature of political systems, on the one hand, as a warning against getting involved too much in other ways (which I think is how we tend to become involved, because we are much more oriented toward taking economic and military action than toward trying to deal with some of the important, complex, and difficult problems of politics). On the other hand, if we are going to become involved, then there is a great deal of logic in trying to put first things first in terms of attempting to promote the development of a more broad-based type of political system—recognizing quite clearly that we can do very, very little in this regard but that if we are going to do anything else, we have to do that first, the country involved has to do that first. If we cannot promote the development of more effective political systems, then the thing to do is to stay out.

SIR ROBERT THOMPSON: One should not become involved politically. The prospect of going in as a political reformer frightens me more than anything else. I would not touch political reform in these territories with a barge pole—and I certainly would not touch it with an American political scientist.

I am not against political reform or political change. All I say is, let the people do it themselves—don't get in on the act. Any measure of aid you give in the form I have suggested is bound to effect, in the long run, political and social changes, and these should be allowed to occur in the people's own time in the country concerned—not tomorrow morning in your time.

SAMUEL P. HUNTINGTON: After Sir Robert's remark about barge poles and political scientists I ought to rise to a point of personal privilege. I waive that, however, to speak, not on behalf of political scientists, but again on behalf of the priority of politics, a very fundamental issue we have touched on. The crucial point here concerns the basic nature of the problem in Vietnam, which, I submit, is entirely different from the problems in Malaya or in most other cases that involved a prolonged insurgency.

As one looks at the program of priorities Sir Robert has advanced, he gives first priority to building up the administrative structure—taxation, communication networks, economic assistance, including social services and a rural aid program—in that order. This is pretty much precisely what we have tried to do—not very effectively—in Vietnam. It is an administrative, technical, and economic approach to what is essentially a political problem.

The reason it doesn't work in Vietnam is, I submit, not because of any inherent defects in the way in which we went about it, but simply because it is only at best marginally relevant to the major problem there, which is one of a lack of political organization and social cohesion. All of Sir Robert's measures will do very little or nothing to promote solutions to that problem.

In fact, I think it can be demonstrated quite clearly that these types of measures in many cases have done a lot to undermine the promotion of political organization and social cohesion. An administrative program like Sir Robert's presupposes the existence of a political system, which is precisely the thing lacking and causing the problem in Vietnam.

There has been too much emphasis on the problem of insurgency and counterinsurgency. Obviously insurgency is present in Vietnam. On the other hand, what is important is what is lacking there—any sort of effective, organized political system within which and through which it is possible to respond to this insurgency. This is what makes nation building, or whatever else you want to call it, the first priority —a priority which cannot be met by an administrative or technical approach.

This gets me directly to some of the points Sir Robert made earlier about leverage. I think there were some moments in the game when we had leverage. We did have some leverage at the time we first influenced people to the side of Diem. We had no leverage on Diem, none at all. Nothing we said or tried to say was credible to him. We could have exerted pressure, however, with the next group. President Johnson had some leverage at the moment he first came in. True, he was not the elected President, but as an elected Vice-President who succeeded to the presidency, he did have a great deal of support within the country. In looking back on it now, I think just after the succession there was a period of a month or so when he could have exerted some leverage on the government in Vietnam. We also could have exerted some leverage when we began bombing. This was a major step in our involvement in Vietnam for which we could have exacted some price.

But after we put in combat troops, we lost our leverage. In point of fact, one of the interesting aspects of progressive involvement, I think, is that our leverage decreases as our involvement increases. Our stake in this thing gets so high that nothing we can say or do to gain leverage will be credible to the government we are trying to help. By then we are in deeply, and insofar as they are concerned, it becomes increasingly our problem.

CHESTER COOPER: I want to remark on some points Sir Robert and Mr. Huntington just made. First, with regard to "leverage," what influence can the United States bring to bear as it becomes progressively involved in the affairs of another state—a state which is in some trouble, or presumably we would not have gone in, and also a state with a not very effective government, at least by our standards?

When we talk about counterinsurgency, one of the missing ingredients in the analysis—and it is hard to believe that there are any missing ingredients in a concept that has been so intellectualized and overkilled—is the whole question of how the United States can get the government it is attempting to help to do the sort of things the United States thinks should be done, without, on the one hand, either taking charge or, on the other hand, going along with existing arrangements and being very much stymied in the process.

The theory of counterinsurgency probably would work well if we were back fighting the American Indians. In that situation we would be confronting an insurgency directly. We would be the primary party, and all the theories, developed so carefully, could be put to work. In point of fact, this suggests one reason why, I think, the differences between the Malayan and Vietnamese situation really are quite fundamental. In Malaya you were fighting the insurgents directly; you were not trying to do it through another government which you had to negotiate with, meet with, threaten, force, etc., for several hours every day. This is what we face in Vietnam.

Now, if we cannot succeed by these means in Vietnam, one alternative is to take over. However, in one sense I don't think we are that smart. And in another sense, if we took over, we would be in a worse situation than we are now.

Related to all of this is the assumption that we know what we are doing when we go into a place like Vietnam. Well, I am not sure that we do. It is not our fault, really, because Vietnamese society is at least as alien to us as China was. In the case of the Chinese, we at least had a history of a couple of generations. On the other hand, we had no history in relation to dealing with the Vietnamese. The first Americans that many Vietnamese saw were American advisors. Also the first Vietnamese that almost all of us ever saw were at the 1954 conference.

STANLEY HOFFMANN: Let me go back to a point you made, Professor Huntington. I was struck by the formalism of your recipes. If I understood you correctly, you are saying there are two kinds of things that can be done. To promote social reform is one, but it ends up being very hard to control and possibly destabilizing. So you pass on to the next, political institutionalization. There you have a set of recipes, a set of techniques, which strike me as very much a projection of the American conception of politics with the usual underestimation of the potential of conflict.

This raises the question, first of all, as to whether we should do this. In other words, is it really in the American national interest to engage in social engineering thus conceived? From the point of view of good old-fashioned power politics, is it in America's national interest to go around the world building up the kind of techniques and institutions you propose? It may be in the recipient's interest; it may be in ours; but we cannot assume that it will always be in both. Ours may well differ from theirs, and doing good to others because one thinks it is good for them is a bizarre definition of one's national interest.

The second question, which is really more serious, is, can we do it— can anybody do it? Here I must go back to Mr. Ahmad's point. These institutions, these forms, are really envelopes. What will happen to them depends entirely on the kind of things—people, organizations, social forces, ideas, expectations, events—that will go into them, and we cannot determine what will go into them.

Your whole approach is one which never mentions the word "nationalism." You don't seem to recognize that, after all, there is a difference between, on the one side, telling somebody literally what values to create, what the national will should be, what social and political policy should be and, on the other, giving limited technical advice on economic development. Political institutionalization or nation building are largely phenomena growing out of what Mr. Ahmad calls "will," or what one might call "national" or "political self-respect." It seems to me very difficult for any foreign nation to do very much in this area, except give the kind of advice which is likely to be misleading if it is largely a projection of its own national experience.

I must, then, add that of all the nations which are, shall we say, not primarily well-qualified to go around the world and give this kind of advice, the United States stands out, exactly because of what has made American history on the whole so different and in many respects so fortunate. This has opened up a kind of communications gap between "us" and "them." In many ways your statement exemplifies the very problem you are trying to solve.

DANIEL ELLSBERG: I am also very disturbed by several lessons Professor Huntington has drawn from experience. This, by the way, does not lead me at all to think one should avoid learning lessons; I think that that is essential, and it is not at all too early that there be efforts such as the one we are on.

Professor Huntington has generalized that the more extensive the American involvement in the politics of another country, the more progressive is its impact on that country. He several times alludes to a possible relationship between intervention and reform.

Now, the first thing that strikes me about this proposition is that Vietnam itself provides a spectacular counterexample. The period of our intervention in Vietnam—which includes the period from 1950 on, and especially from 1954 on—cannot be described in general as a progressive or reform-oriented interval by any means.

One thing, perhaps, that might have misled Professor Huntington—it has misled a lot of other people—is the amount of *talk* there has been about reform, generally from lower-level staff members, and, occasionally, official pronouncements. When he refers to the stress on reform by people in State and CIA, he is mainly talking about the Foreign Service officers who accompany visitors to Vietnam. But this does not characterize very much of what their superiors have said in official, internal policy statements and decisions, and it characterizes even less what we have effectively done.

Stress by the United States government on reform in Vietnam has been virtually entirely verbal; and after the long period we have been in Vietnam it hasn't had much impact. Verbal stress, it turns out, does not create psychological stress in the minds of the people we are advising, or any real impulse for reform. We have obviously not been an effective influence for reform in Vietnam. Talking about land reform or talking about anything else has meant essentially nothing.

In fact, if you look at examples that seem to support Huntington's case, they can be much more precisely defined. The critical factor is not presence but occupation. It is as simple as that. When we Americans occupy a militarily defeated country and are not plagued by a continuing resistance in the country, experience shows a considerably progressive and reform-oriented impact. But experience does not show whether those efforts would have survived a resistance movement. We have not been tested on that.

Incidentally, I know that the historical examples of United States occupation misled many people in the Administration in their predictions of the benign effects of a great American build-up in Vietnam. Many of them had had experience in military government in places like Korea, Japan, or Germany, and this led them to think of us as inevitably a force for reform. But lacking in Vietnam the responsibility we had in occupied countries for the long-term political and economic development of the country, we were in no sense effectively a force for reform. Therefore, to accept your proposition, Professor Huntington, would surely lead us greatly astray in countries where we do not propose fully to take responsibility.

SAMUEL P. HUNTINGTON: I disagree with you on the specifics of Vietnam and the nature of our impact. If you want to go back over the period since 1954, the more we have become involved, the more we have had precisely the sort of impact which the proposition states we will have.

When you talk about occupation, that is precisely the point. This is an extreme case of American intervention. The logic of your argument seems to suggest that if we only did go in and take over Vietnam and run it the way Korea was run or Japan was run, we would have these effects. Here it seems to me you are focusing on an extreme case and building an argument for even more intervention.

DANIEL ELLSBERG: I certainly do not want to be misunderstood in my remarks. I was interpreting your proposition. I believe it is wrong to say that there is anything like a smooth function relating intervention and a progressive impact.

As we have increased our presence militarily, economically, politically, and in every other way, we have, of course, demolished the society of Vietnam. From a very long-term view, this is what is happening right now. Out of this ruin, perhaps, one might say some benefit may come—at great cost. However, in any case we are perceived by the Vietnamese correctly as having supported, first, the French regime and, second, the Diem regime—hardly progressive reform governments, whatever else they were. Finally, we are seen now as having saddled them with a deplorable military regime with essentially nothing to recommend it. This has been our impact, and it is creating intense anti-Americanism.

As for occupation, I am scarcely suggesting that is the solution. Conceivably it would have led to more reform, but that isn't the only criterion anyway. I do not believe it would be acceptable either in Vietnam or in the United States, nor should it be.

Even with respect to the past, I would again ask whether the occupation of Japan or Germany could have had the reforming effect it did, had it been confronted with an ongoing insurgency.

LUIGI EINAUDI: We all agree that in many ways the American presence abroad has contributed to undermining traditional societies. Paradoxically, there is some evidence, at least in Latin America, that those Latin Americans who score highest on various scales of modern attitudes of independence and so forth also tend to score fairly high in their criticism of American policy. This leads me to the proposition that there is a substantial difference between political development and politics. Surely we do not intend to equate political development directly with support of or opposition to the policies of the United States?

Regarding interventions, I want to suggest two questions that should always be asked at the outset. First, what do we know about the country? I come to a knowledge of Vietnam, to the extent I come there at all, by way of Latin America. It is very depressing to discover that my rare colleagues who have extensive experience in both Vietnam and Latin America all assure me it is infinitely easier to know what is going on in Latin America than in Vietnam. What I find peculiarly depressing is that we never seem really to know very much about what is going on in Latin America.

Second, I would ask not only what do we know about the country but what can we do about it—and this not simply in terms of the constraints of American politics or even the constraints of American budgets, but rather in terms of the effect of our short-range interventions on long-range political development. In the 1950's American analysts noted that in a number of countries there was a long-range need for a noncommunist safety valve for the expression of political dissent. As a result, sums of money were apparently provided through various covert channels to individuals and organizations who gave promise of being able to further this aim—a perfect example of political engineering. Unfortunately, in a number of cases about which Latin Americans came to me to complain, when some of these avenues of dissent contradicted short-term American policy interests, funds were cut off. This strikes me as a practical constraint on any American policy of sponsoring long-term institution building. Of course, the existence of difficulties does not necessarily mean one can avoid intervention, any more than one can stop policy-making, but the cautionary weight of these examples is evident.

After hearing your remarks, Professor Huntington, I was reminded of an editorial that appeared in one Latin American paper right after the announcement of the Alliance for Progress. The editorialist commented that it was difficult to choose between those Americans who tell us what to do because it is good for the Americans and those Americans who tell us what to do because it is good for us. If we are always to be dictating, we are likely to face certain disaster as we move into a world in which we no longer have the predominance of power we enjoyed briefly after World War II.

THEODORE DRAPER: I read Professor Huntington's remarks with a kind of double-take reaction. At first I thought he had settled everything nicely because he seemed to suggest that we need not expect any more military intervention until after 1980. If he had stopped there, he would have been ahead. However, he then proceeded to tell us that we have to get in even more than we have gotten in before, that we have to go from promoting social reform to developing the political institutions of the countries in which we intervene, and the development of political institutions requires a party system.

The question arises: if we are going to develop political institutions, are they going to be institutions like our own or not? Our people, at best, can help to develop institutions like our own. We get into trouble at this point—do the local residents want our type of institutions? Are their background and conditions the same as ours? Now, if the institutions we are going to develop elsewhere are not like our own, then we are really helpless because our people simply have no experience with anything else.

In the end, however, Professor Huntington seemed to regard political intervention as if it were a case of self-denial on our part. Whenever we do not intervene more than we do, the reason is, not that we are denying anything to ourselves, but because it is simply beyond us. It is, in the fashionable word, "counterproductive"—it does not work, it hits back at us. Now, when you recommend the impossible, you are really recommending not doing it; and, therefore, by advocating intervention to the point of developing other people's political institutions, Professor Huntington has actually, in an inverted way, presented a persuasive anti-interventionist position.

My feeling is that the only way to get out of this contradiction is to think of intervention as a last resort. It is a most desperate and dangerous thing to do. It is invariably based on political failure. Therefore it should be done only as a very last resort in a situation of extreme danger to the United States. When you have that kind of situation, most of these problems are not so acute, and on the other hand, when you don't have that kind of situation, these problems become insoluble.

SAMUEL P. HUNTINGTON: I would like to congratulate Mr. Draper on getting the message.

JAMES C. THOMSON, JR.: I am a sort of innocent because I am not a political scientist or economist and am barely a social scientist at all. I am really troubled by terms like "modernization," "development," "political development," "institution building," "stability," "nation building," and the like. I don't know what they mean. However, as I grope for their connotations and for the assumptions behind such words and concepts, it seems that the United States is the model being offered—that "development," for instance, means becoming more like us.

But then I am confronted with the remarks of Mr. Ahmad about the uniqueness of our historical experience. This, in turn, makes me troubled about using ourselves as a model. For example, why not use Maoist China as a model? Why not Gaullist France? Or why not Burma, which is a striking model of aggressive and determined non-development? And why, further, is it "a bitter truth," as Professor Huntington puts it, to discover that probably the most stable government in Southeast Asia today is the government of North Vietnam and, beyond that, that it is not only stable but responsive to the needs of its people?

This brings me to the subversive thought that perhaps North Vietnam might be a more appropriate model for modernization, political development, institution building, nation building, and so forth, than others, and, in fact, might be given an opportunity to be such a model, at least among the Vietnamese people.

JOHN RIELLY: External assistance in political development can be successful only where the shared values of elites in the relevant countries are relatively high. The principal value of the United States that has been portrayed most widely is that of minimizing instability. But it is not predetermined that the United States government or the United States population equate stability with progress. I think there is an understanding today, at least in some quarters, that our counter-insurgency programs of the past few years have ended up supporting forces of the status quo in most cases and that the programs must either be totally discarded or completely changed.

It is true that political participation is more difficult to sell to a native elite than economic development. This does not mean that it is impossible. It seems to me that there are cases where the values of the elites are sufficiently similar that external assistance in political development can be effective. For example, there is a sufficient similarity between the values of the elites of West Europe, the United States, and Latin America that assistance in political development can be effective. For the most part, all three would agree on the necessity of participation by the people, of economic progress, and of a certain degree of peace and order. In such circumstances, if a Latin

American government requests assistance in political development from West Europe or the United States, they should be prepared to respond.

The great mistake that has been made, it seems to me, is that we have become very much involved politically in areas over the world, particularly in Asia, where local elites do not share the same values with us. In the case of assistance, in political development, the United States should be extremely reluctant to become involved at all in Asia, and to a lesser extent in Africa. In regard to Latin America, we should be aware that perhaps the similarity of outlook is greater between elites of Europe and Latin America than between those of Latin America and the United States. Therefore, we would see our own purposes best served in many cases by encouraging Europeans, who already show a great ideological affinity and who in some cases actually have tools and institutions to do the job.

SAMUEL P. HUNTINGTON: Let me respond to three points raised. The first is: under what circumstances, if ever, is it in our national interest to become involved in the politics of other societies? It seems to me quite clear that the most successful intervention is no intervention and that, particularly in what I view as the coming phase of American introversion, our capacity to become involved in other societies is going to be limited. In other words, our perceived interests in doing so are going to be limited, and, therefore, the primary rationale for becoming involved at all in other countries is that such involvement may be the only alternative to becoming involved later in a much bigger way.

Obviously we should only intervene in other societies when it is in our interest to do so. And I would define our interest in very narrow terms. In some cases our interests may coincide on specific issues with those of other elites, and in other cases they may not. But I think it is a mistake to assume that you only can have effective cooperation between elites when they share the same philosophy and the same basic values. I think it is quite clear that groups can work together for shared specific objectives, even when they do not share many other things.

The second issue concerns the question as to whether we can do it, and I must say I was a little amused by the seeming assumption that I was urging the promotion of two-party American liberal democracy in other countries. I don't think you can find this anywhere in my statements. I have argued that we have promoted very different kinds of political institutions in various countries around the world. On the evidence, we are not limited to promoting that which is a mirror reproduction of our own system.

I think quite clearly that in any given case what we will be able to do will be very limited, and the type of social forces and political institutions which it will be in our interest to promote will obviously reflect the nature of the particular society.

Finally, there is a question as to whether even this sort of limited political involvement may not lead, as Mr. Ahmad suggests, to larger involvement. I think this is quite clearly a danger. But it is one which can be minimized to the extent that these involvements, as I tried to suggest, are kept reasonably limited, discreet, and covert. Many of the problems of our involvement in other countries in the past decade or so have come from our choice of means, in which we relied very heavily on massive economic aid programs, military assistance, and military intervention.

It is quite possible that one of the side benefits of a shift toward introversion in our society will be less public concern about foreign policy. This development in our domestic politics, which may make more limited forms of foreign involvement necessary, may also make them possible in the sense that there will be less public attention and concern directed to these issues.

EQBAL AHMAD: Professor Huntington, I was rather surprised at how you have squeezed out of the "kiss of death" argument regarding American aid to foreign political institutions. You conceded that the legitimacy of any political party advised and supported by the United States or by any foreign power will suffer. You therefore suggested such support and advice should be kept covert. Now, really, doesn't that impose a certain character on a political institution that is supposed to invite political participation and be responsive to its membership, a political institution that is being based on something people who belong to it don't even know about? It would seem to me that this covertness in itself would compromise the institution at its very inception. It would involve the kind of compromise of principles from which one can go on making more and more. Doesn't the idea of covertly supporting a participatory political institution sound like a contradiction in terms to you?

SAMUEL P. HUNTINGTON: The answer is no.

JOHN MCDERMOTT: Just by way of preface, I am not exactly sure that it is going to be possible in this country to continue to maintain the covert quality of some of the operations. You have now the growth of a very substantial guerrilla scholarship on foreign-policy matters— young men and women who think nothing is more fun than to go through the abstracts to find out what kind of contracts are around and to expose them. Part of the trouble at Columbia, I think, grew out of that. I think this is a new political fact which has to be taken into consideration.

Now, I want to go to a different point. I was really very happy with Professor Huntington's remarks until he began to speak of promoting political development. Then I wish he had clearly introduced a distinction—which may be there but should be clearer—between political systems in which the relationship of governors to the governed are command relationships and those in which they are bargaining relationships. It seems to me that Professor Huntington is envisioning command relationships of governors to the governed. The kinds of political organizations he seeks are what the New Left today calls "co-optive organizations."

In this regard, I was very much interested in Edward Thompson's very good book *The Making of the English Working Class,* which is now a kind of underground rage. I think Huntington's assumption is that the resources for political development do not exist in the masses. For him, political development requires inputs from elites, people with ideas, consciousness, etc. Thompson's book suggests quite the opposite. He talks, for example, in his book about the importance of popular myths, such as the myth of the freeborn Englishman, which enables people subject to new economic and political experiences to organize responses by themselves. It seems to me that in the underdeveloped world we might begin to look for some of this. Miss FitzGerald and I were talking earlier, for example, about myths of the Vietnamese rural classes, which I have a feeling have played a similar role in Vietnam to the myth of the freeborn Englishman in the development of the English working class.

Thompson speaks also about the experience of organization—the ability to form committees, put out broadsides and leaflets—which came out of dissenting churches in Great Britain. He talks about the growth of primitive notions of class, mainly conceptions which identified a group of people who were then thought to have some sort of solidarity against another group, and, lastly, he talks of relationships to sympathetic auxiliaries in middle and upper classes.

I don't think that creation of political institutions in other countries is a technical problem.

SAMUEL P. HUNTINGTON: Neither do I.

JOHN McDERMOTT: And I don't think it is a problem which can be very effectively attacked from the outside. On the contrary, I am very much bothered, for example, by your insistence that you work down from the elite toward the masses, that you look for elites within certain structures who have a stake in the modernization processes. The army is always one of these; I gather that people who are culturally westernized are also a fairly good one these days. The assumption is that somehow this process will work down the pyramid to the mass base.

It seems to me that unless one can design political interventions which do not start at the top of the pyramid and try to work down to the base but do it the other way, you run into the problem that you are building command systems and not bargaining systems, because you do not increase the capacity of the masses to deal with their own elites in periods in which the elites have powerful drives to make profound changes in the country—changes which, unless an organized people can respond to them, may force violent responses. This is even a lesson which is true today at Columbia, where the university administration simply was unaware that its student population had a strong independent opinion on certain questions. The vehement response of students here in our own society, where presumably we don't have great cultural and other barriers between young and old, took people totally by surprise.

If you don't establish bargaining relationships, you are in trouble.

SAMUEL P. HUNTINGTON: I just cannot find any place where I committed myself to building from the top on down, although, in fact, this may be necessary in some circumstances and in some systems, depending upon the nature of the system.

It seems to me that what you were getting at is the necessity in most societies to develop some sort of structures, probably some form of party systems for mass participation and for the decentralization of power. I agree. I think it is particularly necessary in Vietnam, where to a very large extent our problem has been precisely due to efforts to build from the top down, without capitalizing on the assets which exist in the form of local and grass-roots organization.

A LOW POSTURE: ISOLATIONISM, INTERVENTIONISM, AND BALONEY

§§ JAMES C. THOMSON, JR.: To ponder the effect of Vietnam on future United States patterns of intervention is to treat a twofold subject: on the one hand, what might be the effect—an exercise in pure speculation; and on the other, what ought to be the effect—an exercise in preachment. Neither speculations nor preachments offer much in the way of answers, but they can sometimes raise useful questions.

There seems to me one central lesson to be learned from the Vietnam conflict: never again to take on the job of trying to defeat a nationalist anticolonial movement under indigenous communist control in former French Indochina.

Now that is a lesson of less than universal relevance. I cite it nonetheless to stress Vietnam's uniqueness—and, alas, every situation's uniqueness. I cite it to caution against all attempts (including my own) to formulate "guidelines for future interventions" on the basis of Vietnam. And I cite it in full realization that many Americans will assuredly learn other "lessons" from Vietnam and that many of those lessons will be the wrong lessons—for instance, that America has no proper role in Asia, or that we should never intervene anywhere, or that we should at least steer clear of the less developed world, or that we are inherently and incurably imperialist when we move beyond our shores, or that we should never again trust foreigners.

Two further cautionary comments. First, I find myself uneasy with the phrase "United States patterns of intervention." Most "patterns" discerned by historians, critics, and observers of American foreign policy seem to me to do damage to the realities of a pluralistic government in a multiregional world. Washington's attitude toward Latin America (particularly the Caribbean region) and its willingness to "intervene" there will probably remain very different from its stance toward Africa. The Middle East touches a different set of responses, mainly rooted in domestic politics. Similar distinctions must be made for West Europe, East Europe, South Asia, and "the Far East." Furthermore, times change, perceptions of threats change, leaders change, and so does their rhetoric. "Patterns" are generally the product of hindsight or polemics; to impose them is usually to overlook diversity and disorder in the policy-making process. It is also to overlook that crucial ingredient of policy, the accident factor.

A second cautionary comment. Future United States interventions—whether patternable or patternless—will be deeply affected, not merely by our involvement in Vietnam, but by both the reality and the appearance of a Vietnam settlement. Washington's ability to intervene will depend at least in part on the post-Vietnam mood of the electorate and its Congress. A Vietnam settlement that looked quite soon like a "sellout" would surely cause political recriminations at home; but whether those recriminations would lead to irresistible demands for renewed and escalated intervention, or whether they would instead lead to a revulsion against foreign adventures, is quite unknowable. The most that can be said is that a settlement that had the *look* of nondefeat and sustained that look for a while would leave Washington somewhat freer to intervene or not in future situations. If executive flexibility is our goal, our Vietnam settlement had better look "honorable." If, on the other hand, our goal is to apply some brakes to the allegedly interventionist momentum of our national security apparatus, a case might be made for a settlement that bore the clear look of a nonsuccess. As indicated above, however, such a result would entail a risk.

Against this cautionary backdrop, I turn to the speculative question: what *might* be the effect of Vietnam on future United States patterns of intervention? Here we already confront at least two radically different forecasts.

On the one hand, one hears the recurrent prediction that "more

Vietnams" will in fact occur and that they will produce more American interventions—whether in Thailand, Burma, Guatemala, or Bolivia. The proponents of such a view are a curiously mixed lot: among them, cold warriors in Washington, Maoists in Peking, and large sections of the New Left, both here and abroad. Ironically the central repositories of the now familiar thesis that Vietnam is the ultimate test of the theory of wars of national liberation seem to be Washington and Peking. Other capitals have a more sophisticated comprehension of the unique mix of factors that makes Vietnam a less than conclusive test of anything much. Nonetheless, the fact remains that many believe the communists eventually will raise promising insurrections in much of the underdeveloped world and that Washington will certainly counter with intervention. Those of the New Left who are convinced that interventionism is endemic to our federal apparatus certainly hold to this view; and so, I dare say, for rather different reasons, does an influential body of America's military men and conservatives.

One hears, on the other hand, a strongly conflicting forecast that the result of our Vietnam involvement will be a national withdrawal into "isolationism" or "neoisolationism." Many of the proponents of this view are deeply concerned internationalists who fear that the American people will abdicate their global responsibilities in revulsion against our Vietnam experience.

Such a fear is understandable. The Congressional revolt against foreign aid seems an ominous harbinger. Yet the forecast itself may mislead through semantics. "Isolationism" is a strong, loaded term. Its historic connotations are irresponsibility leading to tragedy: America's rejection of Wilson and the League, and nonintervention in Manchuria, Ethiopia, and Hitler's Europe. It also conveys, one feels, a sharp sense of guilt on the part of the interwar generation. And, indeed, many of those who warn of "neoisolationism" are men who reached adulthood in the 1930's.

Yet is "isolationism" actually what such men see ahead? Closer questioning reveals no real fear that America will withdraw from the United Nations, or that we will abrogate our treaties, or that we will cut back on our foreign trade or dismantle our network of diplomatic relations. Too much has changed since the interwar period: the revolution in communications and transportation and the advent of nuclear weapons, to cite only two central developments. A return to "isolationism" seems out of the question.

What, then, is the real concern? On the one hand, some seem to feel that we will fail to help resist "aggression" and thereby feed the "appetites" of aggressors; President Johnson said in July 1965, "We did not choose to be the guardians at the gate, but there is no one else"—and who will be there next time if not us? Others, however, have a different fear: that the United States will cease its efforts to bridge the dangerous gap between the very rich and the very poor, the white and the colored, the minority and the majority of the world's people. Clearly the first concern relates to a willingness to intervene, and the fear implicit is a fear of "noninterventionism." As for the second concern, what is foreseen is an abrupt termination of our postwar governmental programs of assistance toward "modernization." Both noninterventionism and an end to foreign aid are aspects of a somewhat reduced overseas involvement—a lower posture in world affairs. But they are not "isolationism."

It is interesting to note that the two predicted consequences of our Vietnam involvement—either a retreat into pseudo isolationism or continued and even escalated interventionism—seem reflective of two traditionally conflicting themes in America's view of its role in the world. I have in mind, on the one hand, those who from our earliest days saw America as a beacon and an inspiration—a "city built upon a hill"—and, on the other hand, those more activist types who, with Jefferson, believed that the American Revolution was "intended for all mankind" and should be exported. With the turn of the century, mission and manifest destiny became "imperial democracy." But throughout the process there have been ardent and eloquent anti-expansionists, anti-imperialists, and noninterventionists arguing that who we were at home was far more important than what we did abroad. (In recent years this division within our ranks has found new expression, infused with Anglo-Saxon snobbery, in variant approaches to the less developed world: on one side we have Mr. Acheson, who seems to say that the peoples of these regions are such children—and so recently out of the trees?—that we must take them by the hand and do it for them; on the other we have Mr. Kennan, who seems to say that these peoples are, after all, so different from you and me that it is hopeless to try and do much of anything for them.)

Now between these two general forecasts—"more Vietnams" and "isolationism"—one must note that there are the makings of a further middle option. We have seen so far only brief glimpses—the formulations are few and preliminary. But the glimpses include the Johnson Administration's noninterventionist policy toward Indonesia both before and after the abortive communist coup of September 1965. Neither an Indonesia that was apparently sliding under communist party control nor an Indonesia that had become fiercely anticommunist could tempt intervention after our Vietnam experience. A policy of nonembrace and multilateralism has (so far) replaced the old interventionist instincts of the 1950's. A more cautious approach was similarly evident in Washington's response to two crises on the Indian subcontinent: the frontier war with China in 1962 and the India-Pakistan war of 1965. As for the Middle East war of 1967, self-restraint again seemed to prevail—though Israel's lightning victory prevented a real test of Washington's interventionist instincts. Finally, the Congressional uproar over sending planes to the Congo was widely viewed as a strong reminder that the legislative branch is hypersensitive to the danger of "more Vietnams."

Out of these glimpses has come one recent attempt within the Administration to formulate a new approach toward intervention, at least in the Asian region. This is found in the May 7 speech at Pomona of Dr. Morton H. Halperin, of the Department of Defense. Halperin proposes three principles that seem to him to embody the "United States attitude toward intervention": (1) self-help, (2) regional responsibility, and (3) residual United States responsibility. His elucidation of these principles may be, one hopes, a first step toward the officially approved formulation of a middle course that reflects lessons learned from the Vietnam conflict.

I turn now from speculation to preachment—an attempt to answer the question of what ought to be the effect of Vietnam on future United States patterns of intervention. A simple answer comes easily: Vietnam ought to make us more careful. It should make us look before we leap. It should even make us look before we step. But the simple answer tells us next to nothing. What kind of guidelines should we offer to future United States policy-makers on the subject of intervention?

It seems to me that the baffling aspect of the question involves something other than the European balance of power where, for better or worse, ground rules have been established on the basis of the United States–Soviet nuclear balance, the NATO–Warsaw Pact symmetry, and a divided Germany. Here patterns of deterrence, negotiation, and conciliation are pretty well established, at least for the foreseeable future.

It is in those regions of greater chronic instability, the underdeveloped world, that the question of intervention becomes most pertinent and baffling. Instability makes great powers nervous, and the itch to intervene is heightened by concern that if you do not, your great-power adversaries will—or, alternatively, that they already have, so you had better join in to prevent an upset of the regional balance of power.

It is perhaps traditional concepts of "balance of power" and "power vacuums" that mislead us in these instances. All too often they reflect a bipolar—or tripolar—view of the world that overestimates one's adversary's ability to establish and maintain control and underestimates the power and resilience of indigenous nationalisms. This view is a legacy of the cold war. But it neglects the rising tide of polycentrism in the West as well as in the East.

What seems clearly needed is a more realistic response to instability in the less developed world. What should be the ingredients of such a response?

First, we must early ask ourselves whether the nation or region in question is of any direct relevance to our national security. To put it another way, would "hostile" control of that nation or region pose any real threat to our national security (as opposed to our pride or self-esteem)? If the question were applied, not only to Vietnam, but to all of mainland Southeast Asia today, my answer—and the answer of most Asian specialists, I dare say—would be "no." If it were applied to Japan, on the other hand, my answer would probably be "yes"; "hostile" control of the economic and potential military strength of Japan would add significantly to power that could be used against us.

Second, we must early ask if the instability of a nation (or a region) is caused by overt aggression across an internationally recognized frontier or by something else—either indigenously rooted insurgency or foreign-supported insurgency. If the answer is international aggression, we should join with others through the mechanisms of the United Nations and other instruments of mediation to end the aggression and to reconcile the parties. But if the answer is insurgency, then a further set of questions must be asked.

Third, then, what is the nature and source of the insurgency? Contrary to much official rhetoric over the past decade or so, insurgencies —rebellions, even revolutions—are neither inherently iniquitous nor, even if iniquitous, automatically to be resisted by the United States government. At the risk of offering a banality, much insurgency (including foreign-supported insurgencies) is rooted in genuine economic, social, and political grievances—in resistance to widely sensed injustice. At what point should America side with "duly constituted local authority" or "legitimate" regimes (the source of the legitimacy does not usually bear close examination) in order to preserve "stability" against insurgency? The answer takes us back to question one.

If, in fact, the overthrow of the legitimate government will pose a direct threat to our national security (in Canada or Mexico, for instance), our intervention should presumably be wholehearted. But such clear-cut cases are rare. And so an additional question must be asked of the far more frequent marginal cases: is there a chance that with a moderate amount of American assistance the "legitimate" government will succeed? If not, we should not try. Yet here we move into the jungle growth of ignorance, poor intelligence, wishful thinking, and competing constituencies within the United States government. For in raising the key question of our chances for success, we bring to bear human frailty and human illusions—qualities that have repeatedly led us astray in Vietnam. We also confront here the reality of the cultural gap between our own society and those of many parts of the less developed world. We confront, as well, the inapplicability of many of the instruments of our technology (not to mention our politics) in such alien cultural environments. I, for one, am dubious about our ability to bridge such cultural gaps in the foreseeable future.

Out of such pessimistic thoughts a fourth question emerges, one that should be early asked of situations of instability: what multilateral mechanisms are available to help treat instability and ease crises in the less developed world? Too often in the past such questions have been asked too late, if then; "more flags" for Vietnam was an afterthought, as was resort to the United Nations.

Clearly one way to avoid deepening unilateral involvement is to multilateralize the effort from the start; and one way to avoid the embarrassment of one nation's defeat in a losing or at best unpredictable effort is to engage as many others as possible from the start. Surely multilateralism should be the *sine qua non* of future American interventions: multinational efforts to assist developing nations, multinational efforts to cope with insurgency, and multinational attempts to resolve open hostilities. In a polycentric world of resilient competing nationalisms, unilateral intervention is less necessary than ever, less useful than ever—and more obnoxious than ever. Unless you can get others to come along, don't go in yourself.

Other pertinent and more familiar questions should also underlie any guidelines for future interventions. Some are suggested in Dr. Halperin's useful formulation. Is the nation that seeks outside assistance helping itself? Is it carrying the major burdens of its own security and development effort? Is it working with its neighbors "to deal with the economic and political causes of instability"? These are questions, of course, that were frequently raised in the years of our Vietnam involvement; too often, however, they were unanswered, falsely answered, or the clear and gloomy answers were ignored.

Vietnam suggests a further question for future interventions. In my view, our Vietnam relationship has been profoundly and increasingly complicated by what I have earlier referred to as rhetorical escalation and the problem of oversell. To what extent can such rhetorical escalation and oversell—allusions, for instance, to our "national honor"—be avoided in future instances of necessary intervention abroad? Is it endemic to our democratic system? If so, we are in for severe trouble; we will be incapable of limited but sustained involvements and particularly involvements that show little in the way of short-term success. Here again one cure can be multilateralism —a sense of joint enterprise with other nations rather than a sense of the American flag in solitude and, often as not, in trouble.

There is one final issue that must be treated in any consideration of the future of American intervention. This is what Ambassador Reischauer has referred to elsewhere as America's "moral imperative to help those who need help." Or as Dr. Halperin said at Pomona, "The presence in the world of sick and hungry children, and of peoples striving to improve their standard of living and to increase the measure of human dignity afforded to the individual, arouses our sympathies for reasons almost entirely unrelated to American security." Now, no one can doubt that this "moral imperative to help" is very much part of our bloodstream. That moral imperative can lead us, however, into entrapment: too close an attachment to—even, through our rhetoric and our press, glamorization of—regimes through which our assistance is necessarily channeled; too close a tie to the often Western-educated (and therefore attractive) elites who temporarily administer the recipient nations but may be gone tomorrow; and eventually, a philanthropist-mendicant relationship that sooner or later arouses the nationalist ire of the mendicant, not to mention the philanthropist's outrage at "ingratitude."

Here again one obvious solution is multilateralism: the channeling of our largesse through intermediate bodies that can muffle the collisions and avert the embarrassments of bilateral relationships. It will be no easy matter to convince the American people and their Congress to put foreign aid in the hands of such intermediaries. In many circumstances, however, the lesson of recent history may well be that no foreign aid at all is better than most bilateral aid.

But multilateralism on the receiving end may not be enough. A more far-reaching solution may well be in order. For what we have seen in the decades since World War II is not a new phenomenon. The export of American benevolence under "the moral imperative to help" is a very old national tradition, a tradition rooted in the efforts of generations of religious mission boards, educational institutions, and eventually foundations to transform, reform, and modernize other societies. What is new in the postwar years is, not merely a massive increase in the export of benevolence, but also the nationalization of the export. Today's reformers and modernizers are largely representatives of a state of vast wealth and power. With them go the flag and prestige of that state. Private reformers still abound, to be sure; but their efforts have been submerged by the programs of the state.

In this context one might ask if the quantitative change has not produced a qualitative change—if the escalation of international reformism has not altered the character of the enterprise. Private citizens could afford to "fail"—to be thrown out, to allow nationalism and even communism to run their course. But states tend to find failure unacceptable. And those states that find failure most unacceptable of all are those imbued with concepts of mission and manifest destiny.

In recent years America's new efforts to eradicate poverty at home and transform its cities have been pushed toward a restructuring and decentralization. In the years ahead it may well be necessary to restructure, decentralize, and even denationalize our overseas aid undertakings. In a sense the Peace Corps has pointed the way. What might be the prospects for the creation of semipublic foundations on the Washington end of the export of benevolence—to disentangle our overseas aid programs from the flag, our prestige, and the "national honor"? In so doing, we might more easily avert future situations where a righthearted imperative to help would lead us into wrongheaded impulses to intervene.

Speculations and preachments bring me to a final hopeful guess: that America will in fact assume a lower posture, post-Vietnam, without withdrawing from the responsibilities of power—but with the responsibilities defined in less grandiose terms. For we will realize that not only are we not alone as "guardians at the gate," but that there are actually a great many gates, most of them characterized by a brisk and healthy two-way traffic.

§§ EDWIN REISCHAUER: I accept Professor James Thomson's cautionary comments but feel that he both underplays and overplays the most important one. We are still too far away from a final denouement in Vietnam to know whether or not we will have an "honorable"-looking settlement, as Professor Thomson seems to assume, or something that at least in retrospect is tagged a "sellout" or possibly even a simple "pull-out" because American public opinion refuses to continue to tolerate a seemingly endless and hopeless war. Each of these endings would give a very different spin to the ball of American politics, producing quite different attitudes toward future involvements in Asia and the less developed world in general.

On the other hand, while the twist of the ball may still be unclear, the general direction in which it will go, I feel, is much clearer than Professor Thomson admits. The "central lesson" of Vietnam—at least as the American public perceives it—is already, I believe, quite obvious and much more widely applied, whether rightly or wrongly, than Professor Thomson implies. We may still re-escalate the present war if the negotiations fail; but assuming that some sort of Vietnam settlement is achieved, I find it hard to believe that even a relatively strong "sellout" case would produce "irresistible demands for renewed and escalated intervention" in other parts of the world. Vietnam may be a "less than conclusive test of anything much," but at least it has shown the limited ability of the United States to control at a reasonable cost the course of events in a nationally aroused less developed nation. That this "lesson" has sunk home in this country can be seen in the strongly anti-interventionist reaction in the Administration, in Congress, and among the public to the Indonesian, Congo, and other recent disturbances, as correctly cited by Professor Thomson.

This "lesson" can and, I believe, will lead to the broader conclusion that no external power can control (and thus exploit to its own advantage) less developed nations which are large enough in population and have enough national consciousness to be real national entities. I believe that we are moving away from the application to Asia of the "balance of power" and "power vacuum" concepts of the cold war, and in the process we no doubt will greatly downgrade our strategic interest in most of the less developed world. This is the direction in which we are moving, I believe, but just how far and fast we move is still to be determined by the specific outcome in Vietnam.

At this point "neoisolationism" becomes a real question and not the series of straw men that Professor Thomson so easily demolishes. Those who have used the term have never meant to suggest a return to the 1930's type of isolation from Europe and the other advanced parts of the world. This indeed is unthinkable and impossible. Nor have they meant a more cautious attitude toward intervention in internal instabilities in less developed nations. This is coming and will not, I feel, be labeled as isolationism. Their fear is the very realistic one that the United States will move, not just to greater caution about intervention in the affairs of less developed nations, but far beyond this position to virtual unconcern with their fate. The result could be a dismantling of the capacity to intervene in the cases where intervention may indeed be in our national interests and an unwillingness to give economic aid or take other measures that would contribute to the long-range development of the less developed nations.

This, I feel, is no idle fear. Past aid programs have been wheedled out of Congress largely on the basis of our alleged great strategic stakes in the less developed world. Cold logic, however, will increasingly show that we have few if any immediate, vital, national interests in the less developed world, either strategic or economic. And added to logic will be the emotional responses to our present crises at home and abroad. The Vietnam fiasco is beginning to produce the conservative response that if Asians do not appreciate our efforts in their behalf and are not willing to do their share, they deserve to be left to "stew in their own juices." The liberal response is that we should concentrate first on the great ills of our own society (the beam in our own eye) before trying to help distant people with their ills. Cultural (possibly even racial) biases strengthen both positions, as Professor Thomson suggests. Even he admits that "the Congressional revolt against foreign aid seems an ominous harbinger." I cannot see why he does not take the threat of this sort of "neoisolationism" more seriously or discuss the possible answers to it.

The only reason for not adopting an attitude of unconcern toward the less developed countries that I find in Professor Thomson's paper is the argument based on America's "moral imperative to help those who need help," which he quotes from me, only to warn against it as an attitude that could lead to dangerous cultural imperialism. I cited this "moral imperative" as an element in our whole culture; but if this were indeed the only reason for our concern, I suspect that we would move for all practical purposes to the "neoisolationism" Professor Thomson discounts.

I would suggest two reasons why the United States has very real interests in the stability and development of the less developed nations. The first is that no clear line exists between our very immediate interests in the security and stability of the advanced nations (such as those of Europe, Japan, and Australia) and conditions in the less developed world. For example, a complete disruption of all the oil lands of the Middle East might spell catastrophe for Europe and Japan. Spreading chaos which reduced the capacities for trade of the countries of South and Southeast Asia would be hard on a country like Japan, for which trade with these regions is important. While we can guarantee the defense (both nuclear and conventional) of Japan and Australia from across the Pacific Ocean, we cannot defend from such long distances the sea lanes on which both depend. Neither could we so defend South Korea, the loss of which to a hostile power might seriously affect Japan's stability. If basic unconcern with the less developed areas led to an abandonment of our capacities or will to intervene on occasion in those parts of the world, this might have a serious secondary effect on areas of the world that are immediately important to us.

The second reason is very long range and less easily defined but probably more important. In a rapidly shrinking, ever more closely integrated world in which interrelations and mutual influences grow constantly stronger, vast discrepancies of wealth and opportunity between various regions and nations and the resentments and hostilities these breed become increasingly dangerous to world stability as a whole. The problem actually is a new one—in a sense only a cloud on the horizon—but predictably it will grow to dangerous proportions, just as the discrepancies in wealth and opportunity in our own nation, which in a simpler day constituted no great problem, have through neglect produced an explosive crisis in this more complicated age. If we fail to work toward closing the international gap in wealth and opportunity, we may some day face an insoluble problem.

I thus come to an advocacy of the same middle course between overinvolvement and complete unconcern which Professor Thomson reached more easily by not attempting to justify it. I am less sanguine, however, than he that we will be wise enough to take this middle course. The arguments for it are either complicated or very long range, while the arguments for the "neoisolationism" of unconcern are clear-cut and emotionally appealing.

On the optimistic assumption, however, that we will attempt to find our way down the middle course, I would accept most of the specific points about it that Professor Thomson makes, though I would formulate the basic principles to be followed in somewhat different terms:

(1) We should distinguish clearly between our capacity to intervene and our commitment to do so, maintaining the former (at least to some degree) but minimizing the latter. For example, we should maintain the Seventh Fleet in the western Pacific, thus protecting the freedom of the seas and giving us the option to intervene against aggression, thereby probably inhibiting it to some extent, but without committing ourselves in advance. Prior commitments to less developed nations may be necessary in some cases (in East Asia, South Korea probably needs such a commitment, and Taiwan and the Philippines are also possible exceptions because of a long historical involvement on our part and their easy defensibility, as islands, from

aggression), but such commitments should be regarded essentially as liabilities rather than assets.

(2) As a general rule, intervention in internal instability or civil war should be avoided. Exceptions might be countries that are both very small and highly strategic, if such exist. If a regime—with our aid, in case it is worthy of it—cannot handle internal problems of this sort itself, we probably could not do it for them. The chief problem we would face is to be sure that we maintain a strict line between aid to a beleaguered regime and intervention in a civil war. Depending on the case, the line beyond which we should not go might be (a) purely economic aid, (b) weapons, (c) military and constabulary training and advice.

(3) As another general rule, we should attempt to assure that any intervention against aggression is international in character, but we cannot assume that this can always be achieved and there may be cases where we would have to intervene unilaterally. For example, a North Korean invasion of South Korea, a definite possibility, might not elicit an international response but might demand a unilateral American intervention.

(4) No intervention should be allowed to become open-ended. As Vietnam has shown, we must retain the ability to stop the escalation of our involvement if our initial efforts do not produce the expected results.

(5) Economic and technological aid—which to my mind should be the main thrust of our policies toward the less developed nations, rather than military defenses—should be handled in such a way as to avoid our own political and emotional commitment to specific regimes and to minimize their fears of our domination. For both purposes the internationalization of aid mechanisms and the use of semipublic foundations would be helpful, as Professor Thomson suggests. I would also add the concept of divorcing planning and operations in the development process from the providing of funds and materials, putting the former completely under the control of the aid recipient and relegating the aid giver to the role of banker, who provides the funds and materials for development programs and, when needed, the funds for hiring the necessary planning and operations staff, but who is not himself directly involved in drawing up plans or implementing programs.

CHESTER COOPER: Jim Thomson makes the point that much will depend on the nature of the settlement in Vietnam. But much will also depend on the timing of the settlement, regardless of the terms. If a settlement can, for example, be reached before Inauguration Day, then it will have one effect. If it can't be—if in fact the new administration has to make the settlement—it will have another effect. If the new administration can approach the world with a Vietnam settlement behind it, no matter what that settlement is, it will have a lot more elbow room than if it has to make the settlement and if it then has to justify its settlement by acts elsewhere in the world to show that it is still concerned. If the new administration has to justify a settlement that is very soft in Vietnam, we may have some rather precarious times ahead of us. If it doesn't, if it can start with a clean slate and approach the world somewhat more objectively, I think that the new administration, whoever the President is, is likely to have a more serene time of it, and the American people are also likely to have a more serene time of it.

EDWIN REISCHAUER: I liked very much Jim Thomson's point that the lesson to be drawn from Vietnam is a lesson about intervention in Vietnam. This is the humanist crying out against the social scientist, the humanist who sees things as unique. It is the specialist crying out against the generalist. We have overlooked the uniqueness of things everywhere.

To have a wise policy anywhere, you have to know what you are doing; you have to have specialized, detailed, historical knowledge, or else you will not have wise policy.

Beyond this, while I think we all agree that the bureaucracy has distorted our decision-making process, the basic theme of this conference has been that misconceptions, wrong ideas, have perhaps been even more responsible, and they have only been compounded through institutional weaknesses.

We not only tended to underestimate the difficulty for the antagonist to reverse his course, but we have grossly underestimated his will and his intentions. In fact, we hardly even thought about those things. When we decided that bombing would bring him to his knees, to negotiations, we considered it a test of will in which apparently the only variable was our own will. We never put in the other person's will. This is much like one other great miscalculation we made in the postwar world, one made by General MacArthur when he kept going in North Korea as a test of will, thinking he knew how Orientals operate and believing they respected power and determination. He made a fantastic blunder.

These two instances do have a certain similarity which suggests a danger. There may be a racial element involved in these assessments, or to put it in less sensational terms, at least a cultural element—a tendency to disregard the Asian, either for cultural or racial reasons. We are not too far from the nineteenth century yet.

SIR ROBERT THOMPSON: I would like to say how much I agree with Messrs. Thomson and Reischauer. I have always feared that Vietnam might produce United States isolationism. This risk, in my view, has been made even severer by the fact that we may not have seen the real end of this war yet. While we all hope there can be a satisfactory conclusion, I am very much afraid that at the present moment we still could be heading for a catastrophe. What the effects will be within the United States worries me enormously. There has been dissent and disunity on the war up to now, but what might the dissent, disunity, and recrimination be like if we ended with a catastrophe in Vietnam?

I also agree that the gap is growing between the rich and the poor countries of the world. And the one thing that really worries me about violence—whether communist-inspired or not, and especially in highly populated agricultural countries—is that we are rapidly moving into a situation where food is going to become the major world problem, particularly if there is disruption of production in these agricultural countries. I am therefore more worried about what I would call the food button than about the nuclear button in relation to the long-term dangers in the world.

The only other point I would like to refer to is the previously proposed distinction between military intervention and other forms of involvement. I really don't think the military side can be separated from the economic or political. For example, the great problem in military intervention is what you tell your general to do. I would dearly love to see the directive—if there was such a directive—that was given to General Westmoreland in Vietnam. What was he told to do? If the directive simply says win the war, then you are telling the soldier to use all his professional means, and you cannot dispute those professional means with him because he is the professional. If you do not tell him to achieve particular political results, then if the physical means of power are divorced from the responsibility for the political end result, you are bound to get into a mess. To a certain extent we saw that at the end of World War II, where we focused on winning the war rather than on achieving certain political results.

Coming back to one other point, I think that I probably know as well as anyone the differences between Malaya and Vietnam and the power and control we had in Malaya. There the general who was given the directive had the power; but then he also had the political responsibility for the results. However, although technically and constitutionally he had the power to give orders, to make the major decisions, this was not a power that could be mechanically exercised —he had to carry the people of Malaya with him. Where control was vital and really counted was in carrying out those orders. He could control implementation and could see to it—if he gave a tough order which might have harmful effects—that it was implemented delicately to get the maximum effect at the minimum cost.

I would like to leave you, therefore, with two thoughts with regard to power: that you cannot divorce power and responsibility and, secondly, that the whole secret of power is not to use it.

LEROY WEHRLE: Three general points. First, I think there is a great deal of contemporary truth in what we are saying today. But a great deal of what we say reflects our immediate reactions to the bitterness and tragedy of Vietnam; over a long period of time these suggestions regarding United States foreign policy will not wash as well as they seem to wash right now.

Implicit in many of the things we say is an image of a world which is more orderly, nicer, and easier to handle than it really is. I agree with Professor Reischauer that the world is progressing at such a rate that none of us knows where it is going, what is going to happen, or whether we can deal with it even if we learned more about it. The world is much more interconnected. Things that happen in one place snap back immediately elsewhere in somebody's face.

But despite our limited knowledge, and the desirability of understanding ourselves and others more, we still have to get up each morning, say to ourselves we do not understand enough, and then go out and try to deal with the world. To say that because of the tragedy of Vietnam we no longer should be interventionists or activists, or whatever words you want to use, is to miss a larger meaning which the world thrusts at us. I think that the balance between activism and restraint which American foreign policy has struck during the last twenty years is still the right one, refined perhaps by the lessons and mislessons of Vietnam.

Second, there are two lessons I would take away from Vietnam. First, know thy country. Second, keep thy leadership in place. In other words, we must know the people of the country we are assisting, their history and their capabilities. Also it is obvious and fundamental that we find good leadership to conduct American policy in such a situation, and keep this leadership in place for a considerable period. To change ambassadors and other top officials frequently makes impossible a continuity of policy and a tough monitoring of the large American bureaucracy executing policy.

The United States government, like all of us, makes mistakes, sometimes learns from them, and sometimes doesn't. We should not take as a datum of policy that it cannot learn, for this is clearly wrong and the implications of such a conclusion are severe.

HANS MORGENTHAU: A great deal can be learned from a consideration of the intrinsic mistakes which led us into this involvement. First of all, I think one can learn that counterinsurgency is not just another military technique—it is not something like placing machine guns in a different way to have greater military effect. Counterinsurgency is an attempt to defeat and stamp out a genuine revolution, or what is called a "war of national liberation." We cannot succeed in counterrevolution, short of the destruction of the indigenous population, as long as the insurgents can at least base their activities upon the indifference, if not upon the active support, of the indigenous population.

Another lesson one can learn from the Vietnam war concerns the relationship of massive, material, military power to the subtle and almost intangible problems one faces when one deals with an enemy who, if only because he cannot help himself, must rely upon different techniques to which this massive military commitment is utterly irrelevant. In other words, we are in the position of a man who has been attacked by a swarm of bees and who can defend himself only with a submachine gun. By the law of averages he is going to hit a bee from time to time, but he is not going to have a very effective defense.

Thirdly, one can learn from the Vietnam war lessons which have been brought home to me during a prolonged recent stay in India—that there is, indeed, an enormous difference in psychology and attitude between a white nation which, with the best of intentions, tries to reform an Asian nation and the Asian nations themselves. Time and time again cabinet ministers and other prominent people in Asia have said to me that the United States does not care if Asian lives are profusely expended, but that it makes a great deal of difference to Asians.

I remember vividly a dinner party I attended at which a prominent member of the Indian cabinet and other leading intellectuals were present. They all said that the Tet offensive was the third great historical event in the relations between Asia and the West. The first was the Russo-Japanese war of 1905. The second was the defeat of the French, Dutch, and English by the Japanese during World War II; this was the third. This was the last colonial war in which a Western power was fighting on the soil of Asia and failing.

Now, then, let me say a word about intervention in general. Obviously, as others have said, it is quite impossible to lay down abstract principles to tell you under what conditions you ought to intervene and under what conditions you ought not to intervene. One cannot do this any more than one can establish guidelines telling you exactly when you should go to war and when you should not go to war, when you should deploy your navy and when you should not deploy it, when to send an ultimatum to a foreign power and when not to send an ultimatum. This is not a question of abstract principles but of the concrete circumstances of the case to be decided by prudential judgment.

It would certainly be wrong to conclude from the Vietnam experience that the United States should never intervene in the affairs of any other country, but it would be just as wrong to say that we should dispense with taking the lessons of Vietnam to heart and intervene again whenever there appears to be an occasion to stop communism.

The asserted danger of impending isolationism is in good measure, I think, the result of United States government propaganda. I found in India a very strong ambivalence with regard to the Vietnam war.

On the one hand, there is hardly anybody in a responsible position who supports our activity in Vietnam, but on the other hand, almost everybody is mortally afraid that if we disengage from Vietnam, we might disengage from Asia altogether. I think this danger has been conjured up by spokesmen for the Administration, who have made it appear that the United States has only two choices, either to stay in Vietnam or to get out of Asia. However, in my view, those are not the only two choices at all.

I have opposed involvement in Vietnam from the very beginning, from 1961 onward, not because I am opposed to the involvement of the United States in Asia, but because I have always considered this particular involvement under these particular circumstances to be politically unprofitable and militarily preposterous. However, to argue against a particular move on the Asian continent is not tantamount to arguing against the vital American interests in the maintenance or, if need be, the restoration of the balance of power in Asia. The United States has been aware of this interest and has put it into action, beginning with the "open door" policy, through our opposition to Japanese imperialism, to the ill-conceived policy of peripheral military containment regarding China.

Therefore, the ultimate and perhaps most fruitful lesson which can be drawn from the Vietnam experience concerns the policy the United States ought to pursue in Asia, which ought to be neither piecemeal military intervention on the mainland nor disengagement altogether. This, I think, is the real problem for the future.

CHESTER COOPER: I have several points concerning intervention. Many years ago I did an analysis of the concept of strategic importance in an effort to try to come to grips with it. I discovered at that time—and there were fewer such countries then than there are now—that you could find in the literature that reached high places in our government some fifty countries that were designated as being of vital or critical strategic importance to the United States, in one form or another, by one or another government agency. Depending upon what your criteria are, you can make a case that a lot of countries all over the world are of critical strategic importance. But even if you wanted to intervene in every place judged critically important, you just could not do so. Therefore, if you are going to base your decisions regarding intervention on the judgment of whether the area is critically important, you had better take another look at the standards we use in measuring this whole concept of strategic importance and at some principal choices that have to be made.

Having said that, and with due respect to Mort Halperin, if we are deciding whether we want to intervene in a country, examining whether that country is helping itself or a neighbor is helping it involves pretty subjective determinations. Moreover, there are many countries who are trying hard to help themselves, and whose neighbors might be helping, in which we still might not want to intervene. Possibly they may be too far away, or they might not have enough leverage in our own government and Congress. On the other hand, and regardless of the lessons of Vietnam, there may also be other countries in which we may decide—for reasons perhaps altogether different from whether they are helping themselves or their neighbors are helping them—that we will intervene.

All standards for intervention are going to be very difficult to apply. But by the time you heed Jim Thomson's caveats regarding what we should do before we intervene, future United States intervention is made very unlikely. But I suspect that the world we are going to confront after Vietnam is going to be one that will be a very tough one for us to live in alone.

If we can draw a lesson from Vietnam in terms of intervention, I suspect it is that the threshold will be higher for future intervention, that the alarms will have to be louder and more traumatic, that the case for United States security being affected will have to be somewhat more convincing. I am not arguing whether we should intervene or not. I am suggesting the kind of standard likely to emerge after Vietnam, and life being what it is, this standard will have a life expectancy of only five years or so.

JAMES C. THOMSON, JR.: I thought Mr. Draper made a very useful point earlier in trying to put military intervention in a separate category. He would place the beginning of our military intervention in Vietnam at about 1964–65. I gather he feels that our intervention in Vietnam from 1954 up through about 1961 was not military intervention. I would accept this distinction, except for what I would describe as the "slippery slope phenomenon," which makes me deeply worried about economic aid and the like. It strikes me that in our reaction to situations of instability overseas, there is a built-in progression from economic, technical, and internal security types of assistance to military intervention when the initial nonmilitary intervention doesn't work. The slippery slope phenomenon gets compounded by our great-power sense of omnipotence and grandiosity.

EDWIN REISCHAUER: I wish we could get away from the word "intervention" to describe economic aid. This puts it very much in the wrong way. Intervention, to my mind, does not build toward our long-range interests; it reflects only short-range interests in terms of regimes that are there today or vote in the UN tomorrow, things of that sort. However, these are not ultimate interests on our part.

We should view our role in economic aid in an entirely different way. We should not raise great hopes that we can reconstruct other societies by giving economic aid or that we can construct democratic-leaning regimes and things of that sort. But we can contribute to institutional development and economic growth in ways that local people appreciate, and this in turn can contribute at least peripherally to these other objectives.

STANLEY HOFFMANN: I am particularly glad to hear the remarks of Professor Reischauer in relation to economic aid. If we are not able to put marks on the famous continuum of policy and to distinguish between providing plant seeds, on the one hand, and intervention for political development or military intervention, on the other, then I think we are really lost.

If we consider that all this is interconnected, that the only choice we have is between buying a whole loaf or nothing at all, then American Stimsonianism and New Dealism are likely to be replaced by the neoisolationism Mr. Reischauer and I are both worried about. To avoid this one must have a new look at the world and a new look at what kind of interests the United States has.

In some parts of the world I would call the interests we have noncompetitive, interests we share with practically all other nations. We have interests as a rich, industrialized nation in avoiding general chaos. Economic aid flows from such interests. If we are afraid of the slippery slope that Jim Thomson was talking about, then indeed we should try to master multilateral techniques of aid so as not to be tempted by the siren of involvement and intervention. But we might be mature enough to know that economic aid is not necessarily a prelude to grandiose interventions to reshape the outside world.

What worries me ultimately in listening to some of the discussion is a sense that we have not yet realized enough of what I call the foreignness of foreigners—that when one acts abroad, one is treading on mined ground. Mr. Reischauer and Mr. Fairbank have, I think, a tendency to believe that this is particularly true when we deal with Orientals. However, our dealings over the past twenty years with that famous Oriental general, de Gaulle, leads me to the conclusion that what is involved is a more general faith, or belief, that we can affect the will of others, whereas others really cannot affect our will. This is a very deep trait, one which we have to learn to modify.

JOHN McDERMOTT: I am concerned with the rhetorical gap, wherein the words we use—the same words Messrs. Ellsberg and Thomson used within the government—make Professor Schlesinger happy, while their policy results kept Mr. Pool happy.

The relevant distinction is not between political and military intervention but between coercive and noncoercive policies. Very small political and economic coercions shape rapidly and imperceptibly into major coercion. The mainstream liberals are even blinder to this fact than the military brass and the national security bureaucracy.

To reformulate, we should think of intervention as a large baloney. We should recognize that the trouble with the interventionist baloney is that when you start cutting off the left end—which you may call economic—you very, very shortly get up to the middle, and then to the right end—which is called military. And then you have no more baloney, which is where we are right now.

This suggests a good operating rule for staying out of Dutch in the world: if we would not do it in the Netherlands, then we should not do it anywhere else.

FRANCES FITZGERALD: I would adopt an even more stringent operating rule than Mr. McDermott. If we want to stay out of Dutch in the world, then we must be much more careful in the developing states than in the Netherlands, because the Netherlands have the ability to say "no" to us and to usher us out. This is hardly the case in Vietnam.

Our relationship there to our Vietnamese allies, despite enormous amounts of human contact, is basically unsatisfactory, primarily because it is unclear to the Vietnamese exactly what the nature of the relationship is. They do not or cannot see us exactly as colonialists, but on the other hand, they cannot see us as equals either. There cannot be a bargaining relationship involved.

Our dominant relationship with them is not exactly coercive—much as we may wish it were—because they refuse to be coerced by us. Instead of being our puppet, the Saigon government is rather more like a sort of tar baby. It has nothing to do any more with its own people—it is now entirely concerned with managing what comes from the outside, with managing us.

I would imagine this has been the case since the fall of the Diem regime, although I am not personally familiar with the period prior to 1966. Part of the reason why some people in Saigon today are mourning the fall of the Diem regime is that Diem had one crucial ability which all the subsequent leaders have lacked—the ability to say "no" to the United States. This is what made him somewhat of an effective governor in his own country.

What has happened in Vietnam since Diem is curiously totally reversed. In fighting us, the NLF and Hanoi have become much more like us than the government we support, and they will be able to respect us more in the end than the present Saigon government will simply because they can see us as equals. There is an important relationship there. They see us as enemies, and that, of course, is a very clear and firm relationship. When the direct conflict is over, there is a possibility to form another sort of relationship with them; whereas there is no longer that possibility with anything we might call the government of Saigon.

In terms of Professor Huntington's argument, my experience in Vietnam suggests the extreme caution one has to use in proceeding with any sort of political manipulation of anybody else, if only because one cannot tell what the extended ramifications of one's acts will be. The effects you actually create are usually very different from the ones you expect. And when one puts oneself into a situation, it becomes very difficult to continue to see it objectively.

EDWIN REISCHAUER: I just want to put forth the rather old-fashioned point of view that the human mind does have power over baloney. This must reveal my humanist background—that I think we are not yet completely victims of machines and social scientists. Of course, I am talking in relation to the comments made by Mr. McDermott and not the usual baloney. I am not sure we have much control over that.

Mr. McDermott has suggested that innocent aid-giving, the loan of seeds, for example, leads on and on into political intervention, into a Vietnam-type war, and that this is inevitably one big baloney—that once you have sliced part of it, you go right down the whole thing. This isn't necessarily so at all. In this connection, you can perfectly well conceptualize three baloneys, and probably more in many cases. You can have the strictly economic kind of baloney and the political baloney, as well as the military-intervention baloney. These, in turn, might be composed of several little baloneys. You might have baloneys on training, advice, and things like that.

What I am trying to say is that we have a perfect possibility of controlling many of these things if we just see the problem. The trouble is that we have not yet seen the problem. We have thought of involvement as being an inevitable continuum, and so we have made it that.

I would like to make a couple of other points. I think we are obviously moving toward a feeling that there isn't much balance of power at stake in most of Asia, and not many areas of strategic importance to us. In this regard I am sorry Roger Hilsman is not here, but let me take as an example his fascinating chapter on Laos. He devotes one paragraph at the beginning of the chapter to saying that Laos is a strategic place. He backs that up with a vague statement that one could build a road through there which might affect something. He then goes on in the rest of the chapter to deal with what you can do about this strategic place. I believe we are presently moving away from this kind of blind assumption of the importance of small countries. And we obviously are not left with just the choice of complete interventionism or complete isolationism. I think most of us realize that there must be roads in between, and these are what we are trying to define.

I think the word "isolationist" also is a bit unfortunate because it has been used in so many different ways. As Professor Morgenthau pointed out, it has even been used to characterize anybody who had doubts about the Vietnam war. However, I think the way we have been using it here has been quite different—to describe people who are really unconcerned about Asia and the other less developed parts of the world. In the Chinese tradition of rectification of names—finding the right word for the right thing—I would suggest we use the word "unconcerned" rather than "neoisolationism" to describe this attitude.

EQBAL AHMAD: I would like to take off from where Professors Reischauer and Morgenthau have left us. It seems to me that the specter of neoisolationism has been bothering all of us for the last two days. It seems an unnecessary concern. Unnecessary, first of all, because neoisolationism is probably as unlikely to come about today as is the hope of returning to the virtues of village life in many parts of the world. It is difficult to conceive that Americans will become, given the present situation, somehow isolated from the rest of the world, and therefore we have to think in terms of new forms of relationships rather than in terms of isolationism, even if some people like to talk about it.

First, it seems to me that the United States has been unable to grasp the force of nationalism in the "third world," and insofar as it has been grasped, the policies America has pursued have been basically antinationalist. It has been supporting nationalist movements only during the phase of self-determination, but when nationalist movements have acquired social and radical content, the United States response has been negative.

Second, I would like to repeat that nationalism is probably the greatest force in the underdeveloped countries and in a certain sense promises to keep these countries independent of great powers. Therefore, I would expect that the more radical and revolutionary and modernizing a regime is in the underdeveloped countries, the more likely it is to assert its independence in an operative matter. Here I would include regimes like Cuba, North Korea, and, for that matter, North Vietnam.

Another point is that social conflict is likely to occur and even sharpen in our part of the world in the coming decades. The United States' interest probably does not lie in influencing the outcome of these social conflicts. United States interest basically lies in confining these conflicts within national and regional boundaries. In fact, domestic insurgency does not have to be contained. Why talk about containment of insurgency altogether? It should be permitted maximum freedom from foreign interference in redefining what kind of societies we want to be. That we shall be very nationalist and very self-assertive, I think, should be taken more or less for granted.

Therefore, from this argument I would argue that United States policy should lay greater stress on demilitarizing the "third world." I think the United States should put as much stress on demilitarization of the "third world" as it puts on great-power disarmament, perhaps more. The great powers should agree, if possible (and I think it will be possible), not to supply heavy arms to the underdeveloped countries. The denial of such heavy arms might be the first and probably most important step in keeping these conflicts somewhat more confined, perhaps less destructive, and also away from big-power interferences. The three great powers—I include China—can in the meantime maintain commitments to certain countries to defend them against attack from other powers. After all, South Korea has a right to be defended if it so desires, and, for that matter, so does India.

Lastly, and to constantly maintain the distinction between aid and intervention, the danger of the slippery slope syndrome—instead of leading us to decide that economic aid per se should be stopped altogether—should lead us to talk about what mechanisms of economic aid might be best in a variety of situations to give us substantial protection from the dangers of incrementalism. Jim Thomson's suggestion to denationalize aid might be very effective in this regard.

Throughout, I have been arguing for a certain kind of disengagement and pleading against the extreme fears of social revolution that exist in the United States, which somehow lead the United States to believe that any kind of social revolution or insurgency necessarily has to be contained. Expecting orderly change at the moment is likely to bring large numbers of disappointments and frustrations.

STANLEY HOFFMANN: I agree entirely with Mr. Ahmad's point, with one small exception, to which I will come.

On the whole we can distinguish, at least intellectually, two kinds of interventions, one of which we have practiced with some proficiency over the years. This category has been what I would call negative interventions. We did not exactly know what we were for, but we did know what we were against. We intervened essentially against a threat, and we have sometimes been quite successful— Guatemala, Iran, and what have you. As for this category of interventions, I would argue that in the future we at least ought to define more rigorously what it is that so threatens us that we feel we have to intervene either by political subversion or by military action.

The second category is intervention to do something positively. Here again a plea for modesty and limitation is in order. There are a few things we know we can do, particularly in economic aid. However, I am quite convinced, especially after listening to this discussion, that we cannot intervene effectively to build up somebody else's political process. Here we are dealing really with a completely different kind of baloney altogether.

Let me add that for any negative and positive interventions to be successful, we generally need to meet the essential conditions set by Mort Halperin. On the other hand, I agree with Mr. Cooper that there may be occasions when governments can't sufficiently help themselves alone and still should get American aid. But I would hope that one lesson of the Vietnam war is that we will never again interfere militarily or with a high degree of political involvement on behalf of governments that do not know how to defend themselves. If we have not learned this, then I really don't know what we have learned.

This does not mean that we are going to deal with an easy world. Here is my point of disagreement with Mr. Ahmad. I entirely agree with his principles, but if we settle for a world of great domestic turbulence and nationalism, as I think we must, then there is a contradiction between accepting nationalisms and demilitarizing (or denying weapons to) other nations, because they will insist on the right of sovereign states to have weapons. We should consider the kinds of troubles we may have if we refuse to go along with them, while continuing to arm ourselves.

ALBERT WOHLSTETTER: Jim Thomson suggests that the trend toward isolationism is reduced by our continuing participation in the UN. I doubt that anyone here really regards this as enough for avoiding isolationism. In fact, there is a United Nations kind of isolationism. Burton Marshall remarked some years ago that there always has been a close similarity between the anti-UN isolationism typified by the Bricker Amendment—which would simply withdraw, stop the world and get off—and the tendency to wish that the UN would handle all the problems of military aggression that trouble us, that *somebody* up there on the United Nations Plaza would deal with this complex, diverse, quarrelsome world; but not us. There is, however, No one Up There who can do it.

The multilateralism Thomson discussed can be broken into two parts. First, "inter-adversary" arrangements, like the UN. These are multilateral in one sense. They involve many nations, including some present enemies as well as some present friends; and they are potentially universal. Then there are alliances. These are multilateral in the sense that they involve many nations. But they include only present friends and they are usually directed at specific enemies. If in either of these two sorts of multilateral arrangement the U.S. commitment to help party X is conditioned on simultaneous help to party X by Y, Z, W, *et al.,* party X may find the commitment worth very little. And so might a potential aggressor. (As in the case of the League of Nations, or the Suez Canal Users Association, and unlike NATO.) So therefore might we.

In many cases where we want our commitments to be valued, they will not be credible at all if they depend on there being a crowd of helpers which we simply offer to join. We say now that we will respond to an attack on Germany or any other NATO country as if it were an attack on us. We don't say that if Germany is attacked we will wait to see if the United Kingdom presses the button. Or vice versa. If we did, neither our allies nor our adversaries would find the commitment very persuasive. No matter how we label the phenomenon, we are shrinking away from involvement if we say, "Let's not go in unless others do." If we make that a firm condition, it is a recipe for paralysis.

The paper by Mort Halperin that Jim Thomson referred to is thoughtful, and, for a government official today, I think it represents some things that are new. However, Jim has seized on a point in the paper that is both old and weak—the hopeful reference to regional self-help. Since the war both the Republican and Democratic establishments have accepted a kind of regionalism that seems to me quite unthinking. In the current world, mere geographical proximity or connection by land routes is totally irrelevant for establishing common economic, political or military interests. As a matter of fact, it has always been a very poor criterion of association. Communications by water have frequently been cheaper than communications over land, and this has long been true. In an era of 300,000-deadweight-ton tankers, of aircraft carrying several hundred thousands of pounds in payload or carrying passengers at several times the speed of sound, of messages sent by satellite, it will make no sense to treat proximity or land connection as if it were an essential in determining the usefulness of cooperation. We keep pushing Japan into assuming a role in regard to any number of Asian nations in which it has only the faintest interest, simply because they are all in Asia. It should be obvious that Japan's interests will be linked increasingly with such distant places as the United States and Europe.

JAMES C. THOMSON, JR.: Well, I have some bits and pieces but I do not have a closing benediction.

My first bit relates to semantics. I wonder if the purveyors of baloney in the room would mind if, to avoid unnecessary ambiguity, we shifted the image to salami or liverwurst.

With regard to the possibility of isolationism in today's world, Mr. Reischauer proposes the term "unconcern," which I think is a very useful way to put it. However, as my own policy prescription, "de-activism" or "disengagement," I think, would be more appropriate; actually the phrase I use is the Japanese term "low posture"—a "low-posture foreign policy."

EDWIN REISCHAUER: I think everybody would be for a low posture.

JAMES C. THOMSON, JR.: I appreciate what I take to be Mr. Wohlstetter's refinements of my thesis, and I accept them. While it may be true that multilateralism is a "recipe for paralysis" in some cases, I would infinitely prefer "paralysis" to certain types of interventionism.

When I read papers like Mort Halperin's, I keep finding words like "America's commitments," and passages to the effect that of course we cannot disregard our commitments. I would like to propose as a partial brake against future interventions not that we disregard our commitments but rather that we more soberly and deftly try to re-examine, sort out and selectively de-emphasize the accumulated commitments that are the baggage each new administration inherits from its predecessors.

In 1961 we gave ourselves little latitude in East Asia and in many other parts of the world, not merely because of inherited commitments, but—regrettably—because of rather rigid interpretations of those commitments. The Secretary of State urged such rigidity. I would hope we could gradually revamp our understanding of certain commitments without selling our allies and friends down the river or causing them undue alarm.

This brings me to my final point. My hope, out of all of this tragedy, is that America will somehow be a chastened nation in the aftermath of Vietnam. This is the first war we have watched so closely on television. This is a war about which we have more volumes of printed literature than any previous war. The record of our failure is available to the general public as never before. I hope we will go through a chastening period in which we will be knocked out of our grandiosity, a period in which we will see the self-righteous, illusory quality of that vision of ourselves offered by the high Washington official who said that while other nations have "interests," the United States has "a sense of responsibility."

I hope that we may also rid ourselves of what Mr. Schlesinger referred to as "Stimsonianism" as well as the evangelical liberal tradition overseas, a tradition represented here by our distinguished colleague who aims to create "a world in which the political systems of all states are democratic and pacifically oriented." It surprises me to still hear such grandiose objectives proposed.

If Vietnam can result in a reduction of grandiosity on our part, it should likewise result in a discovery that we are, in one sense, quite similar to everyone else—we have our own problems; look at our cities. But it should also make us discover that, in another sense, we are also very unlike others and that in this highly diverse world there are diverse routes to development.

My hopes are strengthened, I might just add, by a conviction that at least some of the new generation of Americans emerging from our colleges and universities will continue to be activists and, hopefully, will become makers of foreign policy. I do not think that these are people who will permit us to remain on the closed track of the cold war era.

Contributors

EQBAL AHMAD Assistant Professor in the School of Industrial and Labor Relations, Cornell University; author of several pieces on revolutionary warfare. He will go to Vietnam this fall as a Fellow of the Adlai Stevenson Institute.

RICHARD J. BARNET Codirector of the Institute for Policy Studies in Washington, D.C.; former official of the Department of State and Deputy Director of the Office of Political Research in the Arms Control and Disarmament Ageny during the Kennedy Administration; former Fellow of the Russian Research Center at Harvard and the Center for International Studies at Princeton; author of several books, including *Who Wants Disarmanent?* and *Intervention and Revolution: The United States in the Third World.*

CHESTER COOPER Director of the International and Social Studies Division, Institute for Defense Analysis; Special Assistant to Ambassador Harriman, responsible for planning the U.S. negotiating position on Vietnam, 1966–67; senior member of the National Security Council staff, responsible for Asian affairs, 1964–66; member of the American delegation to the Geneva and Laos Conferences.

THEODORE DRAPER Research Fellow at the Hoover Institution on War, Revolution and Peace, Stanford University; author of *The Roots of American Communism; Castroism: Theory and Practice; Abuse of Power;* and *Israel and World Politics.*

LUIGI EINAUDI Staff member, Social Science Department, Rand Corporation and lecturer in political science at the University of California at Los Angeles.

DANIEL ELLSBERG Rand Corporation consultant to the Department of Defense on Vietnam on projects relating to pacification and politics in Vietnam; formerly Special Assistant to John McNaughton, Assistant

289

Secretary of Defense for International Security Affairs (1964–65); member of Edward Lansdale's Senior Liaison Office in Saigon (Aug. 1965 to Dec. 1966); Special Assistant to Deputy Ambassador Porter.

JOHN KING FAIRBANK Professor of History and Director of the East Asian Research Center, Harvard University; author of many books, including *The U.S. and China.*

FRANCES FITZGERALD Award-winning journalist who has written articles on Vietnamese society and the war appearing in the *New York Times Magazine,* the *Atlantic Monthly,* and elsewhere. Since her last ten-month stay in Saigon, she has been working on her forthcoming book.

COL. FRED HAYNES U.S. Marine Corps. Currently Military Secretary to the Commandant. Served in three wars, most recently in Vietnam as Commanding Officer of the Fifth Marines and G-3 of the Third Marine Amphibious Force in the northern five provinces; decorations: Legion of Merit with two gold stars, Bronze Star Medal, Vietnam Army Distinguished Service Order, Vietnam Cross of Gallantry with Palm; former Director of Near East and South Asian Affairs OSD-ISA 1965–1966.

STANLEY HOFFMANN Professor of Government, Harvard University; Research Associate, Center for International Affairs; author of numerous books on international affairs including *Organisations Internationales et Pouvoirs Politiques des Etats, Le Mouvement Poujade;* and *Gulliver's Troubles.*

SAMUEL P. HUNTINGTON Professor of Government, Chairman of the Department of Government, and a member of the Executive Committee of the Center for International Affairs at Harvard University. Current Chairman of the Council on Vietnamese Studies of the Southeast Asia Development Advisory Group; consultant to the Policy Planning Council of the Department of State and to the Agency for International Development. His publications include: *The Soldier and the State: Theory and Politics of Civil-Military Relations* (1957), *The Common Defense: Strategic Programs in National Politics* (1961), *Changing USA/ USSR* (1964), and *Political Order in Changing Societies* (1968).

GEORGE MCTURNAN KAHIN Professor of Government, Director of Southeast Asia Program, Cornell University; Director of Cornell Modern Indonesia Project, Cornell University; author of *Nationalism and Revolution in Indonesia* (1952), *The Asian-African Conference* (1956); coauthor (with John W. Lewis) of *The United States in Vietnam* (1967); editor and contributor, *Governments and Politics of Southeast Asia* (1st ed., 1959; 2nd ed. 1964); editor, *Major Governments of Asia* (1st ed., 1958; 2nd ed., 1963).

HENRY KISSINGER Professor of Government and faculty member of the Center for International Affairs at Harvard University; former consultant to the government on foreign affairs, especially on matters of defense; author of several books, the most recent, *The Troubled Partnership: A Reappraisal of the Atlantic Alliance.*

JOHN MCDERMOTT Associate Editor of *Viet-Report* and lecturer in politics and international relations at the New School for Social Research; author of *Profile of Vietnamese History* and of articles in *The New York Review of Books, The Nation, Dissent,* and other periodicals.

HANS MORGENTHAU Professor of Political Science and Modern History at the University of Chicago; Director of the Center for the Study of American Foreign and Military Policy; served as consultant to the Department of State and the Department of Defense; author of numerous books, including *Politics Among Nations* and *Politics in the Twentieth Century.*

RICHARD M. PFEFFER Fellow of the Adlai Stevenson Institute and Research Fellow in Comparative Law at the Law School, University of Chicago; member of the New York Bar; author of articles on comparative law and political development which have appeared in the *China Quarterly, World Politics,* and *Pacific Affairs.*

WILLIAM R. POLK Director of the Adlai Stevenson Institute of International Affairs; Professor of History and Director of the Center for Middle Eastern Studies, University of Chicago; former member of the Policy Planning Council of the U.S. Department of State; books include *Backdrop to Tragedy: The Struggle for Palestine* and *The United States and the Arab World.*

ITHIEL DE SOLA POOL Chairman of the Department of Political Science, Massachusetts Institute of Technology; member of the Defense Science Board, Department of Defense; conducted research for the Defense Department in Vietnam in 1966–67; author of articles and books on international relations, including *American Business and Public Policy: The Politics of Foreign Trade* (1963); contributor and editor of *Contemporary Political Science: Toward Empirical Theory* (1967).

EDWIN REISCHAUER University Professor, Harvard University; former American Ambassador to Japan from 1961 to 1966; has written widely on Japanese and East Asian history as well as on American Far Eastern policy: *Wanted: An Asian Policy* (1955) and *Beyond Vietnam: The United States and Asia* (1967).

JOHN E. RIELLY Foreign Policy Assistant to Vice-President Humphrey; former Foreign Policy Assistant to Senator Hubert Humphrey, 1962–1965; with Department of State, 1961–62. Doctorate in political science, Harvard University.

ARTHUR SCHLESINGER, JR. Albert Schweitzer Professor of the Humanities, City University of New York; former Special Assistant to President Kennedy, 1961 to 1965, and briefly to President Johnson; author of *A Thousand Days: John F. Kennedy in the White House* and subsequent winner of the National Book Award for History and Biography and the Pulitzer Prize for Biography; latest work, *The Bitter Heritage: Vietnam and American Democracy, 1941–1966.*

SIR ROBERT THOMPSON Deputy Secretary and Secretary for the Defense of Malaya, 1957–61, guiding the successful campaign against the guerrillas in that country; head of the British Advisory Mission in Vietnam, 1961–65; author of *Defeating Communist Insurgency* and other works.

JAMES C. THOMSON, JR. East Asian specialist at the Department of State and the White House between 1961 and 1966. Now teaching history of U.S.–East Asian relations at Harvard; Faculty Associate of the Institute of Politics. He has written on Chinese communism in the 1930's, on post-1949 U.S. China policy, and will shortly publish a study of *American Reformers in Nationalist China, 1928–37.*

LEROY WEHRLE Deputy Assistant Administrator for Vietnam, Agency for International Development; former Associate Director of AID Mission and Economic Counselor of Embassy in Vietnam, 1964–67; previously with AID in Laos; senior economist, Council of Economic Advisors, 1961–62; doctorate in economics, Yale University, 1959.

ALBERT WOHLSTETTER University Professor of Political Science, University of Chicago; consultant to the American government in three administrations; principal work in systems analyses in the field of international security affairs, particularly relating to nuclear policy; currently working on distant interests, capabilities, and commitments of the major powers.

ADAM YARMOLINSKY Professor of Law and member of the Institute of Politics, Harvard, 1966 to present; former Principal Deputy Assistant Secretary of Defense for International Security Affairs, 1965–66; Special Assistant to the Secretary of Defense, 1961–64.

Index